MONEY AS ORGANIZATION, GUSTAVO DEL VECCHIO'S THEORY

Modern Heterodox Economics

Series Editor: Carol M. Connell

Forthcoming Titles

Financial Crisis and the Failure of Economic Theory
Ángel Rodriguez, Jorge Turmo Arnal and Oscar Vara Crespo

MONEY AS ORGANIZATION, GUSTAVO DEL VECCHIO'S THEORY

BY

Gianfranco Tusset

Routledge
Taylor & Francis Group
LONDON AND NEW YORK

First published 2014 by Pickering & Chatto (Publishers) Limited

Published 2016 by Routledge
2 Park Square, Milton Park, Abingdon, Oxon OX14 4RN
605 Third Avenue, New York, NY 10017

Routledge is an imprint of the Taylor & Francis Group, an informa business

BRITISH LIBRARY CATALOGUING IN PUBLICATION DATA

Tusset, Gianfranco author.
Money as organization, Gustavo Del Vecchio's theory. – (Modern heterodox economics)
1. Del Vecchio, Gustavo, 1883–1972 2. Money. 3. Monetary policy.
I. Title II. Series
332.4'01-dc23

ISBN-13: 978-1-84893-425-2 (hbk)
Typeset by Pickering & Chatto (Publishers) Limited

CONTENTS

To Eleonora and Renata

ACKNOWLEDGEMENTS

The scientific experience of Gustavo Del Vecchio was an experience of 'intellectual freedom'. I became aware of this several years ago, as I started reading his many articles and books, grappling with ideas and analyses that seemed free from any theoretical tenet, from any ideological constraint, from any methodological imposition. Del Vecchio thought that economic science was the result of successive stratifications, and this left him free to try new approaches, to explore new avenues. He recognized only one obligation: although economics is and remains a thought experiment, it must explain reality and be anchored in facts.

Some years later, my re-reading of Del Vecchio transmitted the same nonconformity to me. This book is an attempt to condense and discuss Del Vecchio's monetary and economic topics, maintaining the intellectual independence that he demonstrated throughout his long scientific life.

I would like to thank Nerio Naldi, Stefano Solari and Alberto Zanni, who read parts of the manuscript or provided me with useful material. I also thank the participants at the various history of economic thought conferences where I presented part of this work for their helpful comments. Thanks to Adrian Belton for his valuable linguistic support. Any errors remain entirely mine.

Finally, I am grateful to the following publishers for permission to reproduce already-published articles of mine: Cambridge University Press for the article 'The Organizational Properties of Money: Gustavo Del Vecchio's Theory', *Journal of the History of Economic Thought*, 34:2 (June 2012), pp. 243–60. Taylor and Francis for the article 'The Italian Contribution to Early Economic Dynamics', *European Journal of the History of Economic Thought*, 16:2 (June 2009), pp. 267–300. And Franco Angeli for the article 'Italian Economists and the Discourse on the Entrepreneur', in M. E. L. Guidi and D. Parisi (eds), *The Changing Firm. Contributions from the History of Economic Thought* (Milan: Angeli, 2005), pp. 305–19.

INTRODUCTION

Biographical Notes

The purpose of this short introductory chapter is to familiarize the reader with Gustavo Del Vecchio by furnishing some biographical details, offering some early notes on his views and briefly describing the cultural environment in which his thought matured. This is followed by a general outline of the book.

Gustavo Del Vecchio was born on 22 June 1883 to Cesare and Bice Cavalieri at Lugo di Romagna, a small town with an ancient Jewish community near Ravenna (Italy).[1] His uncle, Giulio Salvatore Del Vecchio, was an economist and statistician, but Gustavo seems not to have been influenced by him, and he never cited his work.[2] As a consequence of his father's murder in 1888, his family moved to Bologna, where Del Vecchio received his primary and secondary education. In 1900, Del Vecchio enrolled at the Faculty of Law, La Sapienza University of Rome, where he also attended courses on political economy and statistics. Moreover, he studied philosophy of history under Antonio Labriola, a philosopher, first Hegelian and then Marxian, whose influence explains Del Vecchio's youthful interests in Marx and historical materialism.[3] Indeed, although Del Vecchio was a true liberal economist, an interest in Marx's analyses can be detected in all his work.

Del Vecchio then returned to Bologna, where he continued his studies until he graduated in law in 1904. His degree thesis on monopoly was first commended and then published in 1905 with the title *Net Product and Monopoly* (*Prodotto netto e monopolio*). At Bologna, he was introduced to monetary themes by Tullio Martello, a disciple of Francesco Ferrara, who was known for his liberal and anti-socialist views.[4] After his graduation, Del Vecchio spent some time studying at the University of Berlin, where he wrote a passionate obituary of his master Antonio Labriola.

During the 1910s Del Vecchio wrote some of his most important articles, and notwithstanding his scientific commitments, he volunteered for military service in the First World War. In 1920, Del Vecchio was appointed professor of political economy at Trieste. Then, from 1926 to 1930, he was professor of economics and public finance at Bologna, and from 1930 to 1938 at Milan 'Bocconi', where he was rector from 1934 to 1938. His Jewish origins obliged him, after the adoption of racial laws by the Fascist regime, to resign his academic position in 1938. During the early 1940s, he voluntarily taught young Jews banned from schools in Turin.[5] Then, on Giovanni Demaria's advice, he took refuge in Switzerland, where he lived in a refugee camp from November 1943 to July 1945. Notwithstanding the harsh custodial conditions, his sister Celestina recounted that he gave lectures to the other inmates of the camp.

On his return to Italy, Del Vecchio regained his position at Bologna until 1948, when he became professor of public finance at La Sapienza, Rome, where he remained until his retirement in 1958.

Immediately after the Second World War, he was summoned as an expert by the Ministry for Reconstruction from June to December 1945, and he was then Minister of the Treasury from June 1947 to May 1948 in the fourth De Gasperi government, in which Luigi Einaudi served as Vice-Prime Minister and Minister of Finance. Del Vecchio was a close collaborator with Einaudi, and also his close friend. Management of public expenditure obliged Del Vecchio to deal with lobbyists, towards whom he showed a rigour typical of a 'technician', not of a politician. He preferred to leave the latter role to Einaudi. He did not leave writings about his political experience, except for a lecture included in a 1950s textbook where he stressed that the 'freedom of market solves many problems that no law can remedy'.[6] He opposed rules constraining economic and monetary trade, and he advocated liberalization of the price of gold or flexible exchange rates. When reporting to a parliamentarian survey committee on unemployment, he wrote that the factors responsible for rising unemployment included 'protectionism, the monopolistic positions of firms and workers' unions, and the inexorable expansion of bureaucracy'.[7] In May 1948, he was also appointed *ad interim* Minister for the Budget. From 1948 to 1950 he held the position of IMF Governor.

From 1925 to 1938 he was editor of *Giornale degli Economisti*, the most important Italian economic journal at the time, and sat on the editorial boards of various others, among them *Beiträge zur ökonomischen Theorie* and *Econometrica*. He was a member of numerous societies, including the Econometric Society and the Lincei Academy.

Del Vecchio died on 6 September 1972, in Rome.

Del Vecchio's Style

In order to identify Gustavo Del Vecchio with a school or a line of inquiry or with a specific approach to economics, rather than proceed with comparison between his thought and the main schools, it is advisable first to briefly describe his intellectual style. One of his contemporaries wrote: 'In the main, his attitude is somewhat eclectic but he very cleverly manages to combine elements from different doctrines into a new independent theory',[8] which is a perfect description of Del Vecchio's style. Classical, neoclassical, historicist and evolutionary economists, all offered important insights that Del Vecchio gradually incorporated into his view and theory. Certainly, he was a liberal economist, he believed in the virtues of the market and opposed state intervention when it meant restrictions on the freedom of trade; but his rejection of any dogma eventually brought him to the belief that the economy is not governed by natural laws.

Del Vecchio was too far from individualistic or egoistic principles to adhere to individualism as the main basis of economic investigation. He was a subjectivist, but he rejected maximization as the general method of interpreting economic behaviour. Maximization was typical of static analysis, but, as we shall see, he persistently looked for a dynamic perspective.

Put briefly, Del Vecchio had an *evolutionary* vision of the market, meaning that he envisaged a continuously changing, not necessarily growing, economy. On this view, he gradually developed a scientific approach that can be defined as one of 'economic becoming', and in which the most significant economic variables underwent constant transformation. Since monetary variables were no exception, they were presented as immersed in the flow of time that inevitably conditions, if not transforms, the analysis itself.

This evolutionary dimension obliged the analyst to abandon an individualistic reading of the economic agent and to approach the latter from a relational perspective. As explained in Chapter 1, economic relationships are a crucial object of economic science. Absolute values inevitably become relative ones, and as economic relationships evolve through time, they replace maximizing practice as the fulcrum of economic analysis.

This view grounded on relationships was replete with theoretical consequences. The economic world resulting from this approach was imbued with uncertainty and lacked any point of anchorage. Del Vecchio called everything into question. There was no certain fact. All was in constant change. He superseded the reassuring neoclassical dogma with an approach in a world of uncertainty where the economic sphere blends with the non-economic ones, and economic boundaries constantly re-draw themselves.[9]

At this point, we can correctly define money as nothing but a relationship. Better, money is an institution devised by society to make economic relationships among individuals more effective and less uncertain. There is nothing new in this view, even if uncertainty is a constant feature of Del Vecchio's treatment in its entirety and not just of his monetary theory.

Finally, on considering insights as relationships instead of absolute values, and time and uncertainty instead of static representation, one understands why

Del Vecchio, from his very early writings onwards, emphasized the role of organization, or better of self-organization. Lastly, variables like money become tools for the market's self-organization. This explains the title of this book, *Money as Organization*: by allowing the coordination of economic actions,[10] money enables the economy to improve its level of organization. Clearly, as we shall see, this entails re-consideration of the value of money, and its analysis through stressing its functional meanings.

The Theoretical Environment

As already mentioned, Del Vecchio combined theories of diverse provenance. His references to the writings of David Ricardo were constant. Nevertheless, he considered William S. Jevons's work to be a cornerstone for the evolution of economic thought in its entirety. If, on the one hand, he assumed English liberal thought as a guide for his reflections, on the other he cited Carl Menger as a pivotal reference in the building of his subjective approach. It is not by chance that Del Vecchio has frequently been associated with the Austrian School. And, finally, one cannot ignore the role played by the German economic literature in his scientific training.

Accordingly, the correct way to construe Del Vecchio's thought is to view him as an economist who drew largely on all economic schools, but who also grew within a particular cultural tradition, that of Italy. Although the Italian economic culture did not produce a well-defined economic school, it comprised the excellent works by Ferdinando Galiani, Antonio Genovesi, Pietro Verri and many others in the mid-eighteenth century, the unprecedented analysis by the liberal Francesco Ferrara in the mid-nineteenth century, and then Vilfredo Pareto's and Maffeo Pantaleoni's master works between the late nineteenth and early twentieth centuries. And besides these giants, there were the empirical and statistical approaches that left their imprints on Del Vecchio's work in its entirety.

Del Vecchio has been cited as one of Léon Walras's early followers, at least in regard to monetary topics. This point will be developed below, but we may anticipate that the comparison with Walras is not the best perspective from which to understand the theory investigated here. Del Vecchio drew specific methodological and analytical components from English liberal thought, the Austrian school and German historicism, among others, and mixed them with features typical of his cultural tradition.

To clarify the use made by Del Vecchio of the main economic schools, it is useful to consider two or three categories, cultural more than economic, that provide a 'snapshot' of the scientific environment in which Del Vecchio's thought matured. The aim is not to survey Italian economic culture in the late nineteenth and early twentieth centuries, but rather to provide some 'domestic guidelines' with which to understand why Del Vecchio developed his 'eclectic' approach. A concept which usefully introduces the Italian political economy of that time is the notion of *pluralism*: we may state that the then domestic economic culture was prone to pluralism and resistant to any scientific reductionism.[11] Particularly with regard to the early economic dynamic theories, so dear to Del Vecchio, the variety of views and proposals did not result from what can be termed the 'chaos of pluralism'[12] accompanying every scientific innovation; it was instead the natural response to the appearance of new research areas focused on *economic change*.[13]

The early years of the twentieth century were marked by a strong interest in statistics,[14] as demonstrated by the technical innovations produced by Italian economists.[15] However, those economists-statisticians – Rodolfo Benini, Corrado Gini, Costantino Bresciani-Turroni, among others – did not provide technical constructs alone. They contributed to the debate on the 'view' and the method best suited to economics, and specifically to early economic dynamics. Del Vecchio himself credited Benini with having shaped an 'economic sociology with a statistical basis',[16] and wrote that Benini had defined 'inductive political economy',[17] by which he meant that the new research area made use of multiple regressions and statistical tools to provide an economic view of a *complex agent*. This 'complex agent' was not 'the abstract and extreme one depicted by deductive economics', but rather the 'continuously changing man who had a religious, political, and ethical characterization besides the economic one'.[18] Furthermore, the scientific basis for analysis of complex agents was assured by the fact that those agents could be traced back to 'types'. According to Benini's political economy, the law of demand could not be indifferently applied to peoples at different levels of development.

'Statisticians must be qualified calculating scholars as well as careful observers':[19] this was the idea shared by many other statisticians-economists of the time, among them Bresciani-Turroni; and it was taken as the guide for striking the 'exact balance between statistical research and theoretical thought'.[20] Del Vecchio belonged to this tradition of scholars, whose 'examination of facts to identify causes, interdependences, effects, and not to provide pure description, was never distorted by doctrinal preconceptions but nonetheless anchored to theoretical bases'.[21]

The balance between *statistics* and *economics* found its expression in analysis of the business cycle. According to Benini, Camillo Supino Bresciani-Turroni, Del Vecchio, Giovanni Demaria and Marco Fanno, the business cycle was not caused by a single economic variable; rather, it was the outcome of the interaction among many 'small' oscillations, each of which could be traced back to a specific economic or non-economic cause. 'Causal realism', 'empirical connections', 'synthetic links among real world events' became crucial topics in the Italian debate on the method suitable for analysing economic change.[22] It thus yielded theoretical proposals grounded on composite complementarities among research methods. Del Vecchio's inductive-deductive-inductive sequence is a representative example.

We may conclude these notes by saying that an Italian way to deal with '*scientific realism*' came to the fore. It was epitomized by Bresciani-Turroni's endeavour to strengthen theoretical analysis with accurate statistical inquiry in order to reconstruct all the links among effects and possible causes, while avoiding any reductionism that might obfuscate the variety of factors influencing economic change. This realism was also apparent in Del Vecchio's thought. It may have been less anchored to statistical and empirical research, and it may have been more *scientific* according to the weight that Del Vecchio gave to pure research and experimental inquiry.[23]

These preliminary notes must perforce consider the role played in Italian economic culture by two masters of economic theory: Vilfredo Pareto and Maffeo Pantaleoni. Thus far, we have depicted an economic atmosphere that valued statistics, facts and realism – that is, methods and tools which were far from the pure economics of Pareto and Pantaleoni. Certainly Pareto and Pantaleoni were among the best known Italian economists and, as we shall see, they exerted a crucial influence on Del Vecchio. But, they weighed more on Del Vecchio and other Italian economists for their proposals distant from pure economics. In regard to Pareto, the Paretians themselves were attracted more by the wealth distribution law than those of pure economics. Moreover, Pareto's late sociological work exerted large influence also on economists.[24] Analogously, Pantaleoni's pure principles of economics were undisputed, but his followers, including Del Vecchio, wrote mostly on his economic dynamics, that is, on the less neoclassical Pantaleoni. We may say that the then Italian economic culture absorbed from Pareto and Pantaleoni the features judged more consistent with the existing flow of ideas, rather than being oriented and conditioned by them.

Del Vecchio's Book

Between 1909 and 1917, Gustavo Del Vecchio wrote a 'virtual' book in which he expounded his ideas on monetary circulation. The book was virtual because Del Vecchio disseminated his views through a conspicuous number of articles, some of which, in 1932, were collected into a book entitled *Researches in the General Theory of Money* (*Ricerche sopra la teoria generale della moneta*). However, the virtual book, and not the concrete one, is our concern here, because the intention is to investigate the contents of those articles in order to extract Del Vecchio's essential monetary theory, and then locate it historically and comparatively. During his subsequent long career, Del Vecchio integrated, supplemented and reviewed the contents of those articles, but he never disavowed nor substantially improved them. On the contrary, they were re-published in their original versions.

The aim of this book is to re-evaluate critically Del Vecchio's contribution to monetary theory, and to make it known outside his country, also considering that very little of his work has been translated into other languages. The history of monetary theories can only be enriched by wider knowledge of this author, whose main work made its appearance between those of two giants – Léon Walras on the one hand, John M. Keynes on the other – and who was a contemporary of other great thinkers, such as Knut Wicksell, Friedrich von Wieser, Irving Fisher, Ludwig von Mises and Ralph G. Hawtrey, to name only a few.

The virtual book can be given concrete form by citing the articles of which it is composed.[25] A list of articles in chronological order follows, including the publications strictly focused on monetary topics and those concerning kindred subjects:

'Principles of the Economic Theory of Money' ('Principii della teoria economica della moneta') (1909)
'Theory of Capital Exportation' ('Teoria della esportazione del capitale') (1910)
'Disposable Capital and its Circulation' ('Il capitale disponibile e la circolazione del capitale') (1911)
'The Gold Premium' ('Il premio sull'oro') (1911)
'The Economic Theory of Credit' ('La teoria economica del credito') (1913)
'The Periodic Changes of the Discount Rate' ('Le variazioni periodiche dello sconto') (1913)
'Statistical Inductions for the Theory of Circulation' ('Induzioni statistiche per la teoria della circolazione') (1913)
'The Theory of the Discount Rate' ('Teoria dello sconto') (1914)
'Contributions to the Doctrines of Circulation' ('Contributi alle dottrine della cricolazione') (1914)
'On the Economic Theory of Crises' ('Sulla teoria economica delle crisi') (1914)
'General Outlines of the Interest Theory' ('Lineamenti generali della teoria dell'interesse') (1915)
'Crucial Issues on the Value of Money' ('Questioni fondamentali sul valore della moneta') (1917).

I also include a 1925 article which adds significantly to the previous set of essays: 'A Chapter of Monetary Theory' ('Un capitolo di teoria monetaria') (1925) and a 1928 short article in German on entrepreneurial risk, 'Untersuchungen sur Theorie des Unternehmergewinnes' ('Investigations on the Theory of Entrepreneurial Profit'). To be mentioned is that Joseph A. Schumpeter, who cited Del Vecchio in his *History of Economic Analysis*, pressed for the publication of a compendium of his monetary articles in German, a book that appeared in 1930.[26]

It has been necessary to disassemble and then reassemble Del Vecchio's theory of money and circulation in order to pick out the *fil rouge* leading through his general approach to money and circulation. To bring his original view on these topics into focus, one must enter a maze of implied meanings, cryptic sentences and hinted-at developments, which are finally laid out as displayed in the following chapters. But, can Del Vecchio's monetary theory be summarized in a few key words? Relationships, groups, credit, money effectiveness, price expectations, interest, uncertainty and finally organization: these certainly are key concepts animating his theory of monetary circulation.

Chapter Overview

Chapter 1 provides an overview of how Del Vecchio developed his interest in political economy. It would be rash to speak of a 'method' because Del Vecchio largely ignored the methodological aspects of his inquiries, even though his writings were full of methodological implications, from the relationship between theory and history to the role attributed to dynamics. Precisely because he did not strictly adhere to a specific economic school, his method played a crucial role in defining his personal theoretical research.

Chapter 2 introduces monetary topics, starting with Del Vecchio's subjective views on utility and value of money that steered his analysis, and finally induced him to anchor individual decisions in expected prices. Here, crucial relationships make their appearance: first of all, that between current value and expected ones; but also that between the individual and social dimension, and the subjective and objective perspective, as testified by the connection between subjective and social value of money.

Chapter 3 reconstructs Del Vecchio's aggregate view on the demand for money. Some of the most original features of his monetary theory are developed here, beginning from the idea of the 'selling group' drawn from Richard Cantillon. Other categories considered by Del Vecchio are those of monetary effectiveness and distribution of money. Certainly, what emerges is a distinctly imaginative approach to monetary circulation.

Chapter 4 explores another crucial aspect of Del Vecchio's theory: namely credit; and with credit, the banking system, whose role assumes specific importance derived from Del Vecchio's early acceptance of multiple issues of money. Credit is used as an instrument to stabilize the economy, weakening the relation between stock of money and prices.

Chapter 5 focuses on the other protagonist of this monetary story: the interest rate. Del Vecchio's concern was to give a psychological representation of this variable able to influence the other monetary variables, but not saving. To be mentioned in particular is the theory of accumulation, which Del Vecchio built by assigning a crucial role to behavioural variables besides monetary ones.

Finally, Chapter 6 sheds light on the last factor influencing Del Vecchio's interpretation of economic relationships: radical uncertainty. Not in disagreement with the then Italian theoretical debate on entrepreneurial errors, Del Vecchio argued that entrepreneurial choices are in the end surrounded by irreducible uncertainty.

1 MAKING ECONOMIC RELATIONSHIPS DYNAMIC

'Economics studies certain processes instead of making an inventory of wealth'.[1] This youthful statement says much about Del Vecchio's conception of the role that economics must play as a social science. Firstly, economics studies processes, conceived as a set of relationships among agents which changes or evolves over time. Hence economic change lies at the centre of this representation, as Del Vecchio himself had warned with his constant references to the need to include a dynamic perspective in economic analysis. Time is an obligatory dimension of economics, and Del Vecchio's time was irreversible, not mechanical, time. This view can be condensed by labelling it 'economic becoming', where the focus is on the flows instead of stocks. Then, given his interest in general economic equilibrium, Del Vecchio immediately dealt with the difficulty of producing a general scheme which included time. To be noted is that Walras's general equilibrium, with which Del Vecchio's theoretical proposal was connected, was timeless.

But time is not only the legacy of the past. Time implies a forward-looking perspective that calls forecasts and expectations into question. Therefore, subjective choices become crucial for the working of the entire economic system, especially because choices are taken with uncertainty. Moreover, the fact that Del Vecchio depicted the economic capitalism of the time as intrinsically unstable can be read as a consequence of such uncertainty.

However, differently from subsequent views, uncertainty was not explained by monetary variables. On the contrary, money plays a crucial role in the working of the economic system. In 1954, Del Vecchio wrote: 'When economic analysis ignores monetary phenomenon, we do not have economic science'.[2] Money was obviously associated with the circulation of goods, but money was also 'other', in the sense that it played a specific role in this evolving process, which was a process of organization, if not self-organization. Hence process, relationships, time, money, uncertainty and expectations are the prime ingredients of the complex theoretical artefact called 'economic becoming', much more than equilibrium, stability, veil or optimization: a set of ingredients destined to be gradually enriched.

The next section presents Del Vecchio's methodological inquiry starting from a long-standing issue: the relationship between theory and history. The following two sections take the reader into the dynamic world that informs all the analysis considered here. First the concepts of 'economic change' and 'economic dynamics' are treated. Then 'economic relationships', a peculiarity of Del Vecchio's approach, are examined, to conclude by combining dynamism and relationships in the last section, which seeks to give an organic interpretation of the overall method.

Theory and History

Gustavo Del Vecchio was extremely careful to relate theory to economic reality, but he never clarified or investigated the epistemological implications of his nevertheless original analysis. He did not devote a paper to economic method.

Del Vecchio conceived economics as a *unified* science. It is a 'constant, continuous and evolutionary work', which can be compared to a 'multi-level building' where each further level must be 'solid and harmonious' with 'the existing ones'.[3] On recognizing that David Ricardo established the 'general principles' on which abstract reasoning can be grounded,[4] one may maintain, on the one hand, that Friedrich von Hermann tried to make the Ricardian scheme more 'flexible' by introducing first the 'decomposition' of the classical concept of profit into its elements and then subjective features;[5] and, on the other, that Del Vecchio recognized the need to make Ricardian economics more 'unified'. In other words, he maintained that Ricardian economics should still be regarded as the source of pure economic theory in its entirety, including both production and distribution analyses. Consequently, the only way to improve economic theory is to build on previous results, bearing in mind that theoretical effectiveness does not lie in a stronger connection between theory and facts: theory does not describe facts, theory means thought experiments about economic reality. Afterwards Del Vecchio wrote: 'Economic theory is an empirical-experimental theory, not a historical-political or ethical-political doctrine',[6] meaning that the linking theme of his reasoning was the evolution of economic theories, which he treated as thought experiments (*esperimenti ideali*),[7] and as such all worthy of interest. Although mental, the idea of experiment is crucial in Del Vecchio's thought. 'By experimenting, thought stops being a presupposition or a paradigmatic anticipation of things; rather, it becomes concrete, because it grows with things'[8] – not Del Vecchio's own writing, but his Marxist mentor's, Antonio Labriola, to whom Del Vecchio owed his conception of history.

It is essential to remember that Del Vecchio recommended the use of different analytical instruments, according to whether the concern was theoretical or historical. This does not conflict with the concept of complementarity between the two domains, i.e. theory and history, since the need to develop two or more kinds of analyses strengthens, rather than undermines, the 'unitariness' of economic science. This complementarity between theoretical and historical features made Del Vecchio's analysis very close to a theory of capitalist economy, where history is based on a scientific idea of economics.[9] His theories on capitalist accumulation and economic crisis offer good examples of this approach. Let us consider the former.

Del Vecchio inferred the basic nature of accumulation from savings and even more from individual initiatives. He showed that savings, with the exception of life-pensions, 'escape' any economic criterion. This is because the bulk of savings, which are fundamental for economic life, are decided independently from hedonistic calculus and, therefore, regardless of changes in the interest rate.[10] In fact, the supply of savings is decided by extra-economic factors such as the dynamism of social classes, the economic business trend, political revolutions, monetary changes and technical innovations.

Accumulation also depends on the behaviour of firms or, in other words, on the demand for capital. According to Del Vecchio, the main task is to show the linkage between growth of a firm's capital and the lengthening of the production process. He argued that a change of capital involves not only its measurement in monetary terms but also evaluation of changes relative to aspects such as marginal productivity; the expected value of money; the certainty of investments; the demand for and supply of credit. It is evident that Del Vecchio did not restrict his capital theory to exclusively economic factors. According to the above statements, the resulting theory of capital is therefore a dynamic one, but it must be made clear that theory was always kept separate from history.

Del Vecchio constantly developed his theory on accumulation, which, although it was never the topic of a specific work, represented a constant in his thought. Accumulation is intrinsically dynamic, so that it can be related to other dynamic features. This compelled Del Vecchio to put forward dynamic and extra-economic interpretations of traditionally static theories such as those on money and credit. On the presumption that many answers to economic questions lie beyond economics itself, Del Vecchio fully investigated the disciplinary 'borders' of economics. Therefore, heterogeneous and changing relationships represent the core of his economic dynamics. He wrote that by conducting such inquiry we leave the field of economic theory and enter historical synthesis.[11]

On introducing the notion of capitalism, Del Vecchio referred it to early historicism and to development through 'stages' as conceived by Bruno Hildebrand, Wilhelm Roscher and, above all, Karl Bücher.[12] However, because Del Vecchio believed that capitalism reflects a historical period, he raised it to the status of a 'category' or 'ideal type' or 'economic style' in the sense proposed by Arthur Spiethoff.[13] Indeed, the notion of capitalism reflected the idea of economic progress as a movement onto which second-order phenomena, i.e. economic crises, are grafted. Del Vecchio's treatment of economic crises provides another good example of what he meant by a matching between theory and history.

Economies were certainly changing, and economic theory could not ignore those changes. Accordingly, Del Vecchio studied the disciplinary 'frontiers' of economics by focusing on 'residual aspects', and distinguishing them from the 'pure' theory of economic facts. In his opinion, this was the only way to maintain adherence to the economic reality. But it was also the only way to build a 'pure' economic theory though anchored to economic reality.

Del Vecchio's accumulation and crises theories show that he did not subordinate theory to history or, in Edgar Salin's words, rationality to intuition (*anschauliche*).[14] Therefore, his theory was not linked to temporal, spatial, national aspects, as Karl Knies stressed.[15] Del Vecchio treated crises as dynamic phenomena depending on a progressive movement called capitalism. In other words, capitalism was depicted as an 'economic style' *à la* Spiethoff,[16] and crises were symptomatic of this inexorable movement. From this viewpoint, crisis, and not capitalism, is the historical 'fact' which requires theoretical as well as historical methodologies.

The 'political economy of crisis' defines the area of scientific investigation devoted to explaining the different movements of capitalism, of which crises are the inevitable expressions: 'Economic progress and economic crises are both phenomena too important and characteristic of the modern economy to think that they are randomly correspondent'.[17] While nothing could be said about the cycle's influences on long-term trends, it was incontrovertible that crises act on economic progress to provoke a periodic re-organization of the market, including the elimination of non-competitive firms. Therefore, not only are economic crises phenomena deriving from a dynamic and progressive economy[18] characterized by wide fluctuations determined by technology, population, institutions; they are also a necessary component of economic progress because they eliminate those 'pathological phenomena' that intensify during the expanding cycle.[19] Crises are not mere consequences of economic progress; rather, they are its components.

Del Vecchio's insistence on the need for a 'political economy' of crises, instead of a simple theory, is typical of his entire theoretical *modus*. Crises are historical facts characterizing capitalist reality that other economic theories cannot ignore. The five 'research orders' therefore represent the method with which to obtain complementarities between theory and history. At that point, theory must be linked to history, maintaining its nature as a thought experiment, its 'pureness'. The area in which 'pure theory' matches history, in the sense that we can find both the analyses, is that of 'economic change'.

Economic Change

The social dimension, dynamism and effectiveness are original features of Del Vecchio's monetary theory, and their inclusion in that analysis can only be fully understood by considering the theoretical climate in which Del Vecchio's theory took shape. At the end of the nineteenth century and the beginning of the twentieth, Italian political economy was dominated by the conflict between, on the one hand, pure individualistic theory and, on the other, evolutionary and historical approaches. In that theoretical conflict, the young Del Vecchio immediately joined the supporters of pure theory, whose main representative was Francesco Ferrara.[20] But that debate between individualism and evolutionary and historical views intensified the search for new areas of inquiry.

Essential for understanding Del Vecchio's thought is the concept of *economic dynamics*, which was a topic particularly dear to the then community of Italian economists who shaped new paths for economic dynamics by basing them mainly on four different methods: evolutionary, mathematical, statistical and historical.[21] These approaches were more interested in a theory of economic change than in economic dynamics strictly speaking, and they had an analytical criterion in common: time movements should be studied by stating the invariance/change relation. Each theory, whatever its disciplinary affiliation, attempted to combine an invariant element with some change.

This was an early attempt to unravel the alternative between a description without theory and a theory uncoupled from any concrete transformation: that is to say, an economic dynamics as an account of facts and a static economics without any contacts with reality. Synthesizing, the early researchers on economic dynamics moved in the following directions: the abstract analysis that, because of its derivation from mechanics, shed light more on invariance than change; and the descriptive method, which was commonplace among those authors adopting positivist, organic and historical perspectives. The latter, grounded on an initial analogy with biology, adopted evolutionary, finalistic or teleological schemes.

The biological metaphor was commonly cited in the early economic texts on dynamics. This was because it introduced a notion of 'oriented' and 'irreversible' time that, contrary to the mechanical metaphor, was suited to the purpose of representing economic phenomena in their 'becoming'.[22] Evident here is the teaching of Labriola: 'In economics ... time is the measure of the process of production and circulation'.[23]

Discontinuities are virtually ruled out from any global or macro representation when economic systems are posited as changing at a regular rate. Therefore, one of the early ways to deal with economic dynamics was precisely that of considering the evolution of dynamic systems. But individual dynamics were not excluded. While the biological metaphor focused on social bodies, evolutionary economists extended it to individuals. Put briefly, both individuals and groups were included in these early attempts to define the new research area. Finally, this mix of particular and more global approaches found synthesis in what was called the *moving equilibrium*,[24] a view on equilibrium in time common to the marginalist and evolutionary economists of the time.

In Italy, the 'marginalist shift' imposed by Maffeo Pantaleoni in 1890 on the then main Italian economic journal, *Il Giornale degli Economisti*, was bound to marginalize organic and evolutionary views. The latter regained ground in the new research area – economic dynamics – thus maintaining a certain visibility in the economic journals of the time. In addition, it gradually became clear that organicism was not necessarily opposed to Newtonism, with which it shared the focus on the *how* of *changes* instead of the *why*. In effect, Auguste Comte, the both positivist and organicist sociologist, drew the concept of dynamics from Newtonian equilibria.

Del Vecchio mixed three of the above approaches – evolutionary, statistical and historical – maintaining in his thought the rule that 'science is a collective undertaking, and to do science means considering all that came in the past'.[25] He posited that the 'pure' and 'static' Ricardo theory was the 'invariant' part of a discourse that was bound to be enriched by many contributions, which included also what Ricardo did not contemplate, such as subjective methods and historical issues. Del Vecchio was persuaded that if a discontinuity can be discovered in the history of economics, it was neither the marginalist revolution nor that of subjectivism, but rather the emergence of economic dynamics in the early twentieth century.

Consistent with this view, Del Vecchio considered the *Methodenstreit* debate, which opposed deductivists to historicists, as a nonexistent problem:

> In regard to the contrast between deductivism and historicism, we can recognize that economics studies a *fact* that is a historical fact and that the *tool* used for studying it is a *theory* worked out according to the nature of the object.[26]

Del Vecchio discerned in the intersection between historicism and deductivism or pure theory the seeds of the new research area – economic dynamics – whose methodological and theoretical improvement was also required by the continuously changing reality of that time. Therefore, Del Vecchio not surprisingly conceived dynamics as a theory of economic change in which facts and theory are interwoven and not separate, as claimed in the debate on *Methodenstreit*. This view found perfect synthesis in a postulate distinctive of Del Vecchio's and many other theories: dynamic theory should be based on both *invariance* and *change*.

Leaving aside the origins of the invariance/change relation, which reached back to ancient Greek philosophy, it can be noted here that Karl Marx's dialectics between 'law of motion' and 'historical fate' was a version of the invariance/change relation. This assonance with Marx, which persisted thereafter, was due to the Marxist philosopher Antonio Labriola, who had taught the young Del Vecchio. Moreover, Del Vecchio showed here a feature that would signify his scholarly approach: he was a man of synthesis between contrasting polarities. According to Achille Loria, another influential Marxist Italian economist at that time, science (and hence economics) always investigates the invariant principle beneath any change of value and income.[27] Ricardo and John Stuart Mill did likewise by seeking the laws explaining the change of productivity. A different question was whether such an invariance had either a *historical* or a *natural* origin. Marx posited historical invariants, Ricardo natural ones. In this case, the Ricardian Del Vecchio was close to Marx.

Economic Dynamics

It is no accident that Del Vecchio was called the 'Italian Schumpeter':[28] that is, the Italian economist most interested in the study of economic dynamism or, better, of economic becoming. A glance at the main themes developed by Del Vecchio – such as money, crisis, credit and international trade – shows that his static analysis of any economic feature was not only complemented by, but gradually almost substituted with, a dynamic reading of it.

Three sources induced the young Del Vecchio to give central importance to economic dynamics. The first has been considered above: the dialectic between equilibrium and change. In this section we shall deal with the remaining two: Vilfredo Pareto's disputed proposal on general equilibrium; and, finally, the teaching of Maffeo Pantaleoni, a Marshallian economist who contributed to enlarging Del Vecchio's scientific interests to include the changeability of parameters and disequilibrium. Here we shall consider first Pareto and then Pantaleoni.

When defined on a mathematical basis, the above-evoked notion of a *moving equilibrium* intertwining *equilibrium* and *change* had a more theoretical content and, perhaps, provided more elements with which to build dynamics. According to Walras:

> In order to [pass from the static to the dynamic point of view] we need only suppose the data of the problem, viz. the quantities possessed, the utility or want curves, etc., to vary as a function of *time*. The *fixed* equilibrium will be then transformed into a *variable* or *moving* equilibrium, which re-establishes itself automatically as soon as it is disturbed.[29]

This means that Walras presupposed an intra-period dynamics confined to a single adjustment after a change of data. *Tâtonnement* is the process which intervenes to restore equilibrium after a shock, but it does not connect one adjustment to the subsequent one. Del Vecchio had all the tools with which to develop dynamics and a moving equilibrium along Walrasian lines. Moreover, although he has often been depicted as a follower of Walras as regards monetary topics, he chose not to develop dynamics or to investigate economic change within the framework of equilibrium theory.

Similarly, Del Vecchio praised Vilfredo Pareto's intelligence without becoming a Paretian. It is well known that Pareto enriched his works with analogies between mechanical and social phenomena. In the *Cours*,[30] as well as in the *Manual*,[31] Pareto conceived economic dynamics as both *successive equilibria*, which can be studied by comparative statics, and *continuous equilibria*, that is, 'movements of dynamic phenomenon' whose investigation requires analytical instruments based on classical mechanics.[32] Yet, contrary to the prevailing opinion on Pareto, these two are not the only meanings of economic dynamics that he accepted, given that in the part of his work entitled *applied economics* he introduced a third approach to specific dynamic phenomena: the *economic crisis*. All three concepts ought to be considered, not only for the sake of completeness but also in order to understand their subsequent developments by Italian scholars. Here, the third, and least known, approach to economic dynamics matters because the theory of economic crisis was at the centre of Del Vecchio's interests.

Although Pareto was aware of the methodological difficulties in achieving pure economic dynamics, he felt free to develop a dynamics devoid of formal and mathematical constrictions. He named this research area the *theory of crisis*. This theory represented a topic of 'economic dynamics study'[33] pertaining to *applied economics*, i.e. to a branch of economics that Pareto regarded as logically less rigorous than pure economics but closer to actual human behaviour. In the absence of a mathematically consistent dynamic analysis, Pareto judged the theory of crisis, first proposed in the *Cours* and then reproduced in the *Manual*, as the sole 'fully dynamic' theory at that time.[34] This judgement probably explains why the theory of crisis gained such a large following among Italian scholars in the first decades of the century, and thwarted the growth of a sound cycle theory.[35] With this theory Pareto gave a psychological interpretation to crises and thus to the dynamics of such events.[36]

Walras and Pareto both acknowledged that the economic environment, the exogenous 'datum' of the system, could change, but they did not delve deeper into this aspect, except when Pareto explored crisis analysis. Maffeo Pantaleoni, on the other hand, included disequilibrium among the dynamic phenomena to be investigated as outcomes of the economic system's reactions to an exogenous shock. Having established that systems, after a shock restores the initial equilibrium, move towards a new equilibrium, and finally do not converge towards equilibrium, he grouped the first two phenomena involving equilibrium into a single category called *dynamics of first type* (then developed by the dynamic equilibrium line of inquiry), while the phenomena leading to disequilibrium constituted the *dynamics of second type* (developed by scholars of the analogy between dynamics and history). The 'dynamics of first type' involve study of movements appearing in disequilibrium that give rise to an equilibrium position;[37] the 'dynamics of second type' include 'those [phenomena] which do not lead to any equilibrium position visible or foreseeable by us as an effect of those phenomena', so that their study concerns cases in which the economic system remains troubled for a period exceeding a logically acceptable time, or forever, as happens when the shock changes the social character of the system.[38]

The stability of the equilibrium marked the difference between the two categories, since the problem of restoring the initial equilibrium or a new one falls within the paradigm of stability, while the dynamics of disequilibrium lie outside that conceptual structure, being part of the paradigm of change. This dichotomy was corroborated by the two analogies used by Pantaleoni: the analogy with mechanics in his approach to economic continuous equilibrium, and the analogy with biology when he dealt with economic change. Arguing that both equilibrium/stability and disequilibrium/change fall within the domain of economic dynamics, Pantaleoni anchored dynamic analysis to the two pivots of any theory of society, namely stability and change.

When Pantaleoni referred back to Pareto for the dynamics of first type, he emphasized the 'intensity' and the 'length' of economic phenomena that, although not in equilibrium, converge on it, but he nevertheless postulated a logical notion of time. By contrast, a historical notion of time permeated the dynamics of second type. Accordingly, Pantaleoni postulated that the 'initial positions' of economic subjects may vary, for example the distribution of resources fluctuates as well as that of wages or economic opportunities. Since the 'initial positions' of the systems can be defined only if 'related to final goals', they are necessarily unfixed because the goals themselves change as a result of crises, upheavals and other dynamic phenomena. In other words, historical time entails that the 'position' of the economic system continuously changes because of the mutability of its goals.[39]

The main cause of such continuous changes is *competition*. Pantaleoni proposed a theory of social selection in which competition was the 'most active source of dynamism' explaining the movement from one social and economic position to another.[40] His arguments broke down the analytical equivalence between competition and stationary equilibrium by introducing the biological equivalences between competition and dynamism and between competition and selection. Competition is necessary because, by increasing social dynamism it produces a gain, but it also has a cost. The continuous change of the 'initial positions' also determines instability and social resistance, diminishing the net gain of competition: 'it is less than the gain calculated without acknowledging its cost',[41] and such a cost appears when the social aversion to change and the preference for a stationary social system become apparent. By rejecting 'economic dynamism' when it 'involves unknown goals', individuals distance themselves from being *homines œconomici* or 'enlightened egoists'.[42] Consequently, economic dynamism is the dialectic springing from impulses towards change and resistance favouring conservation, both ascribable to social and individual 'motives'. Economic dynamics should thus first study such impulses to movement as well as the individual and collective reactions that they bring about. The assonance between 'habits' and the 'resistance to change' must be emphasized: continuity with the past becomes the distinctive feature of dynamic analysis, according to either the mechanical or the biological analogy. But, as we shall see, Del Vecchio moved beyond this view by focusing on future facts alone.

In conclusion, by complementing Pareto's intuitions on economic dynamics, Pantaleoni shifted the focus to the social 'disequilibrium', or better 'non-equilibrium', associated with economic competition and long-term transformations, providing the basis for a research programme that was to be explored in various ways, even though an actual Pantaleonian school was never established.[43]

Although Pareto is mentioned for his contribution to the general economic equilibrium theory and Pantaleoni is often associated with his *Principles of Pure Economics* and the Marshallian view of partial equilibrium, these two acknowledged masters stimulated Del Vecchio to move in a new direction, and to investigate new areas of inquiry. His interest in economic dynamics was the first reason that moved Del Vecchio away from both the then emerging static approach to economic equilibrium and the historicism characterizing the economists opposed to adoption of mathematical and rigorous methods. Del Vecchio was attentive to history, but he never became an adherent of historicism. Both theory and history were necessary to investigate economic reality: one complemented the other, but history never substituted theory. Rather, here we discover the teaching of Antonio Labriola, the socialist philosopher, who wrote in 1897:

> The nature is in the *praxis*, that is, the historical evolution of man – and saying *praxis* we mean other than the trivial contraposition between practice and theory ... the historical man is always the social man, and the supposed pre-social man is the result of imagination.[44]

Therefore, Del Vecchio considered theories to be the source of logical answers to economic problems. Theories could be treated as thought experiments allowing a type of investigation that (including paradoxes) could be complemented with other more sociological or historical perspectives. Del Vecchio's works are pervaded by a tension due to awareness, on the one hand, of the bounded realism characterizing pure theory and, on the other, of the loss of analytical coherence caused by the presence of extra-economic factors. However, Del Vecchio deemed this tension unavoidable since both the approaches, pure and applied economics, theory and history, are indispensable when dealing with dynamic phenomena like capitalist accumulation.

Economic Relationships

A contemporary of Del Vecchio, Benjamin M. Anderson, wrote in 1917 that

> In general, it is *rights*, rather than *things*, which pass in economic exchange ... Rights, *in personam* or *in rem*, are objects of economic value, and the exchange of these rights makes up the bulk, if not the whole, of economic change.[45]

This quotation is perfectly consonant with what the young Del Vecchio had written in 1905: 'The relationships between certain economic motives and certain economic actions are the centre of gravity of economic science',[46] and later reaffirmed: 'There are not things, but economic relationships',[47] meaning that economic relationships constitute the true object of economic investigation. This view brought Del Vecchio back to Francesco Ferrara and his idea that there is 'nothing to study about wealth as such'.[48] Wealth immediately involves money. And, as we shall see, money itself is a relationship. In 1856, Ferrara had written:

> Nowadays, the topic of money is of second order, in the sense that, once one gets rid of technical and legal aspects, it seems grounded on a few simple principles ... However, a less explored area concerning money remains ... It pertains not to money itself, but to the relations among that tool and exchange rates, capital and the circulation of capital.[49]

Money matters not because gold or some other precious metal represents it, but because of the relations that money generates. The value of goods and things is a matter of relationships, without which it loses its meaning. Ferrara repeated that economics must concern itself with the study of certain relations, the appearance of certain forces, rather than with the definitions or characteristics of certain things. Again: 'The object of economic science is not the growing satisfaction of individuals and groups, but it is the reciprocal persistence or movement of individual position'.[50]

The idea of *relationship* as conceived by Del Vecchio should be clarified and contextualized in economics, but also in *time*: in effect, Del Vecchio focused on economic relationships in time: that is, on the *time coordination* of economic actions.[51] The starting-point is the reasoning that led Del Vecchio to replace the central importance of 'economic good' with that of 'economic relationship'. This process was set out in *Net Product and Monopoly* (*Prodotto netto e monopolio*) (1905)[52] and in 'Intangible Capital and Wealth' ('Ricchezze immateriali e capitali immateriali') (1908),[53] a long essay that Del Vecchio published at the beginning of the century. In 1937, he remarked that, according to a first view, 'economic relationships are relations among goods including services', as stated by static analysis. According to a second view, economic relationships involve psychological features and 'goods are indexes of both effort and pleasure'.[54] Economic relationships have always a subjective origin, the same origin that shapes value. Obviously, this raises the problem of translating relationships to an aggregate or macro level.

Del Vecchio drew the idea of *relationships* from the contemporary German-speaking economists. He reprised the concept as proposed by Friedrich von Hermann,[55] who was, if not the first, one of the earliest economists to point out the importance of relationships in economics. Von Hermann had worked out a theory of economic relationships based on four categories or groups. The first group included the main social or non-economic relationships; the second comprised relations that were goods according to their origin, but not their use, such as the goods furnished by the state without a price being paid for them. The third category contained all the relations involving a passage of wealth from one agent to another, such as credit and entitlements. The fourth group was very similar to the third one and included clientele, monopoly, patents, copyrights, and so on. Even in the last case, entitlements to things or persons counted.

Del Vecchio commented on von Hermann's scheme as follows:

> This distinction appears indeed important for an economic theory of relationships ... although the concept of a relation as a good seems to oscillate among the relationship, the position of agents, the activity explained, and the need that the relationship satisfies.[56]

Put briefly, these non-economic and economic goods generate relationships that condition the choices of any economic agent. Goods may involve 'ownership', 'debt', 'credit', 'entitlements', and so on. But, as we shall see, because relationships shape economic organization, Del Vecchio had a great interest in economic regimes, from pure competition to monopoly, which he considered to be systems of economic relationships – in his terminology, 'economic coefficients'. On the other hand, the idea of relationship allowed him to posit that competition and monopoly are not contrasting regimes; rather, there is continuity between them.[57]

Another author frequently mentioned by Del Vecchio when developing the idea that relationship is a key economic concept was Henry Dunning Macleod.[58] Del Vecchio emphasized Macleod's treatment of economics as the science of the laws governing the relationships among exchangeable quantities.[59] On this view, credit plays a crucial role by displaying a specific relation between two agents: debtor and creditor. This relationship represents a piece of wealth that must be kept separate from the rest, because it involves possession of future goods: according to Macleod, credit is capital. The concept is a subtle one because it implies that credit circulates independently from the wealth with which it is originally associated. This means that 'relationship' gains importance as an economic concept when circulation is treated as a process sharply distinguished from production and also consumption.

Del Vecchio agreed with Macleod because, as said above, he presented economics as a science of processes concerning wealth, and not as a science of the amount of wealth. However, Del Vecchio criticized Macleod's work on the grounds that the distinction between law and economics was lacking or too feeble; a distinction that must be preserved because relationships constitute a crucial concept for economics. Del Vecchio's remained an economic theory without being transformed into a law concerning economy or something similar.

This evocation of juridical causality, besides the economic one, recalls Eugen von Böhm-Bawerk's works on 'titles' (*Beziehungen*) and 'relationships' (*Verhältnisse*): that is, concepts involving a level of abstraction higher than that of material goods where relationships express relative quantities deriving from goods.[60] Del Vecchio was aware of Böhm-Bawerk's criticism[61] of those theories – including von Hermann's – that considered people's capabilities and skills to be economic goods. According to Böhm-Bawerk, only things of the external world and services of those things are goods, while people's attributes cannot be regarded as goods. Consequently, 'relationships' generated by people's qualities, such as human capital, would have no economic meaning. Del Vecchio entirely disagreed with Böhm-Bawerk's assertion.

Del Vecchio also acknowledged that Carl Menger had conducted in his *Grundsätze* a very careful analysis of *quasi*-non-economic goods, i.e. public free goods and individual relationships.[62] He pointed out that the Austrian economist, as well as treating the meaning of the concept of *clientele*, had hinted at a new notion of goods corresponding to copyright and to patent right. Del Vecchio kept these notions in mind when he dealt with the problem of ideas as economic goods.[63]

If economic goods shape economic relationships, the economy can be represented as a set of economic relationships involving individuals and collective agents. A certain number of these relationships contribute to determining each economic fact. Of course, not all relationships are intrinsically economic, only those concerning economic goods or economic choices. Del Vecchio included features such as absolute quantities and the qualities of individual and material production inputs; relationships among quantities of production inputs; the distribution of assets; knowledge about the environment and the effect of people's actions on it; relationships between persons; time as a general factor influencing the whole; and other factors, including economic organization. Finally, also tastes are sorts of relationships between an individual and a good or a service. In short, 'relationships' involve all the factors causing economic facts, both economic and extra-economic, and they represent quantitative and qualitative features that theories assume but do not examine.

Focusing on the economic conception of 'relationship' that Del Vecchio first developed in 1908, when he was twenty-five years old, it follows that commodities and goods are meaningful from an economic viewpoint according to the relationships that individuals have with them. Del Vecchio wrote:

> *a*) nothing is a good from a social viewpoint if it is also a good from a personal one; *b*) a good useful for an individual is also useful for society unless that good is damaging to someone else; *c*) a good cannot be economic from a social viewpoint without being a good from an individual viewpoint as well; *d*) finally an individual economic good could be an economic or non-economic good or also a non-good from a social perspective.[64]

From the relationship standpoint, economics cannot involve anything but a subjective viewpoint where the subject is not *homo oeconomicus* but a historicized individual living in an economy governed by rules. Relationships may change with time, places, cultures, tastes, and they are conditioned by technological, legal and political changes. Whilst wealth has a strictly objective nature, the relationships concerning it unavoidably comprise a subjective dimension deriving from the agent(s) involved. Hence, if we assume a micro or structural perspective, which is the one concerning relationships, the subjective dimension appears.

With the perspective on relationships now clarified, a distinction must be drawn between relationships as economic goods (which can be actual and future) and relationships which are not goods. The following can be considered economic goods: ideas; legal relationships assigning exclusive title to some commodity; the existing or future commodities on which such titles weigh; and legal relationships assigning exclusive title to existing or future services. However, individual qualities cannot be considered economic relationships. Differently, the credit relationship is treated as an economic good because credit is caused by economic factors and has economic consequences.[65]

The focus on relationships was not short-lived. In 1937, he would write that economic theory oscillates between three concepts of economic analysis all concerning relationships:

> One can consider economic relationships as relationships among goods, including individual services. This economic tradition is close to statistical economics and has its main representatives in the physiocrats, Ricardo, Cournot and von Thünen. On the other, less physical side, relationships concern psychological features, and physical goods are expressed as indexes of fundamental psychological relationships, that is, effort and pleasure. This is the original field of pure economics (Ferrara, Gossen, Jevons, Menger), which appears to contrast with classical economics and more mathematical economics (Walras, Pareto and, in certain respects, also Marshall and Fisher).[66]

Finally, economic relationships necessitate a pure theory of capital (Marx?)[67] and money. Del Vecchio's economic theory oscillates between the psychological traditions and the capital/monetary one.

On attempting to give a definitive interpretation to Del Vecchio's focus on relationships – all is relative – we may say that it was his device to keep objectivism and subjectivism together. This was a legacy from his master Maffeo Pantaleoni, but re-interpreted in accordance with Del Vecchio's style. Facts are objective, but they are always filtered through human perception. There are economic variables – goods – aside from economic agents, but they lose their nature as goods if ignored by individuals.

Relationships from an Aggregate View: Economic Coefficients

As long as Del Vecchio adhered to the idea of subjective relationships he treated psychology and law as areas helping to shape that idea. In effect, relationships occur between individuals. But inasmuch as economic relationships assume a social or aggregate dimension, he moved towards an 'engineering-based view moulding economic coefficients'.[68] *Coefficients* are parameters expressing relationships at aggregate level: that is, these parameters quantify the relationship under analysis.

> Relationship is a coefficient concerning the production of goods or services and it could also be a good by virtue of the fact that for each individual what counts is the position in a relationship; for the society as a whole, the relationships itself is an economic coefficient.[69]

Examples include the competitive market, which can be construed as an economic coefficient according to the *level* of competition.

Here, 'objective dimension' means 'social dimension': that is, these relationships are considered not from an individual viewpoint but a social one. Each relationship acts as the *cause* of a specific economic fact. Del Vecchio termed these causes determining economic facts *economic coefficients* (*coefficienti economici*). Examples of economic coefficients include the available production factors; the distribution of wealth; the type of economic organization, more or less competitive; tastes of a society. These aspects are visible only when considering the economy as a whole or a system, and for individuals they are only 'givens' (*dati*). For this reason, Del Vecchio wrote that the economic coefficients explaining specific facts are economic relationships considered all together.[70] Consequently, from an individual viewpoint, only relationships matter. From a social perspective, economic relationships become economic coefficients.

Better understanding of Del Vecchio's original perspective can be gained by recalling that he considered state and bureaucratic apparatuses to be social relationships contributing to the economy's development, i.e., they are just 'economic coefficients'. This means that the institutions are factors able to exert strong influence on economic activities, rather than being economic goods in themselves.[71] From this perspective, public services are intangible goods, as Carl Dietzel stressed in 1855 when he sought to reconcile economic categories with legal and social ones.[72]

Among the objective 'economic coefficients' explaining facts Del Vecchio included *economic organization*, which explains his interest in the organization of markets and enterprises, and in social competition. The set of economic coefficients expressing relationships are indicative of the organization of a given economic system. In 1933 Frank Knight gave a definition of economics that matched Del Vecchio's view:

> Economics deals with the *social organization* of economic activity ... there are many ways in which economic activity may be socially organized, but the predominant method in modern nations is the price system, or free enterprise.[73]

Given its collective or social dimension, organization requires purely objective treatment, but Del Vecchio did not fail to stress that organization is based on relationships involving individuals. Furthermore, this last reference to subjective relationships ensures that 'organization is essentially a dynamic economic aspect' which obliges the economist to investigate market transformations assuming a dynamic view.[74] Organization is what makes a social (meso or macro) group different from a sum of individuals.

As said, although Del Vecchio never wrote explicitly about methodological issues,[75] besides the notion of 'economic coefficients', he also introduced 'infinitesimal orders' (*ordini degli infinitesimi*) in order to weight economic coefficients and establish the extent to which they influence economic facts. Infinitesimal order is a notion that recalls 'density' or something that quantifies the relations among particles. The higher the infinitesimal order, the weaker the link between two entities. As Del Vecchio himself pointed out, the theoretical system is consequently causal, because it is important to determine the infinite number of causes to which the existence of goods as above defined is linked.[76]

He wrote that 'quantitative changes tend to determine qualitative changes',[77] which is obvious unless one understands what Del Vecchio actually meant: any change in the distribution of wealth, income, goods, money, and so on, gives rise to different economic coefficients and therefore relationships. His first important work was titled *Net Product and Monopoly* (*Prodotto netto e monopolio*), published in 1905, and it includes an analysis of the distribution of the surplus among the production factors.

As we shall see, the topic of distribution, as Del Vecchio's frequent cross-references to Ricardo prove, plays an important role in his thought and analysis, also when it is devoted to circulation and monetary topics. It concerns the distribution of what we can generically call 'value', but also of goods and their utility, money included. Perhaps because of Pareto's influence – although Del Vecchio cannot be considered a 'Paretian' – the distributions that Del Vecchio conceived were rarely uniform or Gaussian: homogeneity was not common in his works.

We shall see that the statistical view moulded Del Vecchio's economic view as a whole, and not only because he asserted the utility of empirical arguments. Attention to statistical and distributional analysis induced Del Vecchio to bring aggregates to the fore and to stress the importance of considering the relationships among the components of those aggregates. Put briefly, aggregates matter not only because of their components, but mainly because of the relationships among the latter. This is the perspective from which Del Vecchio's analysis should be considered.

To conclude, an immediate consequence was that Del Vecchio could not strictly adhere to the theory of commodity-based money and assert the direct utility of money as a commodity. Nor could equating the utility of money with the utility of goods purchased fully satisfy him. The focus, he argued, must be trained on entitlement and, more generally, on the economic relationships springing from money: he wrote that 'monetary theory is a set of relationships explaining and linking prices together'. Money is therefore more a relational good than a commodity.

Finally, the notion of relationship enabled Del Vecchio to undertake a *reductio ad unum* of the causes explaining accumulation and interest, i.e. production and distribution. If we abandon the main reason for differentiating the treatment of production and distribution – that is, the *natural* logic guiding the former, the *institutional* logic governing the latter – and adopt the relationships/coefficients couplet, we must consider all economic facts from a unified perspective. Indeed, the idea of relationships is *institutional* in itself and applicable to a broad array of economic facts. As Federico Caffè – one of Del Vecchio's pupils – stressed,[78] Del Vecchio, by means of the notion of relationships, grafted historical and institutional aspects on to neoclassical pure theory, thereby shedding light on economic determinants of distribution which, by contrast, neoclassical theory had marginalized because they involved institutional terms.

A Scientific Realism

To conclude: the relationships that Del Vecchio put at the centre of his analysis are not impersonal (i.e. juridical) relations among atomic individuals in an environment dominated by uncertainty.

Del Vecchio did not have an atomistic view of society, but nor did he treat society as a whole. The idea that some goods are yielded because there are relationships induced Del Vecchio to take a completely economic, and not juridical, view of relationships. He thus safeguarded, on the one hand, his atomic or subjective view of society, and on the other, an overall view on economy and society. Therefore, we cannot fully metaphorically apply the theory of gas to Del Vecchio's view of society, as Alfonso De Pietri Tonelli,[79] a Paretian economist, did in those years. This is because individuals do not interact among themselves as free atomic particles. Individuals are connected by relations that combine to determine global or societal outcomes. Del Vecchio focused on those economic relationships – treating them as economic coefficients – because it is they that mould society.

Del Vecchio rejected atomism if it meant considering economic agents independently from others. Nor did he believe that this involved analysing individual choice as a function of arguments expressing the choices of other agents. Simply, he considered individuals to be necessarily provided with economic relationships whose existence moulds economic society. He abandoned any mechanical analogy, without fully adhering to the biological one. He tried to define the economic variables by considering them as always parts of a whole: in this sense, they are relations. Examples include monetary variables. As we shall see, he preferred the idea of *effectiveness* to that of *velocity of circulation* of money. The latter implies a good (money) circulating independently within a given economy. By contrast, the former expresses something about the outcome of the monetary circulation. It gives us some information about the result of that circulation.

The idea that goods are always *relative goods* means that any individual has a *subjective* perception of goods that *objectively* exist but assume economic importance when related to individuals. Del Vecchio's attention to relationships entailed that subjective and objective views of economic reality were integrated.[80] The above example can help understand this. Velocity of circulation of money has a strictly objective meaning. Effectiveness always involves some kind of velocity of circulation, but the notion is filtered through a judgement on the effects of such circulation. Similarly, the long-term rate of interest becomes a *psychological rate of interest*.

Why did Del Vecchio combine *dynamics* and *relationships*, that is, a temporal and a spatial (relational) dimension? Because these two notions represent the coordinates of his general dynamic (dis)equilibrium mental scheme, according to a realist view of economic theory. As said, he rejected pure economic reasoning alone. He professed a 'scientific realism'[81] reaffirming the utility of theories to interpret economic reality and safeguarding, in this way, both an objective and subjective perspective. Facts do not *follow* theories, and the latter are not abstract constructs alone. Vitantonio Gioia clarified Del Vecchio's methodology thus:

> Del Vecchio perceived realism in a twofold perspective: first, it is a positive intellectual device allowing us to test our statements, without falling into the trap of a radical objectivism admitting an 'absolute' and 'definitive' empirical proof of a theory; on the contrary, it represents a 'limit' because it makes it possible to delimit an area in which the assertions of the social sciences are legitimate. The latter helps avoid the other trap of radical subjectivism.[82]

Del Vecchio applied his realism to the entirety of economic relations. Each economic choice has both a subjective and an objective component. Del Vecchio mixed subjectivism and objectivism, attributing the former to the individual level and maintaining the latter so as to analyse the meso- or macro-level. Money has both faces.

2 VALUING INDIVIDUAL DEMAND FOR MONEY

The name of Gustavo Del Vecchio is often associated with that of Léon Walras, owing to their shared endeavour to develop a general theory of money. In seeking to explain why money is demanded besides its use as a medium of circulation, Del Vecchio investigated the concept of money proposed by Walras in the fourth edition of the *Eléments d'économie politique pure* of 1900, where money is considered according to the service it may grant, that is, the so-called *monetary service*. In this regard Arthur W. Marget wrote:

> it can be said that [Del Vecchio] not only shows acquaintance with the parts of the *Eléments* which deal with the point under discussion [to incorporate the value of money into the general structure], but also that he sees that the whole problem turns upon the question whether, as Walras held, money may be said to provide a 'service' to the individual who holds it, during the time it is being held.[1]

Del Vecchio analysed Walras's equations on monetary services included in *Lesson 29* of the *Elements of Pure Economics*,[2] judging them impeccable from the mathematical and formal points of view.[3] But immediately afterwards he affirmed: 'The problem that Walras has put forward and resolved differs from the real monetary one for both unnecessary and essential features'.[4]

Del Vecchio was inclined to consider the Walrasian services as *outcomes* due to circulating money. The condition to have services is that money circulates. On this point, Bridel wrote:

> the demand for money balances is a special case of the agents' demands for circulating capital. The *services d'approvisionnement* of the circulating capital and hence of the cash balances are related to the goods themselves just as productive services are related to the goods which help produce them. Money balances should thus be analyzed in the same way that fixed capital goods are.[5]

Giovanni Demaria, Del Vecchio's principal pupil, tried to posit money as a fixed more than a circulating capital: 'Like every fixed capital, money offers a continuous service which is represented by the fact that it allows goods to circulate through it: that is, it allows "exchangeability"'.[6]

We are persuaded that this is not the only possible interpretation of Del Vecchio's thought. He was too involved in a dynamic perspective to treat money as a fixed capital and therefore as a stock. Acknowledging that in a dynamic economy the demand for money exceeds that in a static one, he was willing to admit that the excess quantity is demanded *per se*, also independently from the fact that it can cover unexpected changes in production or needs. From the monetary service perspective, this raises the question of the services provided by the hoarded money.

In effect, more than monetary services, it was another of Walras's concepts that reappeared in Del Vecchio: that of *encaisse désirée*. Walras had written:

> The value of all or part of the final products and perpetual net income which the parties to the exchange wish to purchase, and which they desire to keep in their possession in the form of cash or money savings, constitutes their *desired cash-balance* ['*encaisse desirée*'].[7]

Del Vecchio admitted a demand for money *per se*, which comes clearly to the fore at aggregate level, but which can be posited also at individual level when analysing subjective choices. Therefore, it will be clear that Del Vecchio was not so far from Walras's *encaisse désirée*, and the other similar expressions of what Charles Rist called 'the need for money'.[8] However, Del Vecchio added that the money demanded in a dynamic economy is greater than the corresponding money in a static one because of the cash demanded *per se* in a dynamic view.

While the aims at the basis of Walras's and Del Vecchio's need for money are comparable, in that both involve providing money for future exchanges, these personal reserves depend on the level of prices accordingly to Walras, on subjective expectations concerning future prices according to Del Vecchio. But, because any type of reserve or of storage, including money, is envisaged, a commodity or money poses the problem of both its utility and its value: is its value anchored to utility, or is the latter determined by the former?

Del Vecchio tried to solve the puzzle of money represented by the relationship between utility and value, by setting both utility and value in relation to time, and finally concluding that both the utility and value of money acquire conclusive meaning only in a social or aggregate perspective. This does not mean that the utility of money, for example, lacks individual significance. The point is that when seeking to explain the utility of money in a time perspective, it is necessary to consider the relationships among individuals and to investigate how money allows indirect or non-simultaneous exchanges. As we shall see, this occurs for both the utility and value of money. At any rate, Del Vecchio wrote that economics is a science of relationships: that is, it studies coordinated actions.

Although Del Vecchio did not make it clear, it seems that the importance of the aggregate dimension for understanding also subjective behaviours was what induced him in his 1909 *Principle* to put the aggregate demand for money before the subjective one. Contrary to what Del Vecchio did, here it has been decided to reverse the investigation of his thought by starting with the subjective analysis of money demand and postponing the aggregate demand for money to the next chapter. This is because examination of individual relationships can help provide a basis for the analysis of aggregate relationships, in particular the notion of 'group' or 'aggregate' that, in this theory, must not be treated as a sum of individual components.

A review of Del Vecchio's study of utility and value of money will clarify subjective monetary relationships. It can be anticipated here that the arguments put forward by Del Vecchio to explain the relationship between the individual and money were not grounded on indiscriminate application of the maximizing principle to explain individual choices. In effect, the maximizing principle was mitigated by the inclusion of the category of relationships, which imposed a relational analysis.

Nevertheless, it is true that a subjective perspective on money required Del Vecchio to focus on the utility and value of money making use of the marginal approach. It seems that he was moving towards a monetary approach grounded on individual choices, which immediately posed the problem of how much money individuals demand for trades and how much is held *per se*. Although Del Vecchio remained loyal to the transactional nature of money, from the outset he developed an original approach grounded on the role played by time.

In effect, it was when investigating individual choices that Del Vecchio stated the significance of shifting to a dynamic view. On considering the demand for money in an inter-temporal perspective, Del Vecchio showed that a monetary function other than that of acting as a medium of exchange is admissible. Time involves expectations, and the latter play a crucial role in explaining the demand for money not directly linked to immediate exchanges. Therefore, although Del Vecchio at first rejected Walras's notion of monetary service, his subsequent analysis of the value of money in a dynamic perspective enabled him to explain why a need for money independent from immediate transactions exists: it can be explained by assuming an infinite horizon. Once Del Vecchio had reached this conclusion, he moved to shorter horizons, arguing for the full subjectivity of the money demanded. But precisely the reasons explaining the demand for cash refer to a social conception of money.

The first section of the chapter presents the demand for money as a pivotal component of Del Vecchio's monetary analysis. The second section deals with the utility theory of money that Del Vecchio developed from 1909 to 1917. It is followed by discussion on the social utility of money, a concept that Del Vecchio developed in 1909 and then abandoned. The next sections are devoted to the value of money, presented first as an expression of the interest rate, then in its relationships with the expected prices, and finally in Del Vecchio's reinterpretation of money as social value. This discussion is followed by remarks on the individual demand for money grounded on expectations.

The Demand for Money

Having stated that Del Vecchio's interest was mainly in the demand for money, there arises an aspect that must be made clear in order to explain his view on money: this concerns the logical sequence in which he analysed the demand for money. As said, Del Vecchio did not begin with the individual demand for money and then move to the aggregate demand. He started from a macro or aggregate analysis and then constantly alternated his subjective and aggregate (individual and macro) perspectives. His subjective analysis of the demand for money followed, and did not precede, his criticism of the quantity principle.

However, we think that individual analysis can furnish useful insights into an aggregate one, not because principles explaining individual behaviours can be extended to groups, but because relationships, so crucial for Del Vecchio, are first subjective and then must be translated into an aggregate perspective. This accounts for our decision to reverse the presentation.

A first premise – the relationship between gold and paper money – concerns the time Del Vecchio was writing. He pragmatically assumed fiat money as given, showing that he was unconcerned with the debate on the gold standard. It was clear that international circulation obliged the use of gold or silver, but this was a matter of exchange rates, not of paper money convertibility. As we shall see, the value of money depends on its exchangeability, not on its intrinsic value. This is not merely a technical point, because it is indicative of Del Vecchio's distance from uncritical adherence to the then dominant monetary dogmas. In his introduction to the 1928 book, *The Monetary Theories and the Return to Gold*, written by Giovanni Demaria, his most outstanding pupil, Del Vecchio was somewhat sceptical about a return to the gold standard. He thought that the rules could not be dictated by the standard, but rather by 'the free system involving exchange rates, discount rate and in general all that concerns the financial market'.[9] Markets, including the monetary one, are self-organizing entities. In some sense, goods cannot circulate without money (or its substitute, credit): money 'transforms' goods into *economic goods*. By circulating, money (and its substitutes) enables goods to circulate and, consequently, to acquire value. This confirms that exchangeability is certainly a central component of his approach.

From the first pages of his best-known article on monetary topics, the 'Principles on the Economic Theory of Money' ('I principii della teoria economica della moneta')[10] (1909), onwards, Del Vecchio confirmed his adherence to the neoclassical principle that money performs a function as a *medium of exchange*:

> Money … is money if it deserves to be exchanged … only during the exchange is it useful, and even if we can affirm that it is useful since it has value … certainly it is useful when it is exchanged; in less conceptual terms, we can say that its utility coincides with its exchangeability.[11]

The emphasis on 'exchanges' did not rule out functions different from exchangeability. But it is also true that the weight which Del Vecchio gave to 'relations' compels us to put 'exchangeability' at the centre of his monetary theory, and therefore to investigate money as a *technology of exchange*,[12] that is, as a tool or a set of tools enabling exchange processes. This notion of money obliges the inclusion of credit among the instruments of which this technology is composed.

Money remained a 'means', although the idea of money as an asset sometimes made its appearance. Nevertheless, the fact that money (and credit) is used to coordinate different exchanges makes it possible to demonstrate that money has an organizational function which is only indirectly ascribable to exchanges. While Mises wrote in 1912 that: 'The function of money is to facilitate the business of the market by acting as a common medium of exchange',[13] with Del Vecchio we shall find that money does much more than 'facilitate' exchanges: its existence enables the organization of exchanges occurring at different times.[14]

Towards a subjective theory of the demand for money: the utility of money Von Wieser, often quoted by Del Vecchio, had written in 1893 as follows:

> A greater value almost always corresponds with the greater utility, and a lesser value with the lesser utility and on this account transactions which commend themselves in consideration of their utility, commend themselves also in consideration of their value. The service of value consists, then, in representing utility wherever both show the same tendency.[15]

Usually, the utility and value of a commodity are linked by an interdependent relation that can also be broken down in causal terms. That relation appears much more intricate when it is referred to money. Von Wieser anchored the value of money to both current and past prices and incomes:

> The various things which determine the money value to the individual are the following: the amount of money which is at his disposal; the nature and quantity of the goods which can be obtained under the existing market conditions and prices; the utility which those goods are able to give, as also the utility already secured by possessions otherwise acquired; and, lastly, the amount and urgency of the demand.[16]

It is true that the current value of money is conditioned by past judgements, but it is also true that such value is determined by expected future conditions as well. Expected prices condition current decisions determining the demand for money. This will be the next step towards a complete representation of Del

Vecchio's theory of circulation, which put him in an original position in the monetary debate of those years.

We will start from the utility of money, considering it as the outcome of a relationship between the individual and goods, in this case a particular good.

In accordance with the predominant treatment of the utility of money of that time, in 1909 Del Vecchio sought to insert money into the utility function of the agent, which would mean integrating money into the theory of value. The relationship between *final* or *marginal* utility[17] and the value of money became a decisive component of this model, and it proved very difficult. Subsequently, in 1917, he wrote:

> To apply the marginal approach to the *utility* of money means to draw the value of money from its utility. But, it can occur that it is the utility of money that in its turn depends on the value of money. The problem remains unsolved.[18]

Proceeding at the individual or subjective level, the correct understanding of terms like 'utility' becomes crucial. Also in this case, Del Vecchio did not lack originality. He was able to insert a feature that freed the treatment of the utility of money from its mechanical adherence to analysis of the utility of goods, on the basis that money is a totally different commodity that cannot be equated with other goods. We shall see why.

Having clarified the pre-eminence of the demand for money, Del Vecchio claimed that 'money is useful when it is exchanged', with the implication that, at first sight, hoarded money has no utility. It is clear that the utility of money is inextricably bound up with the function that it performs in transactions on goods and services, although in 1913 he stressed the 'psychological and subjective nature' of the demand for money, so that it seemed far from being a demand solely for exchanges. It is precisely in the relation between the utility of money and the demanded quantity of money that one must seek the basis for an economic (pure) theory of money.[19]

Del Vecchio's reflection on the utility of money is not straightforward: it is full of suggestive theoretical insights, often not adequately developed. We can start with his 1909 statement that it is possible to give a quantitative expression to the marginal utility of money.[20] He assumed the known inverse relation between marginal utility of money and its quantity, as occurs with that of the goods purchased, but with the difference that the curve of money was downward, but less so than that of goods. The different gradient of the utility curve in comparison with that of goods derives from the fact that money can be hoarded for future exchanges. This does not contrast with the idea that money when exchanged has the same value as the good purchased.

Not interested in a strictly cardinal measure of the utility of money, Del Vecchio wanted to posit that increasing the quantity of money, the marginal utility of money, although decreasing, did not reach nil utility.[21] Figuratively, we can imagine that the curve representing the utility of money has a long tail preventing it from reaching zero. The analytical consequence is clear: money has utility also when it is not exchanged. Hence Del Vecchio could state that, in a dynamic perspective, demanded money is higher than that corresponding to the static one. At first sight, this involves an exchange between objects with different utilities. But this does not correspond to the truth because the added utility comes to the fore only when money is not exchanged. Therefore, also 'satisfied' consumers or firms may demand money.

Moreover, Del Vecchio stated that the traditional idea that money has a constant final or marginal utility was totally false.[22] It would be paradoxical – he posited – for a good to have nil utility and positive value, as stated in a time perspective. Hence the final or marginal utility of money cannot be nil, and a change of monetary stocks inevitably modifies its final utility.

Utility of Money and Time

Del Vecchio was persuaded that the utility of money involves two dimensions: *mass of money* and *time*.[23] According to Del Vecchio, the demanded mass of money depends on its utility. This is self-evident. But, as said, it is time that contributes to explaining the demand for money not directly connected to exchanges, i.e. the part of money that although not immediately employed for exchange has a positive utility. This does not mean that money satisfies a need different from exchangeability.

Ultimately, this reference to time as the factor explaining the utility of money which is not immediately used for exchanges reintroduces the idea that money performs a service that necessarily has a time dimension. Exchanges matter, but they do so as the objects of monetary services. Therefore, introducing time means admitting that because money maintains its value over time, it can be considered as capital performing a specific service. Consequently, in a dynamic economy, the money that an individual demands is larger than his/her need for exchanges. The theme is interesting because if, on the one hand, dynamic conditions need more money than static ones, on the other, money seemingly cannot perform a service while it is held because it would induce the storing of money instead of letting it circulate.

Del Vecchio proposed the following comparison:

> We think of money as a means of transport ... the final [marginal] utility of which is not the utility of the less useful merchandise it has carried, nor the utilities of the two less useful goods carried in the double direction, but is the sum of the differences between the utilities at the final point and the starting point: so the final utility of

> money is the addition of the differences between the utilities of the goods purchased and that of the goods not purchased.[24]

The same concept can be expressed by saying that money has an incremental utility equal to the difference between the utility perceived by the individual before and after time has passed or a change has occurred.

This quotation shows that Del Vecchio's scepticism about considering money as capital originated from the assumption that money is not hoarded *per se*, but in view of potential future exchanges. Del Vecchio wrote that, in a dynamic economy, money demanded exceeds the current needs because every agent distributes its purchases across an indefinite time period. But he cannot exactly forecast its monetary needs. Consequently, the final utility of money cannot be treated as a constant because it varies according to the time foreseen before money is spent.

If for any individual money matters for exchanges, this is the only admissible 'service'. At aggregate level, that service assumes a meaning that cannot be deduced by summing the individual 'services'. It assumes a different meaning with no correspondence in Walras's monetary services because a different 'subject' is considered. In 1909, Del Vecchio clearly stated that an 'economic subject' is different from the sum of individuals composing it.[25] Thus, only by assuming that the aggregate can be treated as an autonomous economic subject can the idea of monetary service be accepted. Monetary service is an aggregate category, not a subjective one: this is the reason that hindered Del Vecchio from following Walras.

The Social Utility of Money

Although in 1909 Del Vecchio declared he did not accept the Walrasian notion of *service*, as we have seen, in 1917 he reintroduced the concept to explain why money has a use value independent from immediate exchanges. There is, however, a case in which already in 1909 he recognized a monetary service: when money is viewed according to its *social* utility. This is an aspect not subsequently developed by Del Vecchio, but it is nevertheless worth mentioning because it provides proof of the organizational character that Del Vecchio ascribed to money. It is treated below, after a review of utility and value from a subjective point of view, because it exemplifies the oscillation between the individual and aggregate level mentioned above.

Del Vecchio's conception of social utility introduces a German author well-known to him: Karl Knies. In his 1873 *Das Geld*,[26] Knies spoke of 'social use-value', explaining 'the economic value of a good in society [money, in this case, which] is an *average* of its varying use-values to different individuals in the market'.[27] Del Vecchio was well acquainted with Knies's theory, which he frequently cited with reference to the social dimension of money.

We may also mention Benjamin Anderson, who wrote on the 'social mind'[28] in 1917, while Del Vecchio was writing his last important youthful article on monetary topics and recovering monetary services, applying them to the value-in-use of money. In both cases, an absolute value was at stake. Anderson detected three origins of value:

> At the one extreme we have theories of 'intrinsic' value, which would be place economic value outside the wills of men ... At the opposite extreme would be the economists, as Professor [Herbert] Davenport and Jevons, who find no value for a good except in the minds of individual men, so that there may be as many different values as there are different men ... In between these two extremes, is the social value theory of the present writer. Economic value is not intrinsic in goods, independent of the minds of men. But it is a fact which is in large degree independent of the mind of any given man.[29]

Finally, the topic can also be introduced by recalling John Bates Clark's notion of 'social marginal utility', although the sum of individual marginal utilities implicated by Clark did not find full correspondence in Del Vecchio's social utility.[30] Perhaps more important was Wieser's notion of 'public economic value' consistent with Nassau W. Senior's 'intrinsic causes of value'. Certainly, Del Vecchio's social utility definition posed an additional problem since it could not be grounded on average values.

To return to the 1909 *Principles*, Del Vecchio attempted to determine whether a *social* utility of money exists besides its *individual* utility. Although in static conditions money performs a single function, the intermediary one, this does not rule out the possibility that money furnishes a 'further and additional service'.[31] In fact, Del Vecchio hypothesized that money may be held 'because hoarding it represents the satisfaction of a need that is different from the need to purchase',[32] thus opening a new perspective on social utility:

> The individual point of view must be distinguished from the social point of view; it is necessary to know the relationships between the two perspectives and to replace the notion of utility with that of service; finally, studies must be focused on these two aspects: the services offered by money to individuals and those given to society as a whole.[33]

Thus, the monetary service made its appearance when the social dimension came to the fore in Del Vecchio's thought, while, as we will see, it remained in the background on the individual level until 1917. Del Vecchio wrote that it is possible to explain the common tendency of individuals to hold money, although it seems contrary to 'the economic principle'. To understand this point, it should be borne in mind that Del Vecchio treated circulation in a different way from production. While the sum of individual productions is equal to the aggregate amount of production itself, the social utility deriving from the circulation of money is greater than the sum of individual utilities. This is because social phenomena assume a form (*forma*) different from that of individual phenomena.[34]

Social utility arises only by assuming aggregates of individuals exchanging among themselves: 'Money does not present final utility for a group of individuals treated as a single individual, but we cannot say that such utility does not exist when we consider a group made up of single individuals'.[35]

Del Vecchio added:

> In general, the equality of final utilities is a condition allowing economic equilibrium: but, in the case of organizational factors the principle according to which the total utility exceeds the utilities of the individuals ... is true.[36]

Although Del Vecchio started by considering neutral money, in its social dimension it furnishes a *service* that is a factor ascribable to *economic organization*. Money allows the circulation of goods and, according to Del Vecchio, this must be considered a service that appears on treating individuals as components of an aggregate.

Money, therefore, has a social utility that is different from its value; or better, a social service that differs from individual ones. Because individuals are aware of this social service, they hold liquidity. At this point, it is also clear that the individual utility of money is different from the utility of the goods that money makes it possible to purchase. On this Anderson wrote:

> The value of the money, on the one hand, and the values of the goods on the other hand, are both to be explained as complex social psychological forces. But when this method of approach is used, when prices are conceived of as the results of organic social psychological forces, there is no room for, or occasion for, a further explanation in terms of the mechanical equilibration of goods and money.[37]

Moreover, the organizational properties of money clarify why Del Vecchio preferred to treat his proposal as a theory of circulation and not of money in the strict sense. For the same reasons, we cannot assert that Del Vecchio rejected every kind of direct utility of money.[38] Social utility is a direct utility, and monetary service also exists in stationary conditions. It is true that such utility is inseparable from exchanges, even when they do not occur, but individuals, on perceiving both the individual and social role of money, decide to hold it.

The Value of Money

Del Vecchio began to build his theory of money by rejecting the notion according to which money is a metal or commodity whose value is intrinsic to its substance. Del Vecchio set aside theories grounding money on the cost of producing or importing the precious metal, with all its implications as regards its industrial use and its seignorage. The first page of his *Principles* is devoted to rejection of the cost of production as the criterion with which to fix the value of money. Money has a production cost, but this is not the cause of its value. Certainly, the cost of producing gold can condition the value of money, but it is not sufficient to explain why gold has a given price at a given time. There is no intrinsic value of money springing from the fact that money is however a commodity.[39] Neither does the international price of the commodity assumed as international money appear to be the first cause of monetary value, even though Del Vecchio was aware that current and expected productivity in the industrial and mining sector conditions the formation of prices (mainly expected prices) and consequently the demand for money.[40]

Put briefly, neither the cost of production of money, nor the alternative use of money as such or as commodity, nor the use of money in different countries, can be the starting point for a pure analysis of the value of money, although these are all important features.[41] Money is a sign or an entitlement before it is gold or anything else, and as entitlement it must be considered when its value is explored.

Another approach rejected by Del Vecchio can be introduced by recalling that Anderson began his 1917 book, *The Value of Money* thus: 'The problem of the value of money is a special case of the general problem of economic value'.[42] That is, he did not exclude that the value of money could be treated like that of commodities. To be clear, Del Vecchio clearly stated from his first article on this topic onwards that the value of money must be considered a 'different case' requiring specific explanations. The origin of the value of money was wholly different from that of the common goods with which money is exchanged, i.e. it cannot be explained by overlapping the supply of and demand for money.

We shall argue that, finally, Del Vecchio explained the value of money as a time relationship in which subjective and objective features are interwoven. This relationship clarifies that, although Del Vecchio treated the value of money from a subjective viewpoint, he never forgot that money has necessarily a social dimension which makes it different from other goods. The value of paper or fiat money is a market or social fact, not an individual one only, which a reliable monetary analysis cannot ignore. As we shall see in the following chapter, Del Vecchio would provide a satisfactory account of the value of money when he gave account of the social demand for money, not the individual one only. However, it is also true that social value derives its meaning from the fact that individuals perceive that money has value, but that value can be fully appreciated by individuals when they regard money as an instrument of coordination and organization. That is to say, the value of money cannot be imposed by law without social acknowledgement.

Obviously, Del Vecchio recognized the meaning of the value of money as the 'reciprocal of the average of prices', but he argued that it cannot say anything about the origins or causes of the value of money. That was merely an expression of the value of money, and it was treated as such in Del Vecchio's work. The reference to prices recalls the definition of the value of money as 'power of exchange' or the better-known 'purchasing power'; but, as Böhm-Bawerk posited, this means that the value is strictly connected to exchange.[43] What must be established is whether the value of money is explained by something anterior to exchange. Del Vecchio's subjective analysis of both the utility and value of money has precisely this purpose: to understand whether both the utility and value of money originate from exchange only or from outside that realm. As regards utility, we have seen that each agent recognizes that money can be useful besides its immediate exchangeability.

Transposing this conclusion to the value of money, to be noted is what Maffeo Pantaleoni, a teacher of Del Vecchio, wrote in his *Pure Economics*:

> The value of money must be understood in two senses: 1st. In a strict sense, the value of money is its power of exchange expressed in a quantity of money of whatever commodity ... 2nd. The term, value of money, is used, though improperly, to designate the payment made for its temporary use, that is, for a loan of money. This payment represents the value of the use of money, and its termed discount.[44]

But Pantaleoni immediately added: 'We must therefore avoid confusing the *value of money*, or its power of exchange, with the *value of the use of money*, or its rate of discount'.[45]

Subsequently Alfred Marshall would claim concerning the correspondence between value of money and discount rate that 'the "money market" is the market for command over money: "the value of money" in it at any time is the rate of discount, or of interest for short period loans charged in it'.[46]

We find Pantaleoni's view developed in Del Vecchio, who started his analysis of the value of money by stating that the origin of value implies an individual's *need* for money, where that need has the two dimensions envisaged for utility: the *mass of money* required for a given transaction and *time*.[47] The former point falls within the domain of money demanded because of its value: but it seems tautological if the origins of value are not identified. It was clear that what an individual needs is a 'mass' of money. The latter point is less straightforward, although 'time', wrote Del Vecchio, 'is an original and essential character of value, since holding on to money involves some kind of waiting'.[48] The idea that the value of money is intrinsically linked to its hoarding over time gradually took shape according to what Mises in 1912 defined the second function (besides medium of exchange) of money, i.e.: 'as a transmitter of value through time and space'.[49]

The Value of Money and Expected Prices

Reconstruction of Del Vecchio's notion of dynamic facts can aid understanding of his temporal conception of the subjective demand for money and of the value of money. Firstly, in almost all his works, when Del Vecchio speaks of static phenomena he means stationary ones. Indeed, he wrote: 'static phenomena are those repeating themselves identically'.[50] He evidently meant stationary phenomena. Dynamic facts are mainly those in which the economic magnitudes change, also because of variations in extra-economic factors. Economic changes must be considered during the entire time in which they appear, and not only instantaneously. Finally, dynamic phenomena are typically those where current facts differ from previously expected facts.

Even though Del Vecchio was writing years before the advent of a complete theory of expected values or involving expectations – this would happen in the 1930s – he furnished a clear conception of subjective expectations, including them not as marginal but as crucial variables in his monetary theory:

> The future is the presupposition for the present. To state that current value depends on past value is to deny the solution of the problem; on the contrary, to state that current value depends on the future value is to move closer to the solution. Today the value of money is determined by expectations about its future value. Because money at the moment is esteemed for the value that it will have in the future, when it will be exchanged, then the future expected values determine the current ones.[51]

He acknowledged that money draws its value from the future conditions and, more precisely, those future conditions affecting current judgements.[52] Having stated this, i.e. the basis of his theory on the value of money, Del Vecchio stressed what he considered to be the limitations of other theories on money value. The quantity theory's main weakness was that it explained the value of money on the basis of current facts. The theory of cost of production and re-production ignored the demand for money and assumed a virtual value of money that does not necessarily correspond to its real value.[53] Another aspect concerned the velocity of circulation, and the quantity of money could not be considered independent from the value of money, as the classical theory of money had done: on assuming a dynamic perspective, both of them are conditioned by the value.

Del Vecchio first chose to reduce the value of money to a completely subjective notion grounded on individual judgements about the future, where expectations play a role in valuing future variables.

In the article 'Crucial Issues on the Value of Money' ('Questioni fondamentali sul valore della moneta'), Del Vecchio wrote that 'a category of dynamic facts springs ... from the differences between expected and real events':[54]

> We can observe that expectations (*attese*) of higher prices increase the velocity of circulation of money and, indeed, bring forward the effects deriving from a future growth of the stock of money. Expectations of lower prices produce opposite effects.[55]

The importance of (future) time had already been adumbrated by Del Vecchio in 1909, but it acquired a primary role only in 1917, after he had written about crises,[56] the discount rate[57] and the interest rate.[58]

Time and dynamic features are not merely additional, because they mould the functions attributed to money:

> The fundamental element in our treatment of the value of money is not a static fact, neither is it deducible from current conditions nor does it depend on the past phenomena. Essentially, it hinges on the future conditions and most precisely on those among them that influence the current judgements.[59]

Thus, the value of demanded money is determined by expectations about future transactions.

To complete these introductory notes, to be stressed is that Del Vecchio subsequently defined the difference between dynamics in economics and dynamics in mechanics and other exact sciences on the basis of the conception of time adopted:

> We can modestly recall that the use of *time* in mechanics is possible because it is reduced to space, whilst in economics we have to deal with a real and not abstract (psychic and non-physic) time that cannot be treated with the instruments used in physics.[60]

We may say that time in economics does not flow independently of the individual's perception of his relationships and of economic changes. The *psychic* or *psychological time* evoked by Del Vecchio can be translated as *expectation time*, a notion implied by Del Vecchio in his works on the interest rate and crises, years before the concept of *expectation* had been introduced into the economic literature.

Summing up, in comparison with the 1909 *Principles*, in the 1917 *Crucial Issues* Del Vecchio seemed aware that the value of money depends on individual expectations: 'money is worth today what it will be worth in the future without limitation of time'.[61] Compare Del Vecchio's statement with Keynes's subsequent famous sentence in the *General Theory*: '*For the importance of money essentially flows from its being a link between the present and the future* [original italics]'.[62]

In regard to Del Vecchio's key concept – relationships – the current value of money for an individual depends on the value which that individual expects will be attributed to that money in the future.

If exchangeability explains why money is useful for an agent, the fact that money allows the planning of individual future exchanges on the basis of price forecasts explains stored money and, ultimately, its value. Del Vecchio presumed that the demand for liquidity is determined at individual level, where both consumers and firms must cope with the uncertainty surrounding future exchanges values: expected prices.

Subjective Value of Money

In 1912, Del Vecchio reaffirmed:

> The value of money, conceived as the general purchasing power of money itself, does not concretely exist; on the contrary, there are many prices, that is, many terms of trade of money with goods and services. Moreover, assuming other times, the terms of trade with the same goods change. These are real facts, which can be measured, and of which the value of money is only a vague and summary abstract expression.[63]

In 1912, Del Vecchio seemed to have still a long way to go before solving the puzzle concerning the origin of the value of money. Only in 1917 did he devise a solution to the question of the value of money at individual level by moving decisively towards a subjective dynamic analysis. But this was a solution with more than one ambiguity.

The first step along the path towards the 1917 solution concerned Del Vecchio's still unresolved and vague idea of monetary services – the Walrasian anchor. On discussing and criticizing von Mises rather than Walras, in his 1917 article, 'Crucial Issues about the Value of Money', Del Vecchio reformulated his position on monetary services.[64] Von Mises had written in 1912:

> The subjective estimates of individuals are the basis of an economic valuation of money just as of that of other goods. And these subjective estimates are ultimately derived, in the case of money as in the case of other economic goods, from the significance attaching to a good or a complex of goods as the recognized necessary condition for the existence of a utility, given certain ultimate aims of the part of some individual.[65]

It did not matter that 'the subjective value of money is conditioned by its objective *exchange*-value, i.e. by the characteristics that fall within the scope of economics'.[66] Mises did not differentiate commodity-money from other goods: according to him, value-in-use and value-in-exchange coincide:

> In contrast to commodities, money would never be used unless it had an objective exchange-value or purchasing-power. The subjective value of money always depends on the subjective value of the other economic goods that can be obtained in exchange for it.[67]

The purchasing power of money drives all subjective evaluations of money. The objective purchasing power (prices) contrasts with subjective judgement.

For Del Vecchio there were no institutional factors determining the velocity of circulation of money and explaining the quantity of money (purchasing power) that each individual would like to hold, as on the contrary is described in Fisher's *Purchasing Power of Money* (1911).[68] Here the explanation is couched in more choice-theoretic terms, *à la* Marshall, according to a more behavioural view.[69] Simply, Del Vecchio brought all these variables back to the subjective dimension, in order to single out the reason inducing the individual to demand money besides his immediate needs, conditioning its value. Consequently, the first step was to rethink the value of money by adapting it to a subjective dimension. However, problems arose with prices, which were objective variables although presented as expected ones.

Del Vecchio proposed the following solution. The shift to a dynamic view of the subjective value of money meant lengthening the future until any references to objective variables disappear. In such a way, 'the process of monetary valuation turns into an indefinite series of future valuations'.[70] This is the stratagem proposed by Del Vecchio to set up a subjective notion of value of money.

Almost paradoxically, Del Vecchio thought that the problem could be solved by projecting the value of money into remote time: 'Once the current value is substituted with the future value, which is indefinitely remote, the problem is disentangled'.[71]

The value of money as an objective feature remains; but because it is confined to the remote future value, it loses any relevance. With this passage, Del Vecchio pioneered the notion of *perpetuity*, here termed *remote time*. Unfortunately, he did not give an analytical or mathematical definition of remote time, i.e. perpetuity. By moving expectations forward, Del Vecchio reduced the objective character of future processes, transforming the value of money into a subjective variable.

Put briefly, money has solely a subjective value when it is used for transactions cast in the remote future. But this means that money is demanded *per se*, free from any tie with its exchangeability. In such a way, Del Vecchio conceptualized a fully subjective demand for liquidity that evoked the subjective notion of *encaisse desirée*.

Although not established by Del Vecchio, the corollary of this point is that the money cast into a remote future loses any connection with exchanges, with the consequence that the shift to the use-value of money entails that money is demanded as liquidity, and not only as a means for exchange. It is plain that the use-value of money has a completely subjective dimension. The same notion of 'remoteness' became a strongly subjective notion.[72]

This analysis clarifies that Del Vecchio theorized the detachment of money from its strictly exchange function. Indeed, this line of reasoning explained why the value of money is never nil. Inasmuch as money is demanded also as cash, it has value. Thinking of a remote future, it was clear that money is demanded *per se*, as cash without any reference to immediate exchanges.

Obviously, remoteness was a thought experiment to state that money has value independently from any immediate use. It was not necessary to cast expectations in a remote future to argue that money has a value *per se*. However, once the value had been stated from a subjective perspective, the remote future can be substituted with the notion of 'horizon', on the argument that: 'Any objective value of exchange of money is removed from the features causing the utility and the value of the monetary service'.[73] Therefore, casting exchanges in the future makes it possible to state a subjective demand for liquidity and a subjective notion of value.

At this point, it is of interest to reconstruct Del Vecchio's answer to what Mark Blaug[74] and others would term the 'circularity bogey between utility and value of money'. Assuming static conditions, the circulating money corresponds to the money demanded, and the possible excess has no utility and value. Velocity is given, and there is no uncertainty in transactions. But, this was not Del Vecchio's position. On moving to a dynamic economy, things change. If a future horizon is assumed, the demand for money is justified *per se*, without any connection with future variables.

Thus, Del Vecchio could draw as a first general conclusion: 'All these points, together with the elements drawn from our *Principles* and some notes about the real and monetary rates of interest, are enough to resolve the problem of the value of money'.[75]

In the *Principles* Del Vecchio stated the equality among the service provided by money, its marginal utility and the rate of interest.

Value of Money and Rate of Interest

Thus, the psychological rate of interest concurs in determining the value of money. In particular, given a static analysis, the rate of interest directly conditions the value without being influenced by it. At this point, brief discussion is required of Del Vecchio's concepts of interest rate and its relationships with the value of money.

Each agent formulates expectations about future prices and future exchanges. Hence, a theory anchored almost exclusively to the demand for goods is closer to the 'truth', but it has still not reached an 'adequate expression' of the demand for money.[76]

But, Del Vecchio added, each individual forms his own idea of the (real) interest rate according to his needs, the availability of goods, and the historical time. In 1909, and then in his 1915 *General Outlines of the Interest Theory*

(*Lineamenti generali della teoria dell'interesse*), Del Vecchio spoke of an *individual psychological rate of interest*, *i*, that may differ from both the *natural rate of interest* determined by the length of the productive process[77] and the short term interest rate, that is, the discount rate, *d*.[78] Each individual's psychological rate of interest *tends* to the natural rate of interest, but it is not necessarily the same.[79] Thus, individuals take decisions about (future) transactions on the consumption of goods according to their habits and to their expectations.

It may be said that this psychological rate of interest depends on beliefs, trust, habits and forecasts prevailing at the particular moment, according to economic trends and social customs. Only apparently do organizational concerns remain in the background, because any change and 'unification' of markets influences the rate of interest.[80]

In 1909, Del Vecchio provided a first representation of the rate of interest by referring it to the relationships between two economic groups, *A* and *B*, each composed of producers and sellers, which exchange respectively good *a*, which is an agricultural product sold by *A* and that can be purchased in a future time and *b*, an artefact always ready, sold by *B*. In the Böhm-Bawerk's lexicon, the production of *a* is longer or more capital intensive than that of *b*. Thus, the considered exchange is between current and future goods. Assuming that *i* is the long-term psychological rate of interest; *d* is the monetary interest rate; U_A is the weighted marginal or final utility enjoyed by the group *A* which sells *a* on the forward market and buys *b* on the spot one; U_B is the weighted marginal or final utility enjoyed by the group *B* which sells *b* on the spot market and buys *a* on the forward one. To understand the meaning of U_A and U_B we can explicit them as the ratio between the good *b* expressed in terms of good *a* for each group.[81]

Defining the rate of interest *i* as $i = \frac{U_A - U_B}{U_B}$, it can be stated that the system is in equilibrium and exchanges remain constant when

$$\frac{U_A - U_B}{U_B} = i = d \qquad 2.1$$

i.e, the psychological rate of interest is equal to discount or monetary rate.

Given $\frac{U_A - U_B}{U_B} > d$ or $i > d$, *A* and *B* will be interested in increasing the exchanges. That is, *A* judges the cost of borrowing money at *d* for buying *b* lower than the discounted gain from selling *A* on the forward market. Thus, exchanges increase. Differently, the latter are reduced if $\frac{U_A - U_B}{U_B} < d$.

Thus, U_A changes according to the prices or values attributed to the future goods.

One may wonder why the monetary rate of interest, *d*, can differ from the ratio between comparative marginal utilities. Del Vecchio gave an answer in his long essay on the discount rate published in 1914: 'We can suppose that the difference between utilities is not equal to the monetary rate of interest. It can only depend on the fact that the current prices are different from the forecasted ones'.[82]

If p^e denotes the expected prices, their increase Δp^e modifies U_A and U_B with inevitably $i > d$. The value attributed to future goods increases. As mentioned above, this induces people to borrow money, increasing *d*. Because the psychological rate of interest is determined by the forecasts (expectations) on future prices, it follows that the expectations on prices influence the monetary equilibrium. It is easy to suppose that expected increasing prices raise the demand for money, pushing up the discount rate. This process theoretically continues until the equilibrium is re-established: $\frac{U_A - U_B}{U_B} = i = d$ and prices are no longer expected to grow.[83] Anticipating a point developed in Chapter 4, the discount rate may not increase if credit is infinitely elastic and banks are in the conditions of satisfying the increasing demand for loans at a constant *d*.

Clearly, this was not a subjective representation of the rate of interest, but a view grounded on the relationships between groups. The latter are here treated as individuals, following Del Vecchio's statement that relationships prevent consideration of an aggregate as the sum of its parts.

Thus, in a more complex economy, the meaning of $U_A - U_B \neq 0$ is that the difference in weighted marginal utilities induces group *A* or *B* to make use of intermediaries (merchants) to deal with different timings in production and selling. By borrowing money at interest rate *d*, the two groups can regulate their exchanges. Consequently, the change of *d* conditions the access to goods and their comparative utilities.

Consequently, any change of the monetary rate of interest conditions the demand for money for exchanges and, finally, its value. This induced Del Vecchio to state that the rate of interest influences the value of money.

The fact is that the non-alignment between the two interests is the *normal* condition. This is a critical point explaining much of Del Vecchio's thought on these topics because, given the imbalance between the two interest rates, expectations on future prices become crucial for determining the demand for money. We shall return to this point.

It is clear that Del Vecchio resolved the indeterminacy caused by presupposing as many rates of interest as there are individuals by gathering the individuals into groups presenting some common trait. If the rate of interest is a factor influencing the monetary value, it comes to the fore on considering relationships among individuals and groups. Habits and expectations about production, payments and prices determine the utilities within the group, without having recourse to average values. Interrelationships within the group yield the resulting rate of interest.

Anything but a Veil!

Del Vecchio then introduced what was a crucial and original point for that time: the effect of the use of money on the value of the circulating goods. This point was very distant from the common view of money as a 'veil':

> 1) The use of money is a cause of the increase in the mutual value of goods. If the increase is uniform, the reciprocal values are unchanged; but this is implausible because, according to production conditions and the demand for each good, the value may relatively increase or decrease; 2) each yielded good has a value higher than the costs of production, because of the value referred to money; 3) values in a monetary economy are higher than values in a barter economy.[84]

The third point is only apparently cryptic. If money is a social capital yielding a service, that service is transmitted to the exchanged goods.

Anything but a veil! Here, money is a productive or 'circulating' factor bearing on costs. Money makes it possible to improve the organization of the economy, that is, the coordination of indirect economic exchanges, but at a cost. This explains Del Vecchio's point.[85] From a social viewpoint, money is a productive factor yielding a service. This position separated Del Vecchio from Alfred Marshall and Arthur C. Pigou, both of whom stressed that 'the value of all commodities other than money in terms of one another is determined independently of the value of money'.[86]

Del Vecchio developed the point, stating that, if money is a necessary factor implying a price, it contributes to the production/circulation of goods, and this contribution must be named. The most obvious explanation of this cost lies in the monetary interest rate paid by firms to borrow liquidity. One can immediately conclude that money reduces the cost of transactions, but its contribution to the economic system's working must be paid for. In some sense, the use of money *transfers* value to the exchanged commodity.

Del Vecchio analysed the question by formulating a model comprising two economies:[87] the first, C', is a pure non-monetary economy in which exchanges are free and unbounded; the second, C'', is a monetary economy, where money is not a veil, but a limited and expensive instrument. The two economies are similar except for the following unknowns, which are found in C'' and not in C': *a*) the mass of goods *a* exchanged with *b* – these unknowns also exist in a barter economy, but with different values; *b*) the mass of money, *M*, and its value – the value can be known, while the mass remains an unknown; *c*) the relationship between the monetary interest rate, *d* (discount rate in Del Vecchio) and the ratio between the weighted marginal utilities of goods, i.e. the psychological rate of interest, *i*. The question is: if *C*′ reaches the equilibrium state, how does the addition of new unknowns condition the equilibrium in *C*″?

In fact, the unknowns included in *a*) and *b*) can be easily determined once the relationship between the two interest rates is made clear, in accordance with the primacy assigned in this analysis to the long-term rate of interest. In effect, the monetary economy differs from a barter economy mainly because of the variables included in *c*), which require some further comment. The first problem derives from the fact that the monetary economy potentially has *various* monetary interest rates, and not a single one, oscillating around *various* natural interest rates: the former according to the number of banks, and the latter, given its psychological nature, according to the fact that it can vary from individual to individual. Hypothetically, Del Vecchio's scheme includes as many interest rates as there are agents, although a scheme of this kind would be unmanageable.[88] However, considering economic groups instead of individuals, this source of indeterminacy can be overcome.

This is the same as saying, as we shall see in the next chapters, that the various psychological rates of interest may converge towards an objective rate determined by the length of the production process and, finally, that this objective long-term interest rate may be equal to the monetary discount rate. The objective rate of interest is not an average value, but, the rate determined by the most important productive group in the economy (the 'main selling group', as explained in the next chapter). The length of production of this group determines the rate of interest. This is also a way to state that it is the marginal (of one group) value and not the average condition that determines the economic equilibrium or explains economic variables. Del Vecchio resolved in this way the indeterminacy due to admitting a plurality of monetary rates of interest.

Del Vecchio's psychological rate of interest can be compared with the rate of interest theorized by Irving Fisher. A difference is that the American economist assumed the value of money as given and then focused on the interest.[89] Conversely, Del Vecchio regarded the interest rate as a factor influencing the value of money. And the monetary rate of interest is in equilibrium when it is equal to the objective one determined, not by any average, but by the productive groups and, at macro level, by the main important productive group.[90] However, Del Vecchio's economy is an economy of relative not absolute or average values. This point distanced Del Vecchio's theory from that of Fisher.

From a Strictly Subjective to a Social Value of Money

We restart from $\frac{U_A - U_B}{U_B} = i$ because the utilities here represented *contain* the expected prices and we still lack a theory of expected prices. The decisions to demand and hold money depend precisely on the relationships between current and future utilities, and because we exclude a remote future, those utilities are conditioned by expected prices.

Current prices are objective variables that can be treated at meso-/macro-level by means of economic dynamics. Expected prices, which have a more subjective nature, are not derived from the current ones, at least not solely: expected prices are determined by changes occurring in the real economy that Del Vecchio listed as follows: (a) changes in the general productivity of industry; (b) changes in the mining industry's productivity; (c) changes in one country's productivity in comparison to countries producing precious metals. These are all factors observed in production, to which Del Vecchio added a fourth, more monetary, one: (d) changes in the credit system and, more generally, in the circulation system (rules governing the banking system).[91] Although important, Del Vecchio kept the fourth factor separate from the previous three because of the lesser strength of its effect on prices. It was clear that expectations on these changing variables were subjective because they were expectations, but they were grounded on objective factors. Subjectivity and objectivity here combine together.

Gathering the changes of various productivities into a single variable symbolizing productivity, q, and assuming d is the banking rate of interest, we can write the expected prices, P^e as follows:

$$P^e = f(q, d) \qquad 2.2$$

Del Vecchio assumed that any increase in the productivity of industrial production is indicative of higher productivity in longer processes, involving a shift of investments towards those sectors and a dismantling of shorter productions. This leads to an increase of prices in the latter productions as well. In general, any increase in productivity, as envisaged by points (a), (b) and (c) determines increasing expected prices.

The relationship between d and P^e is even simpler because any growth of d is translated on future prices.

As all these productivity and credit changes influence expected prices, they condition the demand for money and therefore the value of money: 'At any time the value of money depends on the future conditions of these elements and on the way in which they are forecasted'.[92]

In this way, Del Vecchio anchored the monetary economy permanently to the real or productive one, even more so if we consider the role that this scheme assigns to expected prices.

Del Vecchio laid the foundations for a theory of expected prices including the effects of the above changes on other typical dynamic variables, such as the discount rate, exchange rates and also financial markets. In this sense the effects of the above-mentioned changes on prices are first-order effects, while the consequences on exchange rates, the discount rate and financial markets are second- or higher-order effects.[93] The lack of reference to any link between monetary stock changes and prices changes immediately stands out: 'The quantity of money expresses an intermediate link only in the whole of the economic relationships. Rather it influences factors such as the change of industrial productivity and changes in credit'.[94]

While those cited above are the main factors indirectly influencing expected prices and then the demand for money and its value, Del Vecchio considered other aspects worthy of attention where the demand for money and, given the supply, consequently the value of money are at stake.

The first concerns money as a *hoarding good*. Money is useful as a static and dynamic reserve and as a reserve in activities linked to credit:

> No fund decreases below a stated level in order to avoid inconveniences. This is the static utility of money. In a real dynamic economy, this level should be higher, because of the greater amplitude of the variations and the smaller capacity to forecast them. This is the utility of money as a dynamic reserve.[95]

Credit is fundamental for circulation because it adjusts itself to the change due to the demand and supply of means of circulation. Moreover, changes occurring in the credit system can modify the circulation itself. Little by little, the social dimension strengthened in Del Vecchio's view on the value of money.

Money can also be treated from the viewpoint of its *storage as value*. Money is an instrument that allows hoarding when investments in securities and real estate investments are not favourable. It is remarkable that Del Vecchio affirmed, already in 1917, that money can be treated as a substitute for financial and real investments,[96] placing it among the crucial factors influencing the monetary dynamics.

Money is also the object of *specific reserves* held by banks and other financial institutions. Those reserves are the basis for credit activity, given that credit can substitute money in transactions.

However, the point is to grasp how 'these utilities' add up to determination of the value of money. Briefly, we may say that those utilities, by modifying the supply or the demand for money, change its value. This is even truer when the changes are time-extended. Pragmatically, if these services increase the demand for money and the supply remains the same, the value of money will rise.[97]

Finally, Del Vecchio was induced to accept that the value of money is connected to the services offered by money, although such services were limited to guaranteeing the exchangeability of goods in an indefinite time. Obviously, these decisions concerning the demanded money are mainly conditioned by expectations about prices. Thus, expectations of higher prices increase the velocity of circulation of money and enlarge the demand for credit and money. Consequently, the discount rate grows.[98] Expectations of lower prices lead to the opposite outcome.

We are finally able to define the exact meaning of the additional or secondary, or also dynamic, services that Del Vecchio attributed to money.[99] As stressed by Giovanni Demaria,[100] Del Vecchio seemingly espoused the neoclassical principle that money performs a function only when it is used as a medium of exchange. Nevertheless, he admitted that money furnishes 'secondary' services as a consequence of being held, even if it is not immediately used for transactions.[101]

In fact, what Del Vecchio did was justify a subjective demand for money due to the fact that money helps individuals to organize their exchanges. He admitted that money can provide secondary services, but he treated the latter only as secondary. The focus remained on exchanges, but on the organization or coordination of exchanges, not on the direct act alone. Finally, it was clear that, as thus conceived, money cannot be demanded or valued from a strictly subjective viewpoint. Money involves relationships and, hence, a social view. Therefore, any subjective value of money cannot prescind from the social function of money.

Concluding Remarks on Expectations and Demand for Money

This long and demanding chapter is concluded with a brief discussion of the notion of expectations developed by Del Vecchio between 1909 and 1917. This was the result of his interest in dynamic analysis, which at the time was taking its first steps in economics. But nevertheless it was an idea that gradually permeated his circulation analysis, becoming pivotal in his study of the monetary effect transmission.

It is clear that *future values* (*valori futuri*) involve a fully subjective formation of expectations (*attese*) grounded on subjective interpretations of the current values of variables. The past matters, but Del Vecchio's expectations were not projections into the future of past values.

Del Vecchio did not dwell on the process of expected values-making: he specified what expectations are not. They are not the transposition of the past to the future; they are not the result of some mechanical or rational process; they are not 'rational' in the sense that they can prove to be wrong. Briefly, expectations are the outcome of a pure subjective or cognitive process of economic reality reading: they are a complete expression of the agents called upon to decide while taking the future into account. These expectations lead, as stated by Frank Knight, to 'uninsurable risk', i.e. to radical uncertainty.[102]

Consistently with his view of economic and monetary equilibrium, Del Vecchio did not link expectations with some sort of equilibrium, subordinating variables like the value of money, the discount rate, the interest rate, to expectations themselves. At that point, also considering that the economic agents envisaged by Del Vecchio were firms, all the economy's workings would be plunged into uncertainty.

Expectations are linked to the use of time in Del Vecchio. No idea of period- or time-bounded analysis is traceable in Del Vecchio's thought. He did not apply the idea of equilibrium (and disequilibrium) to time, as John Hicks and the Swedish School would do later. Simply, time exists because current decisions include variables referred to future, and as we have seen, to the remote future as well. This means that Del Vecchio did not introduce the idea that expectations can be taken as constant for a given time. On the contrary, they can change continuously, thus generating radical uncertainty.

Is it possible to determine how much money individuals, firms or consumers will demand? No. In this lies the meaning of *irreducible uncertainty*, a concept that Del Vecchio had already made clear in 1917, if not before. This point will be developed in the following chapters.

However, finally, in an economy in which the rate of interest, determined as stated above, fixes the mass of money, is it crucial to quantify the stock of money beforehand? In effect, Del Vecchio seemed more interested, first, in establishing how the stock of money is distributed and the flows that such a distribution yields (see Chapter 3), and, second, to stress the role of the banking system (see Chapter 4) in managing that stock of money.

We may wonder from where Del Vecchio drew this view of expectations and the consequent uncertainty. He did not cite authors or sources that can steer us towards the right answer. I hypothesize that, as a statistician, Del Vecchio borrowed ideas from the then debate and research on economic barometers: that is, on research on price forecasts. Del Vecchio had been a pupil of Maffeo Pantaleoni, who on more than one occasion cited the economic barometers already known at the end of the nineteenth century.[103]

3 DISTRIBUTING THE STOCK OF MONEY

Moving to aggregate analysis, Del Vecchio's monetary theory must be read in light of the role that money plays in the self-organizing process connoting a changing economy. Money 'contributes' to organizing the price system of an economy, and to making the relationships between real and monetary variables work. While the mechanism of price formation is set by the characteristics of economic production and circulation, the trend of prices and expectations about them are the outcomes of a complex set of interactions involving both objective and subjective features, both real and monetary factors.

Money matters, not only as absolute quantity, but also if not mainly because it is canalized among the economic sectors or groups. The point was treated in original manner by Del Vecchio in his first articles, where acceptance that money can be demanded *per se* led him also to consider how money distributes itself among producers. Money distribution, a relative notion, more than the absolute stock of money, is the key feature because it embodies the essential relationships explaining the aggregate demand for money.

Del Vecchio grounded his analysis on the dynamic interrelation between, on the one hand, the distribution of money, i.e. how money is stored by some agents, and on the other, the circulation of money. Del Vecchio, in fact, presented his theory as a circulation theory, without directly relating it to money distribution. But, as will become clear on reading this chapter, Del Vecchio continuously oscillated, at least in his early writings, between issues concerning why money concentrates in some groups instead of others and the implications of admitting money as the main means of circulation.

The intertwining between these seemingly contrasting aspects inevitably brings to the fore the relational aspects of the economy, which, given a system of price determination, range from the size of firms, through the role of credit in favouring the circulation of goods, to money as a means allowing payments and reserves. All these aspects create a composite theory of the demand for money. The relevant point is that, in each of the areas, the distribution-circulation pair leads to specific developments that Del Vecchio did not structure in an established theory or analysis.

This approach to investigating how money is demanded and distributed had two immediate consequences. First, Del Vecchio was induced to re-modulate the quantity principle. He had doubts about the causation between the factors implied by that principle: for example, he did not believe that changes in the stock of money necessarily alter the level of prices. Moreover, he also chose an original way to rethink the quantity theory, grounding it on the distribution of money among productive sectors or firms. This view also entailed reference to the effectiveness of money in guaranteeing the circulation of goods. In its turn, the effectiveness of money could be considered an index of the level of competition or of organization of a given economy.

Secondly, considering the distribution of money from a general perspective brings a new concept – that of hierarchy – into the analysis. Del Vecchio put forward a hierarchical view of economic relationships evidenced by the fact that certain firms or sectors drain more money than others. This phenomenon can be read as the outcome of an economy far from perfect competition; but unequal or hierarchical relationships are a constant in Del Vecchio's realistic representation of the economy. This contributed to shifting Del Vecchio's attention away from a general equilibrium analysis, whose interdependence approach was considered effective when applied to production while it was inadequate when referred to circulation. In some cases, causal relationships are better able to explain real monetary facts.[1] However, Del Vecchio was not a theoretician of economic power relationships: it was his realism that led him simply to notice and admit their existence.

Analysis of these two points shows that distribution and circulation are ultimately two sides of the same coin: one cannot be explained without considering the other. The next section brings us closer to Del Vecchio's thought by introducing his notion of monetary equilibrium. The following ones deal with the revision of the quantity principle, at that time being reformulated by Irving Fisher, and the distributional issue of money. Here, Del Vecchio displayed all his originality. The subsequent section examines one particular aspect that is a consequence of the topic treated in the previous section: namely Del Vecchio's criticism of the velocity of circulation of money as a key variable. The sections thereafter attempt to reformulate first the quantitative theory and then the value of money in light of Del Vecchio's thought. The concluding section returns to the issue of money distribution and discusses the monetary aggregates considered by Del Vecchio.

The Aggregate Supply and Demand for Money

Although Del Vecchio constantly interacted with other scholars and their theories, and although he fully engaged in the debate of that time, reconstructing his monetary theory involves a journey in a world of concepts, views and arguments that at that time were not developed by other monetary economists. For this reason, some preliminary theoretical notes are required to convey his view of monetary equilibrium.

Although his early articles investigated individual or subjective monetary issues, monetary equilibrium was presumed, if not clearly developed. Thus, Del Vecchio conceived the idea of aggregate monetary equilibrium, where the supply and demand for money can match, but he did not dwell on this notion. Rather, he seemed to presuppose a supply of money that is always matched by the demand for money, the latter being carefully examined from both the aggregate and individual viewpoints. In 1925, he wrote that the bank system 'transforms' the supply of money in such a way as to adjust it to the demand.[2] Therefore, Del Vecchio's monetary theory is clearly a theory of the demand for money which purposely leaves the supply in the background.

Consequently, as we shall see, in his 1909–17 articles on monetary topics Del Vecchio did not analyse the monetary market from the monetary supply side. He was more interested in the mechanisms which allocate money among different groups, industries and, simply, agents. This is almost to say that it is pointless to examine the monetary supply if the allocation of that money is neglected. Clearly, money reaches its destinations by circulating, so that the two processes – circulation and distribution – cannot be treated as rigidly distinct.

Del Vecchio developed his monetary theory anchored to the demand for money in a period when Irving Fisher's reformulation of the quantity theory directed attention to the money supply. It must be pointed out that Del Vecchio wrote before the 1920s, i.e. the years that saw a substantial growth of publications focused on the demand for money.[3]

This does not mean that he disregarded the role of stocks and quantities. Quite the reverse: although he criticized the quantity theory, the role of stocks of money constantly re-emerged. At that time, the role of central banks was taking shape, with the result that the stock of money was considered to be the response of the issue banks to demand by the market. However, although Del Vecchio was not completely clear on this point, we can hypothesize that, as a follower of Francesco Ferrara, he could not accept that monopoly on monetary issue should be in the hands of a single bank.[4]

In theoretical terms, he looked favourably on a liberalized system of banks; but on practical grounds he recognized and accepted that countries progressively establish a monopoly on the monetary issue and regularize the banking system.

The reasons for the concentration of issue into a few institutes or a single one were of both technical and economic type. By contrast, Del Vecchio believed that such a tendency had solely a 'political and financial basis'.[5] He consequently maintained that the axiom of the monopoly of issue was not justified and was not the most effective solution: 'From the theoretical viewpoint, that statement [monopoly of issue] has prevented the establishment of the real theory of circulation because it considers as fundamental what has only a political origin'.[6] Del Vecchio was persuaded that when the political criterion, which is at the basis of the monopoly of issue, 'reigns' over paper circulation the link between circulation and deposits is definitively broken. However, although Del Vecchio did not go into details on the handling of the money stock, he was clear that the relationships between the money stock, on the one hand, and economic variables like prices or exchange rates on the other, are crucial for the working of monetary markets. Firstly, the causation between quantity of money and prices, and the exchange rate and the discount and interest rates, should be stated. Rather than one-way causation, Del Vecchio preferred to adopt interdependence as the interpretative key. Therefore, the above-mentioned economic variables influence the quantity of money and its distribution. It must be established how variables including prices, expected prices and the interest rate, among others, are conditioned by the stocks of money. Del Vecchio subjected the details of this reciprocal influence to thorough analysis. The price trend influences the distribution of money and thus its effects. Clearly, Del Vecchio was far from stating that the quantity of exchanged money had effects on the price level, either in the short or the long term. We will have to take this aspect into consideration when discussing the critical reinterpretation of the quantity theory that Del Vecchio proposed.

Alternating the individual and aggregate views, he treated them separately to affirm that the logics driving the two spheres were different. It can thus be presumed that the aggregate demand for money as defined by Del Vecchio cannot be derived from the individual one.

This point can be understood by stressing Del Vecchio's statistical knowledge, which undoubtedly shaped his view of economic phenomena.[7] He considered aggregates to be heterogeneous entities: when consumers or firms are considered together, they give form to heterogeneous groups that cannot be depicted as sums of representative agents. Therefore, the aggregate analysis requires methods that are logically different from those necessary for subjective or micro-analysis. It is not amiss to state that Del Vecchio 'assembled' the monetary aggregates by treating them as subjects, not as sums. The overall demand for money by an aggregate can be estimated only by considering the relationships among the components.

The Revision of the Quantity Principle

Beside that of money as commodity, Del Vecchio criticized a second, perhaps more crucial, dogma: the *quantity theory*. Considering the importance of the topic, here his position was not completely plain. More than rejecting the quantity principle, one may say that Del Vecchio rewrote it, starting from the assumption that the quantity principle cannot be considered a monetary theory for two reasons. Firstly, it assumes the quantity of goods as known or as given when, in reality, it is unknown.[8] Second, it postulates that money circulates continuously, which prevents it from being hoarded.

From the outset, Del Vecchio detached himself from the wide acceptance of the quantity theory[9] and sought new concepts confuting the contents of the latter. As we shall see, he refused to consider notions like the average velocity of circulation of money.[10] In 1925 he was even more precise:

> We must replace our considerations on *one* mass of commodities, *one* mass of money and *one* level of price, etc., with *many* heterogeneous masses of commodities, *many* heterogeneous masses of money and *many* levels of prices ... We must obtain a scheme more complex than that given by the quantity theory of money.[11]

The idea had already been put forward in 1909, when Del Vecchio argued that the average velocity is a concept of no utility once the distribution of money has been introduced into the analysis.[12]

The definition of economic averages, like the velocity of circulation of money, was also elaborated by Irving Fisher, in the *Mathematical Appendix* to chapter 2 of his 1911 *The Purchasing Power of Money*.[13] Fisher's mathematical treatment of the topic was indeed more complete and sophisticated than Del Vecchio's. Fisher was also interested in different velocities of circulation of money according to different goods and also to different times, but for the purpose of determining the average velocity. For each period he calculated the amount of money spent by a given person, and the amount of money possessed by that person. Thus, having established the times that money was spent by each person in a year, he could determine the rate of turnover per annum, or the velocity of circulation for each person and then the average of the values for different agents. In this way he obtained the velocity of circulation per annum or a given period.[14]

Del Vecchio's aim was entirely different. He was so deeply involved in investigation of the circulation of money that he could not ignore the fact that, by circulating, money concentrates and remains stored in given sectors, groups and industries, thus reducing the efficiency of the entire system. His rejection of the average velocity was intended to maintain the focus on factors that make monetary circulation easier or more difficult. It might be objected that the possible increased concentration of money is expressed in a reduced velocity of circulation. But, Del Vecchio argued, this change contains no or little information about where and how money can be circulated or hoarded.

The above quotation from Del Vecchio's 1925 article – anticipated by his 1909 statement about the uselessness of the notion of velocity of money circulation – dismissed any idea of a quantity theory and therefore posed the problem of what aggregates fit monetary relations. In fact, Del Vecchio's economic theory was not populated with average values leading to a tidy or Gaussian representation of economic variables.[15]

However, also when hypothesizing a quantity theory comprising one mass of money, one mass of goods and one velocity of circulation of money, Del Vecchio immediately focused on the circulation of money and goods. Money is a stock, but in a strictly monetary economy money matters because it circulates as well as goods. Money and goods circulate at the same velocity, but it is the circulation of goods that fixes the velocity of both. In a scheme where the velocity of circulation of money is ultimately caused by goods, the velocity of the latter contributes to determining the value of money. To put it differently, the factors influencing the circulation of goods become of great consequence for establishing monetary values. But if an average circulation of goods is an argument lacking in logic, then also the average circulation of money, identical by definition, does not have a logically acceptable meaning. Money follows goods, even when they do not circulate in a homogenous way, and when goods are stored also money may be hoarded.

Hence, Del Vecchio's criticism of the notion of average velocity of circulation relative to money was one of the first arguments that he put forward to dispute the quantity principle. As we shall see, this criticism also had a constructive side, which concerned the relation between money stock and prices.

When Del Vecchio wrote that 'the stock of circulating money is independent from its value',[16] he was implicitly stating that the mass of money does not determine its purchasing power: that is, it does not have a direct influence on prices. Analogously, the value of money, conceived here as the reciprocal of the price level, does not condition the velocity of circulation of both goods and money. Thus the quantity theory is nothing but a 'hypothetical abstraction' which may be valid only if both a closed economy and a stationary state are given.[17] Del Vecchio rewrote this equation, assuming the just-mentioned conditions, but also stating that the quantity theory, also when reformulated, is not an explanatory theory because it assumes as given variables – such as the mass of money – that which in fact are unknowns.

Del Vecchio was vague on this point, but it is clear that he considered the stock of money neither as a given value nor as an average quantity because he 'saw' the stock of money once it was put into circulation and then naturally distributed in a non-homogeneous way. In this regard, we stress that in Italy at that time the issue of money was not concentrated in a single bank. Because the destination of money is not known, one cannot foresee a clear effect of stock money change on the level of prices.

Del Vecchio considered his twofold criticism of the velocity of circulation of money, on the one hand, and the causal relation between stock of money and prices on the other, as sufficient to affirm the need to rethink the quantity principle. The latter, as Del Vecchio was wont to repeat, not without rhetorical tones, should be made more adherent to the economic reality. But before considering how Del Vecchio revised the quantity principle, one may wonder why Del Vecchio was so resolutely opposed to the use of average values.

Answers are provided by both his interest in the Marxian view on economics and his attention to statistical distributions. Both induced Del Vecchio to reject what today is termed the 'representative agent' or, more simply, the average value. As a legacy from Antonio Labriola's teaching, Del Vecchio paid constant attention to social inequality and, above all, to the social ladder enabling some individuals to gain better social positions (see Chapter 5). In this regard, in 1925 he wrote: 'A division among classes, as deep as the one that we are experiencing and co-existing with formal juridical equality, is sustainable only because a high social mobility is permitted'.[18]

Dynamism was a requirement for the survival of capitalism. According to Del Vecchio, economic theory (or pure economics) could not ignore this crucial feature of economic reality. But this progressive regime was guaranteed by economic institutions that might fail,[19] so that 'economic recession' might prevail. Del Vecchio's theory in its entirety was intended to be consistent with this postulate stating the centrality of dynamics, more than with mathematical reasoning.

Despite his youthful Marxian interests, Del Vecchio was never a Marxian. On the contrary, he was loyal to liberalism: he believed in individual enterprise, but precisely for this reason he could not ignore the fact that economic reality was deeply unequal, and that it was the cause of movement and dynamism. Individuals were heterogeneous in terms of wealth and money distribution, with the result that the economy, and not only society, was traversed by endogenous pressures for change. To be stressed is that Del Vecchio did not want those pressures to change: he simply recognized them as unavoidable.

The interest in statistical distribution is explained by the mastery of statistical analysis displayed by Vilfredo Pareto in his *Cours*,[20] a text repeatedly praised by Del Vecchio. Combining this feature with his interest in distribution inherited from Ricardo, Del Vecchio regarded the Pareto Law and other non-symmetrical distributions as tools of great interest for the analysis of wealth, but also of money. Given his interest in the Pareto Law, Del Vecchio could not ignore the distribution of both wealth and money. By contrast, because the quantity principle was grounded on average values, it was unconcerned with how money is distributed. When money is assumed as an endogenous variable, it cannot be represented by average magnitudes presupposing a Gaussian distribution. Given an unequal distribution of the money stock, also the other monetary variables, like the velocity of circulation of money, and according to Del Vecchio also prices, are not uniform either. Consequently, they cannot be expressed in terms of averages. Therefore, as shown below, it was precisely his focus on the distribution of money that prevented Del Vecchio from making use of average values. Obviously, this did not stop him from constantly seeking rigour in analysing the monetary variables, to the point that we can say that Del Vecchio's distinctive approach to money and circulation consisted of logical arguments coherent with economic reality plus statistical data.

Finally, a further reason for Del Vecchio's opposition to the quantity theory was his conception of the economic system. As we are told by Robert Skidelsky,[21] 'the quantity theory was the first theory of macroeconomic stabilization', and its acceptance involved the ideas that economic capitalism can be stabilized, and that economic fluctuations threaten the social order and must be brought under control. This – Skidelsky continued – was the view of monetary reformers like Irving Fisher and Knut Wicksell. Yet this aim was not to be found in Del Vecchio, who saw the then capitalist economy as an intrinsically unstable system that cannot be stabilized by means of measures grounded on acceptance of the quantity principle.[22]

The Notion of 'Selling Group'

The first step towards a revised quantity principle concerned the stock of money, considered not from the standpoint of the monetary supply, but from that of the demand for money. Before going into the details of Del Vecchio's treatment of the demand for money, it should be noted that he was writing in a country devoid of a central bank assuring the uniform distribution of money.[23] The latter concentrated according to the workings of the market, i.e. to the characteristics of the market in a country with strong economic differences among its regions. Nevertheless, this analysis raised a problem, that of the uneven distribution of liquidity, which was only supposedly resolved by the central bank's activity. Thus, Del Vecchio's analysis should be read as a reflection on the uneven distribution of liquidity with regard to the individual's monetary needs, where the 'individual' was not a single agent, but a group, sector, firm or industry.

It should first be pointed out that Del Vecchio proposed a theory of money which was neither micro- nor macro-founded; rather, it was a *meso*-theory built on the organization of a given economy into productive/social groups. This was nothing new in regard to the conception of monetary relationships as extensions of productive ones. But the detail that intermediate subjects (firms, productive sectors) were the protagonists of monetary relations was certainly an original feature.

This brief outline is sufficient to show that Del Vecchio's view was not consistent with Irving Fisher's famous analytical expression of the quantity theory.[24]

Therefore, Del Vecchio treated the stock of money as a mass depending on the behaviour of social or productive groups dominant in a given society. Differently from the traditional conception in the quantity theory, not *all* groups received the quantity of liquidity that they needed, but the *main groups* or *group* did so. It is this less direct idea that underpinned Del Vecchio's monetary theory, including its alternative view of the quantity theory.

Firstly, Del Vecchio referred to the volumes of transactions by the main components of the economy (landowners, entrepreneurs, farmers, workmen, domestic servants, and so on), as Richard Cantillon had done when treating monetary circulation in his *Essai sur la nature du commerce* (1755).[25] Del Vecchio labelled those components *selling groups*, by which he meant productive subjects characterized by specific customs and habits concerning monetary circulation, especially payments involving prior and subsequent hoarding. Here, the selling group combines both production and circulation, in the sense that its definition encompasses both the production and sale of commodities. In other words, the selling group is production plus payment(s) received or made. Del Vecchio wrote:

> The selling group is a set of goods as regards how a unit of money is used in a single transaction (not one as average, but one or nothing). The selling group will be determined for each period of time; after that, a unit of money can be used to make another exchange: if this period is very long we have a very high value of money; if the period is very short, we have a very small value of money.[26]

The longer the production process, the larger the amount of money demanded for the initial investments, and the larger the stock of money hoarded after the payments have been received. This clearly recalls the exchanges occurring in Cantillon's economy, where the distribution of agricultural products and exchanges between town and country are brought about in a monetary economy.[27] Here, the longer the production, the more liquidity is involved in that activity. This is the point that matters.

Del Vecchio presented selling groups by hypothesizing, *à la* Cantillon, an economy composed of a class of *farmers* and a class of *manufacturers*, who trade with each other by means of a class of *intermediaries*. Each good is traded two times: the first time involves the producer and the merchant; the second links the merchant to the consumer. In this economy there is no distribution, and the mass of money is homogeneous and divisible. The sole function of money is the transactional one. To be added is that wheat is harvested once a year while artefacts are continuously exchanged.[28] Here, the main selling group consists of farmers who sell their products once a year to merchants. According to Del Vecchio, the mass of money needed for this transaction defines the stock of money of the whole economy; but that money will be used for *all* the exchanges occurring among the different economic classes. The causes of the prevalence of one group's monetary needs over the others must be sought in the then existing power, economic and technical features.

Del Vecchio wrote:

> The main selling group is the one with the most discontinuous production, that is, without a continuous flow of goods ... Discontinuity concerns the circulation and not the production, with consequences on the value of money and the height of the rate of interest.[29]

Therefore, following Cantillon,[30] Del Vecchio centred his theory of circulation on the role played by the largest payments occurring in a given economy. At Cantillon's time, these payments were the rents that farmers paid to landlords. At the time of Del Vecchio, they were those concerning the main industries or economic sectors, but also an intermediary one like the banking system. What remained was the idea that the largest payments shape the circulation in its entirety.

To single out the selling groups, Del Vecchio did not consider an indistinct mass of goods, but rather the 'species' of goods. The simplest case is that in which half of the economy considered yields a species of goods that will be exchanged with one or more other variety of goods. In short, neither the individual nor the country, but the productive (or social) group, is the subject expressing demand for money according to the quantity of goods exchanged.

Put in a slightly different way, the main selling group is the group that imposes the largest monetary transactions on the economy. In so doing, it 'absorbs' the bulk of the circulating money. Del Vecchio specified that 'The size of the main selling group depends on technical and economic conditions, which, in their turn, are moulded by the economic principle of competition'.[31]

The main selling group can be also identified with a transaction that characterizes the entire economy because it involves a sum of money that is larger than those involved in other transactions. That sum of money is employed for that specific operation. But since that biggest payment requires time, money is in the meantime hoarded and borrowed by other minor groups needing money for their smaller but more frequent transactions.

Simplifying, we can suppose three selling groups, *A*, *B* and *C*, where the main one, *A*, corresponds to half the economy and the total of circulating money (Figure 3.1*a*). If one selling group exchanges half of all the goods produced in the economy, the value of those goods is equivalent to all the demand for money necessary for that economy. In this example, the money that *A* receives from selling its goods is sufficient to buy all *B* and *C*.[32]

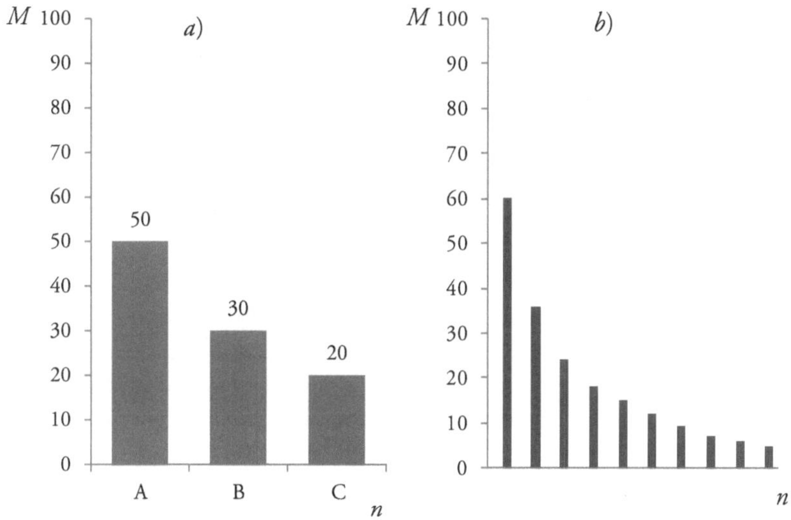

Figure 3.1: Distribution of money among selling groups.

Figure 3.1(*a*) gives an idea of the distribution of money. Shown in (*a*) are the three selling groups *A*, *B*, *C* of different sizes. *A* is the main selling group, and its demand for money is 50. We can suppose that *A*, making one or two payments yearly, lends 50 until it needs liquidity. Thus, 50 originally demanded by *A* circulates by means of the other selling groups that use them for their transactions. Thus, 50 are distributed between *B* and *C*, which receive 30 and 20 respectively. In reality, also when 50 are deposited, they can be borrowed by other groups and circulate as credit.

We can add that because the selling group decides the overall demand for money, it in fact fixes also the money circulating in the economic system: in short, it decides the money supply. This aspect, implicit in Del Vecchio's reasoning on the selling group, is consistent with the preference assigned to multiple monetary issues, but it assumes a different meaning by hypothesizing that the selling group is the banking one.

To return to our figures, in the case of many groups, it is more difficult to determine the demand for money.[33] Certainly, given many selling groups of different sizes, we can hypothesize a money distribution that assumes the form of an exponential distribution as depicted in Figure 3.1(*b*). If we increase the number of selling groups (firms), maintaining the different sizes, we obtain a curve following an exponential law with a long tail of small groups.

Despite Del Vecchio's opaqueness on this aspect, it is apparent that the amount of payments is the outcome of contracts among different agents. Mixed technical and juridical features concur to define the creditor/debt relationship, in which money is a tool, but whose use gives a representation of the economy's workings or also of its organization. It is not money itself that conditions the economic organization; rather, it is the use made of money. After all, by circulating, money shows how an economy performs.

Del Vecchio pointed out that many payments follow a calendar.[34] The paradigmatic example is that of farmers' transactions linked to the seasonality of harvests. Moreover, since industrial payments are more frequent, they do not show the same periodicity. Finally, agricultural transfers connote the monetary seasonality of the entire system.[35] However, although seasonality appears to have been his main concern, Del Vecchio stressed the importance of the unequal distribution of money among social classes.[36] This imbalanced distribution may also concern countries, mainly when they have different production structures: for example, agricultural versus industrial countries. But money distribution may be unequal for political, organizational or other reasons as well. These features prevent monetary variables from being expressed as averages, as Del Vecchio posited.

Briefly, with the introduction of selling groups, the demand for money depends on the behaviour of the social or productive groups prevailing in a given society, and this makes the quantity of money endogenous to economies.[37] Put differently, the demand for money in a given economy is determined by its productive system, by the sizes of its main firms or industries, and also by the level of competition typifying that specific economy. Del Vecchio said that, given prices, the value of goods exchanged is not sufficient information to establish the demand for money and, consequently, its supply. Nor does the velocity of monetary circulation as an average value allow completion of the calculus. What is lacking is an indicator of *how* money circulates in the economic system: this clarifies the reference to Cantillon's selling group as incorporating the quantity exchanged but also some information about how goods are traded. If the timeframe of payments is important, another variable that can furnish this type of information is the *effectiveness* of money, which will be examined in the next section. Here we can anticipate that the effectiveness of money, added to the moved *mass of goods*, completes the notion of the *main selling group*. To prevent misunderstandings, it should be made clear that the adjective *main* does not mean *better* or *most effective*, but refers to the main selling group according to the mass of money exchanged.

Velocity of Circulation and Effectiveness of Money

The notion of 'selling group' obliged Del Vecchio to recognize the existence of different velocities of circulation of money (and goods), thus connecting the demands for money to the production structures. But, not only did he reject the velocity of circulation as an average, because it would be insufficient to give a complete representation of monetary circulation, he also replaced it with the notion of the *effectiveness of money*.

The substitution of the velocity of circulation of money, *V*, with the *effectiveness* of money, *E*,[38] was a pillar of Del Vecchio's rejection of quantity theory. In fact, by means of this concept he attempted to introduce qualitative features besides the *physical* or quantitative ones represented by the velocity.

The notion of the effectiveness of money must be strictly associated with that of selling group. By stating that 'the selling group is a set of goods transacted with a unit of money',[39] Del Vecchio seemingly adopted the definition given to the 'efficiency of currency' by William S. Jevons in 1876: 'By the efficiency of a currency we mean the average number of exchanges effected by each piece of money in a unit of time, such as a year'.[40] If a given stock of money can exchange a larger amount of goods, it increases its efficiency or effectiveness. Jevons then considered the rapidity of monetary circulation as expressing the efficiency of money. Thus rapidity or velocity became a measure of the efficiency of money, the latter depending mainly on technical innovation.[41]

This was partially true in Del Vecchio's theory as well, but with some adjustment, because by means of the effectiveness of money he pointed out that the velocity of money could not be treated as a constant, as claimed by the mainstream thought of that time. He believed that the velocity of circulation of money changed according to the sector and to the behaviour of agents (firms).[42]

Also Irving Fisher used the term 'efficiency' as a synonym for the 'velocity of circulation' of money in his *The Purchasing Power of Money*, defining it as 'the average number of times a year money is exchanged for goods'.[43] Fisher specified that

> The important magnitude, called the velocity of circulation, or rapidity of turnover, is simply the quotient obtained by dividing the total money payments for goods in the course of a year by the average amount of money in circulation by which those payments are carried out. This velocity of circulation for an entire community is a sort of average of the rates of turnover of money for different persons. Each person has his own rate of turnover which he can readily calculate by dividing the amount of money he expends per year by the average amount he carries.[44]

Del Vecchio attempted to go beyond mechanical velocity, which must necessarily be considered an average, to find a more revealing concept. Effectiveness can be better understood if money is treated as more a means of circulation than a means of payment. If money allows goods to circulate, as stated by Marx,[45] it becomes more a *technology of circulation* than a *technology of exchange*. Del Vecchio weakened the notion of velocity, although he preserved the idea that velocity concerns more the demand for money than its supply, as subsequently stated by Marius W. Holtrop in a cited article about the velocity of money: 'the size of the cash-balance is not dependent on the properties of the coins, but on the will of the owner, which is governed by economic motives'.[46] Similarly, the effectiveness of money must be considered a classical notion associating the 'rapidity of circulation' with the demand for money, while the post-classical velocity was related to the supply of money.[47]

Even if Del Vecchio's notion of effectiveness seemed to be synonymous with rapidity of circulation, it assumed a more revealing meaning when Del Vecchio specified that, by 'effectiveness' he was referring not only to the fact that money allows goods to circulate but also to the 'capacity' of money to make goods circulate. This capacity does not derive from specific characteristics of money, but from how money is used given the type or organization of the economic regime. The level of effectiveness is thus 'intrinsic' to the economic regime under consideration; in some sense it is an index of how that regime works. Although Del Vecchio did not discuss the advantages deriving from the use of money, it is indubitable that monetary effectiveness evokes an improvement in the organization that can be expressed as reduction of transaction costs, although obviously Del Vecchio did not make use of such a notion. But money (and credit) allows activities and transactions that do not occur in a non-monetary economy. Money may involve a cost, too, but it allows the economy to work. Del Vecchio believed that money reduced the organizational costs of operating the economy.

At this point we can fully understand the notion of 'selling group', which is not a strictly productive or real notion in that it is also a 'monetary' concept: 'the concept of selling group is ... different from both a distributive group and a mass of circulating goods, because it also contains the effectiveness of money'.[48] In other words, it can be identified by starting from the monetary transactions that a selling group performs. The more money is demanded and hoarded, the less it is effective in that economy. It is immediately clear that the effectiveness of money increases as the size of the main selling group decreases. Thus, it is the *way* in which goods circulate by means of money that defines the selling group. Clearly, as increasing uncertainty demands more hoarded money, it reduces the effectiveness of money.

On the one hand, this confirms that Del Vecchio conceived money as a medium of exchange and not as an asset. But, as discussed in the previous chapter, this did not exclude that money can be demanded *per* se, without any connection with immediate exchanges. If competition means more kinds of goods and, consequently, more selling groups, the effectiveness of money increases according to the expansion of the level of competition. It was no accident that Del Vecchio grounded his arguments concerning the effectiveness of money on Cantillon's rents paid by farmers to landlords. That was a case of the limited effectiveness of money. Hence, the effectiveness of money must be associated with the concept of 'selling group' and with the circulation of goods, which is not a technical question alone, but also a matter of will and economic relationships.

The notion of 'efficiency', with the same meaning as effectiveness, would return in Schumpeter's 1917 article *Das Sozialprodukt*, where the 'income-velocity' is defined by the ratio between the quantity of money in circulation and the income. Stating that the quantity of money is not the 'stock of money but the latter minus bank reserves, 'hoards' and 'reserves' of private individuals, as well as money used in what Schumpeter called the 'capital-sphere' – that is, money used for the purpose of transferring property rights[49] – Marget wrote that Schumpeter conceived 'efficiency' (*Effizienz*), 'as the number of times money enters into income [becoming] automatically equivalent to its definition as the number of times it is spent on consumers' goods'.[50]

After Schumpeter, Pigou, Marget and others, analysis of the velocity of circulation focused on income, where the intent was 'to show how income affects prices'. In this way, money was confined to its intermediary function, without performing other functions that enable exchanges. Moreover, the idea of velocity as average was implicit. Instead, Del Vecchio emphasized that it is the ratio between groups that connotes the circulation of goods and, consequently, of money. In Del Vecchio's theory, 'velocity of circulation of goods' and 'velocity of circulation of money' are equivalent concepts.

The point is this: can money influence the relationship among goods? By using a qualitative notion like the effectiveness of money, instead of a technical one like the velocity of circulation of money, Del Vecchio agreed that effectiveness is the result rather than the cause of such a relationship, the latter depending on the economy's organizational characteristics. Thus, at first sight, money as such does not influence the circulation of goods. A different result emerges if we consider the distribution of money instead of money itself. Not the characteristics of money, but its distribution may condition the circulation of goods. It is sufficient to think of the exponential law set out above. Finally, the distribution of money includes also its storage as bank deposits and their availability to borrowers.

To be investigated in this regard is the use made by Keynes of the notion of 'efficiency' applied to money in his *Treatise on Money*. He wrote that: 'The 'velocity' measured the average frequency with which a coin (or a bank-note) changed hands, and thus indicated the 'efficiency' of the currency for the transaction of business'.[51]

This view brings the 'velocity of circulation' back to the effective money in active circulation 'and not to stultify the conception by watering down the velocity of the money in circulation by including money which was not in circulation at all, but was being used as a "store of value" and therefore had *no* velocity'.[52] This view was evident in Del Vecchio as well, when he linked effectiveness to rapid payments, as opposed to long ones, considered as less effective because they implied the hoarding of money.

Keynes then related *efficiency* (E) to the ratio of Bank Clearings to Total Deposits, maintaining that it differed from the velocity of circulation of cash or cash deposits (V):

> It follows that $E = Vw$, where w is the proportion of the Cash-deposits to the total deposits. It is not inappropriate to call the expression E the *Efficiency* or *Cash-Efficiency* of Bank-Money. For the greater this fraction becomes, the greater the volume of Bank-Money is; – a growth of savings-deposits decreasing, and a falling away, and a falling away increasing, the 'efficiency of Bank-Money for cash purposes.[53]

Hence the efficiency of money embraces the role played by individual and banking reserves, a point extensively developed by Del Vecchio, first in 1909 and then overall in his writings of 1913 and 1914, as we shall see in the following chapters.

Reformulating the Quantity Theory

Considering the quantity principle unsatisfactory, Del Vecchio reinterpreted it from a different perspective.

To summarize, if E is the effectiveness of money as stated above, Q is the total mass of goods exchanged in a given economy in a time t, P is the price index in the economy, Qmg is the good traded by the main selling group, as above defined, and Pmg the price index of that good, then the effectiveness of money is:

$$E = \frac{QP}{Q_{mg} P_{mg}} \qquad 3.1$$

where P and P_{mg} can be assumed = 1. Therefore, the effectiveness of money is the ratio between two monetary amounts of exchanged goods.

$$E = \frac{Q}{Q_{mg}} \qquad 3.2$$

We can suppose that each group makes use of a given quantity of money proportionally to its exchanges. Evidently, the larger the exchanges, the larger the amount of money used. But each demand for money hinges not only on the exchange but also on the frequency of exchanges, that is, on how rapidly that group makes money circulate. Moreover, that rapidity will be conditioned by many factors, including the social and economic role of the group. Thus, the term 'effectiveness' sums up all these aspects better than mechanical 'velocity'.

This is not a quantitative notion alone; it is a qualitative one as well, because the ratio tells us something about the organization of the economy, about the relation between overall production and the role played by the biggest sector or group. In this way, Del Vecchio established a relation between money and the level of competition.

The weakness of this concept lies in its measure when the number of selling groups increases (Q_{mgs}). In this case, the demand for money cannot be established by one group only. In that case, the above equation 3.2 must be replaced by the following:

$$E = f(Q, Q_{mgs}) \qquad 3.3$$

Stating that E increases as the size of the main selling group, Qmg, diminishes but not in a proportional way.

However, having stated that $Q_{mg}P_{mg}$ is equal to the demand for money for the whole economy, from equation 3.2 we obtain:

$$Q_{mg}P_{mg}E = QP$$

If we have two groups only of the same size, it is evident that E is equal to 2 and the overall demand for money, Mmg, is half global production according to the following:

$$M_{mg}E = QP \qquad 3.4$$

Differently, if the selling groups are more than two we have to measure E according to what said above. However, we can write:

$$ME = QP \qquad 3.5$$

that represents the quantity principle according to Del Vecchio.

If the economy comprises more numerous and competitive selling groups, then the demand for money depends on the total quantity of exchanged goods, and the factor E defines the relation between the demand for money oriented by the main selling groups and the need of the whole economy.

This revised expression of the quantity principle is the first general conclusion of these early statements by Del Vecchio: the demand for money is determined directly by the quantity of goods exchanged, but it is so according to the type of economic organization of the economy, here symbolized by the effectiveness of money, E.

Consequently, effectiveness entails consideration of the capacity to influence the entirety of monetary exchanges. Clearly, this concept prevents the use of notions such as 'average mass of circulating money', which becomes a 'nonsense' in Del Vecchio's view. We may add that average concepts are precisely the opposite of the relational concepts emphasized in Del Vecchio's approach.

Hypothesizing, according to Del Vecchio, that the whole demand for money, M, is that of the main selling, M_{mg}, thus $M = M_{mg}$, we can rewrite 3.5 as follows:

$$M = QP/E \qquad 3.6$$

This can be named the *Del Vecchio behavioural equation*. Interpreting Del Vecchio, who never explicitly formulated such a relation, and recalling that M must be considered from the viewpoint of the demand for money, it can be said that the overall demand for money depends on the price-sum of goods exchanged, but also and inversely on the effectiveness of money exemplifying the characteristics of the economic regime, for example, the periodicity of payments, but also its economic organization consisting in the size of production groups, the level of competition, and so on. It cannot be treated as an identity because the stock of demanded money may be different from the ratio between the price-sum of goods and the effectiveness of money.[54]

Reversing Del Vecchio's behavioural equation, we obtain the following equation:

$$E = QP/M \qquad 3.7$$

That is, the effectiveness of money changes according to the excess or the shortage of money relative to the requirement of the economic system. A diminishing E can also mean that the same price-sum of goods requires more money because exchange practices have changed. In short, the organization of trade has changed.

Del Vecchio's idea that the economic system is self-organizing periodically came to the fore. In effect, the so-called 'Del Vecchio behavioural equation' $M = QP/E$ tells us that a relation exists between the demanded quantity of money and its effectiveness.[55] We may resume the notion of effectiveness as resulting from Del Vecchio's analysis: that is, it is a variable containing information about the structure of the production system and the payment system, which is the result of individual decisions as well. The entrepreneur can decide to modify the quantity of hoarded liquidity on the basis of his expectations about risk and the future. Effectiveness is both an *objective* and *subjective* variable. It thus constitutes a sort of ideal bridge between macro- or, better, meso-analysis and subjective or micro-analysis.

Therefore, the behaviour of agents, firms and consumers conditions the effectiveness of money and then the monetary balance. Admitting rising expected prices, P^e, it leads to greater demand for money *per se*.

$$\Delta M = Q\Delta P^e / E \qquad 3.8$$

This point can be stated in different terms. The circulation of a given quantity of goods may require different quantities of money according to expectations about prices. If we hypothesize that a given system can absorb a different stock of money, also at given prices, the notion of average money-velocity loses part of its meaning,[56] being substituted by a more meaningful variable. However, this point will be made clearer in later chapters.

At first sight, the inclusion of the effectiveness of money, *E*, reduces the significance of the same quantity of money: the above Del Vecchio behavioural equation is a sort of *anti-quantity* theory,[57] simply because it envisages a variable that can react to the change of money. If *M* increases, *E* can decrease, maintaining the relation between *M* and *QP*. Although Del Vecchio did not write what we have called his 'behavioural quantity equation' in his 1909 article, he was highly critical of the quantity theory. His entire theoretical construct based on productive groups and the distribution of money is a clear demonstration of his position. Unfortunately, in his subsequent articles he partially abandoned, or at least did not elaborate, his ideas on selling groups and the distribution of money, partially restoring the quantity theory to its position of indisputable importance.

It is evident that the last equation built on Del Vecchio's reasoning differs from Fisher's well-known quantity equation[58] because of the presence of *E* instead of *V*, M^d instead of M^s. That is to say, for Del Vecchio money matters according to its distribution; in the case of Fisher, money matters according to its velocity of circulation. The two equations are quite similar, but their meanings are rather different. While velocity can be treated as a constant, the distribution of money finds expression in effectiveness, which is a behavioural variable.

To conclude this point, in confirmation that, according to Del Vecchio, the quantity principle became a theory of the demand for money, we can express the latter as follows:

$$M = f(\underset{+}{Q}, \underset{+}{P^e}, \underset{-}{E}) \qquad 3.9$$

where the demand for money gets bigger with the increase of *Q* and P^e, while decreases improving the effectiveness *E*.

The Organizational Function

Del Vecchio did not explicitly concentrate on the appropriate stock of money. He stated that the supply of money must balance the demand. But, on admitting that money may be substituted by credit, the issue of the right stock of money arises.

One feature concerns the consequences of the type of organization characterizing a given economic system in terms of demand for money. Del Vecchio did not only deem organization to be 'the main object of economic theory',[59] nor did he only observe that economic organization is more important inasmuch as the economic is dynamic, but he also related organization to firms, which in their turn shape the market. He explicitly focused on the economic organization of the capitalist system, emphasizing both its level of stability and price-making process as its distinctive features: 'After all, in the capitalistic system the economic organization is a relationship among prices, that is, a relation between certain prices and certain others'.[60]

As we shall see, money and circulation play a role in shaping this relation. But two points should be stressed before examining monetary features further. First, the relation between prices is also diachronic, and not solely synchronous: that is, past, current and future prices must be considered. As we shall see, this is an important part of Del Vecchio's circulation theory. Second, prices are determined according to the market regime. Competition is only one of the possibilities. Del Vecchio did not aprioristically assume perfect competition to be the ideal market regime: he admitted, in abstract, a plurality of market regimes ranging from competition to economic centralization.

Within a competitive regime, the entrepreneur assumes a central role because he makes prices with the purpose of increasing his profit, and he assumes some risk. But it is not possible to foresee what type of competitive market will emerge: more or less competitive, more or less fragmented or concentrated. Money is an essential factor in this continuously changing process called 'organization'. The demand for money *per se*, i.e. not directly explained by exchanges, is a basic feature of this organizational process: money allows and facilitates economic organization. Some years later, Del Vecchio would write: 'Each economic activity needs a certain "cassa" [the Walrasian "encaisse" or a "fund"], i.e., a certain quantity of disposable currency, and such quantity changes according to the subject, which could be a household, a firm, a government'.[61] Hence, each economic unit holds a certain amount of money that can be associated with the economic organization.

Moreover, the concept of effectiveness implicitly entailed a relation between exchanged goods and demand for money. Del Vecchio specified that the more the economy is competitive and less monopolistic, the greater its effectiveness and the smaller the quantity of money required. On the other hand, the expression of effectiveness proposed by Del Vecchio – the ratio between the total amount of produced goods and the amount yielded by the main selling group – is indeed a measure of competitiveness. But the effectiveness of money may be different also in the presence of the same type of market, because it is also a consequence of how the economy is organized, either competitively or monopolistically.

Therefore, to return to the initial point, once velocity of circulation and level of prices are given, the stock of money is not determined by the national product or income alone; nor is money solely the product of the need to exchange a given amount of goods. On introducing effectiveness, the stock of money depends also on the characteristics of the productive system. Thus, the way in which the production and circulation of goods are organized is an important factor in determining the demand for money and, given a banking system that guarantees monetary balance, its supply.

For the time being, here we conclude that the effectiveness of money synthesizes the organizational features of an economy.

Reformulating the Value of Money

Anticipating that in a simple economy (few groups) the value of money, V_M, is given by the ratio between the main selling group, *Qmg*, and the stock of circulating money, *Mmg*:

$$V_M = \frac{Q_{mg}}{M_{mg}} \quad 3.10$$

and, as seen above, given $Q_{mg} = \frac{Q}{E}$, we obtain

$$V_M = \frac{Q}{M_{mg} E} \quad 3.11$$

that is, the value of money is equal to the ratio between the quantity of goods and the stock of money, employed by the main selling group but also supplied in the economy, and its effectiveness. Only when this aspect is taken into account does Del Vecchio's following claim (in regard to a simple economy with few selling groups) become meaningful:

> Only the main selling group matters for the value of money; on the contrary, the others might join or break up without any effect on the value because they make use of excess money as regards the goods circulating in that moment.[62]

Given the above assumptions and remembering that the stock of money, *Mmg*, is the circulating money *M*:

$$V_M = f(\underset{+}{Q}, \underset{-}{M}, \underset{-}{E}) \quad 3.12$$

This states that there is a link between the value of money and its quantity, a notion that Del Vecchio never abandoned;[63] and, more importantly, that there is an opposite relation between the value of money and its effectiveness, the latter expressing the various aspects mentioned above.

This is a point crucial for understanding Del Vecchio's specific categories. Because the effectiveness of money is an index of how money is used, the value of money itself must be related to effectiveness. But when a productive group tends to monopolize exchanges, money is held to postpone transactions, and its value rises. Therefore, as productive groups store money or demand it *per se*, money devoted to exchanges diminishes, increasing its value. But, since the value of money depends on its storage, the fact that money is not equally distributed cannot be ignored.

To use different terminology, the value of money is conditioned by the money not demanded for immediate exchanges. Put briefly, Del Vecchio made the value of money depend on the demand for *liquidity*: his notion of 'cassa' or fund. Although 'liquidity' is not a Del Vecchio concept, he sometimes gave the impression that he conceived the demand for money as a demand for liquidity. In 1914 he wrote: 'the demand for money is constituted by the mass that the public stores in each time: it depends on its habits'.[64] The reference to habits – that is, a long-run concept – requires consideration of all the demanded money, not just that determined by exchanges of goods.

At this point, it is also clear that Del Vecchio associated the hoarding of money with characteristics of competition and economic organization. The less competitive (less organized) the market, the less effective is the use of money, and finally the higher is the demand for liquidity and, consequently, the value of money. Expressed in this way, the value of money can be considered an index of the competition (organization) characterizing a given economy.

Del Vecchio implicitly assumed that the more competitive the market, the more effective the use of money. Associated with this is the observation that competition reduces both organizational and transactional costs. The concentration of production therefore probably also entails a less effective use of money and higher costs. Consequently, the existence of concentrated firms leads to an unequal distribution of money which entails a gain in value. In fact, by proposing a monetary theory anchored to the characteristics of the production system, Del Vecchio put forward a theory of the distribution of money. Although not formally stated, Del Vecchio's theory of circulation gradually proved to be a *theory of monetary distribution*, an approach practically unknown at that time.

It must be also clear that Del Vecchio maintained a general approach to the economic system, if not economic equilibrium, at the core of which was the intertwining among production, distribution and circulation. The *quasi*-paradoxical aspect is that only money (liquidity) is the factor connecting these three *momenta* of the economic activity. Money links production to distribution and distribution to circulation, while the latter is linked to production by means of exchanged goods. This is the essence of its organizational character.

The first conclusion that can be drawn from the role assigned by Del Vecchio to selling groups is that the value of money is determined by the amount exceeding the quantity immediately needed for exchanges: in practice, the demand for liquidity. If money is not stored and can circulate, it reduces its value, which, on the contrary, comes to the fore when money is hoarded or for future payments. If money were completely and immediately used for exchanges, it would not gain in value. Evident here is the cross-reference to the value of money as interest rate or discount rate.[65]

This dependency of the demand-for-money on subjective evaluations of future monetary needs, besides the current ones, makes the overall demand for money extremely unstable, which in its turn hampers any application of the quantity principle – with which, however, Del Vecchio disagreed.

A second conclusion is that the distribution of money, and thus its value, depends on the use made of it for immediate exchanges, on the one hand, and for hoarding on the other. Both are linked to exchanges, but with different time scales. If exchanges are postponed, the hoarding of money increases its value. Thus value is implicitly a time variable.

Third, the circulation of money is strictly connected to the goods produced and exchanged, but also to the fact that money is not stored. Money hoardings can make more exchanges difficult, particularly those involving small selling groups.

In the conclusions to his 1909 article, Del Vecchio revealed all his doubts about the correspondence between economic models and economic reality and simultaneously his multiple view of money:

> Real monetary phenomena are very different from the abstract hypothesis establishing that money is a fixed quantity, expressing only a monetary utility, circulating in a single perfect market. In the latter, two goods endowed with a simple and immediate utility are exchanged at given velocity and effectiveness, without any intervention by the banking system. That hypothesis concerning money could be substituted with money possessing many qualities and functions besides that of being a real intermediary in transactions. Money could furnish another utility besides that concerning transaction – that of credit, among others. The velocity of circulation of money is not constant; rather, it is variable, which depends on the conditions of production ... As well as the goods increase yielded, the effectiveness of money changes following the rate between the total of goods and the production of the main selling group. Finally, capital goods are treated as simple goods, according to the idea that many markets are more realistic than a single uniform market, the former continuously changing because of factors such as savings.[66]

Taking account of these points, all of which influence the monetary balance, Del Vecchio asserted the need for a theory of circulation, not a theory of money.[67] The discrepancies derive from the dynamic view that Del Vecchio held even when he was explicitly assuming a static perspective. But he always kept an eye on circulation rather than money alone: money is the main circulating medium; effectiveness concerns the circulating money; the velocity is obviously that of circulating money. The utility of money is connected to its circulation, not to a pre-existing value. By contrast, as will be demonstrated, it is the monetary rate of interest that precedes and determines the value of money.

Del Vecchio's View on the Aggregate Demand for Money

As mentioned above, Del Vecchio rejected average variables like those included in the quantity equation. This raises problems concerning the passage from individual to aggregate variables or, better, in this case from aggregate to individual magnitudes. In this regard, Del Vecchio, although not explicitly, followed Pareto and his statistical analysis developed in the second book of the *Cours* (1896–7). Aggregates and individuals must consequently be analysed as autonomous subjects, although there is a mutual dependence between them. The starting point is recognition that aggregates are composed of heterogeneous individuals. This aspect clarifies the specificity of Pareto's conception of aggregate entity: 'Society as an aggregate is different from the individuals forming it, but this does mean that society can exist independently from individuals'.[68]

Aggregations and society are thus entities separate from the individuals of which they are composed. But sums or averages cannot give the exact magnitude of the aggregate phenomenon; the latter can be better expressed by means of distribution curves like the Pareto Law. Pareto is known for his individualistic approach, which however did not restrain him from granting subjectivity to aggregate entities. In his 1902–3 *Les Systèmes Socialistes*, Pareto stated that 'the features of aggregates are not the sum of those of parties; neither can they be obtained from their juxtaposition ... the outcome of many things is not the sum of them'.[69]

That aggregates must be treated separately from individuals is evident when Pareto introduced references to statistical tools. The application of the latter to the conception of social equilibrium enabled Pareto to treat individuals and aggregates separately while maintaining a strict link between them. In some sense, aggregates were always micro-founded. But it was apparent that social equilibrium could be conceived independently from individuals. In 1994 Michio Morishima noted how, on passing from economic equilibrium to social equilibrium, Pareto's thought was more closely related to the concept of equilibrium in statistical mechanics.[70]

That was a rather common view among the Italian economists from Pareto onwards. Alfonso De Pietri Tonelli gave an instance of this when writing:

> [J]ust as it is not possible to study the movement of each gas particle against the bottle containing it, but it is feasible to deal with pressure and gas mass by means of statistical averages ... so it is not possible to study the impulses of each individual, but it is possible to deal with the uniformities resulting from averages and sums of the actions of heterogeneous individuals belonging to a given social circle or class, according to the random distribution of such impulses.[71]

De Pietri-Tonelli[72] theorized a market characterized by the heterogeneity of individuals. He did so by drawing on analyses based on statistical and probabilistic methods conducted by Italian statisticians and mathematicians during the early decades of the twentieth century. Interest in such topics and phenomena is apparent in the other Paretians: Giuseppe Palomba,[73] who wrote on the equilibrium among heterogeneous economic groups; and Arrigo Bordin,[74] who developed an interesting approach to probabilistic economic equilibrium. Finally, Luigi Amoroso, the best-known Paretian scholar, is cited by economists for his attempts to dynamize Pareto's general economic equilibrium, and by today's econophysicists for his 'generalized gamma distribution' derived from the Pareto Law.[75]

Gustavo Del Vecchio made use of another image: that of a fish tank containing fish moving autonomously. The form of the tank remains the same (society), while the fish are moving. In fact, he added that also the 'tank' changes because the society changes.[76] This was perfectly consistent with the view of theory that he was incubating and which led him to state that 'the new theories are fragmented and not unitary as in the past ... [Such theories] proceed according to the observed facts'.[77] We may extend to Del Vecchio what Pasquale Jannacone wrote about Pareto in 1949:

> Pareto's thought oscillates between a representation of social equilibrium as mechanical equilibrium – a balance of forces – as stated in pure economics, and as statistical equilibrium consisting in continuous balance among the interdependent elements forming a group. Perhaps one depiction may be useful for representing certain problems while the other is useful for others. But, once the social system is considered as a whole, the statistical depiction prevails, as for that matter it does in other fields of the social sciences.[78]

Although not clearly specified, Del Vecchio's equilibrium involves both individuals and groups (see the selling group). It is not the result of actions by 'representative agents', as we would say today, or of aggregates resulting from the sum of agents. When aggregates are considered, equilibrium is the result of the encounter among complex subjects like groups. The statistical reading of economic phenomena may be of help because it allows consideration of aggregates as autonomous entities whose behaviour is independent from that of the heterogeneous individuals involved.

This type of equilibrium fits better with Del Vecchio's theory when we consider that economic organization is focused on decisions by firms and entrepreneurs. If we envisage that each entrepreneur formulates a demand for money, we can obtain a distribution of these demands according to the economic regime prevailing in that economy. In some sense, we extend the idea of selling groups to a more complex and fragmented economy, where the distribution of firms may be uniform but also strongly polarized. In the latter case, many causes can explain the unequal distribution, perhaps with a long tail; but here more than causes it is outcomes that are important.

As we shall see on analysing the concept of the psychological rate of interest, social turnover is crucial when wealth and income are unequally distributed.[79] Del Vecchio listed the possible causes of this inequitable distribution, but rather than focusing on them, he preferred to point out that society and economy constantly change also because of the attempts made by many individuals to improve their position:

> The internal [to society] flows of social turnover are not constant, but they change with the historical moment. Taking this into consideration, we can hypothesize that economic inequality stimulates economic activity and entrepreneurship.[80]

These movements probably do not change the form of the distribution curve, the Pareto-curve evidencing that wealth is concentrated into a small part of the population while the remaining vast majority of individuals are poor. But although an increase in wealth makes the rich even richer, it allows the poor to improve their circumstances.

This view is very similar to the following contemporary definition of statistical equilibrium:

> Over time the distribution of wealth in the economy converges to an exponential distribution, and stays there. Even though the individual economic actors continue to exchange money, and ascend or descend the wealth scale, the overall distribution of wealth in the economy remains constant. Some poor people may get rich, some rich people get poorer, but the overall situation remains the same. A small number of people end up with a lot of money.[81]

It is true that Del Vecchio contextualized this exponential distribution (actually, he meant a Pareto law distribution) in a dynamic context, showing that inequality grows when wealth increases: the additional distribution to the poor makes it possible to maintain social equilibrium. But inequality in distribution must diminish when social wealth decreases; otherwise the social equilibrium may be challenged.[82] Nevertheless, 'a system can be in a statistical equilibrium even when its configuration is continually changing'.[83]

Yet the economic and also monetary equilibrium devised by Del Vecchio fully corresponds to a statistical equilibrium. That equilibrium is grounded on the idea that each individual has money and can exchange it. Money is not a veil, but its main function is to allow exchanges. Exchanging money is the condition for maximizing utility (for minimizing energy in a statistical equilibrium), but the amounts of money exchanged are random: from very small to very large. To reduce this uncertainty, Del Vecchio cited the role of the main selling group and its amount of demanded money, the latter should be sufficient to cover the monetary needs of all the economy. As seen, Del Vecchio implicitly admitted a large heterogeneity of agents, firms or sectors, to the point that money is so unequally distributed that the demand by the biggest actors steers and conditions the behaviour of all other agents.

Before continuing, it should be pointed out once again that Del Vecchio devised a representation of the aggregate distribution and demand for money grounded on organizational as well as institutional features. Aside from reinterpretation of Cantillon's scheme and its relevance to an economic world populated by many sectors and groups, it is undisputable that Del Vecchio raised a problem often concealed by the use of average values: that of the concrete distribution of money among groups, sectors, industries, or other entities.

In conclusion, the aggregate demand for money is a more serious affair than the sum of the individual demands. It is a concept that necessarily involves features concerning organization, hierarchy, habits, expectations, time, and yet others.

4 SUPERVISING MONETARY BALANCE

While the previous two chapters have focused on the demand for money (both subjective and aggregate), this chapter will look at the supply of money, or better, of money and credit, obviously from Del Vecchio's perspective, which in this case, too, does not lack originality.

We must start from two main simplifications that Del Vecchio attributed to the then most widespread monetary theories. The first was that theorists analysed a pure monetary regime without considering credit:

> A perfect monetary regime without credit is not only an unreal system, but it admits a hypothesis that is not useful for building an economic theory of circulation ... An economy without credit is not a first approximation, but it is an absolute falsification of real monetary facts.[1]

It goes against history and experience to deny the role of credit, which does not follow monetary institutions but appears simultaneously with them. By means of credit, banks can sell monetary services even when money is unavailable.[2] In other words, credit provides the same services as money.

Second, monetary theories at that time were static, with no concession made to time:

> The fundamental error of pure monetary theory is to represent the monetary phenomenon as a scheme implying an instant and a unique act. *On the contrary, the extension through time of the monetary phenomena is intrinsic to them and it cannot be disowned.*[3]

An exchange involving money cannot be isolated from what will happen subsequently, i.e. another exchange, and so on. Therefore, money necessarily involves time, even more so if one considers that credit is an intrinsically temporal phenomenon.

If money can be considered an instrument of economic organization, its contribution assumes full significance only if credit is included among the monetary tools. It will be shown that, by mixing the use of money and credit, the banking system can better stabilize the monetary market and the overall economy.

After a long discussion on the demand for money, this chapter concentrates on the supply of money and credit, the latter as a crucial factor deep-rooted in economic dynamics. Del Vecchio was persuaded that credit is not solely a complement of money. It is essential for the working of an economy based on exchanges, and not only because it makes the economy more efficient by shortening the length of production processes. In Del Vecchio's view, the entire banking system acts on credit, and the discount rate assures the monetary balance. Far from furnishing a mere intermediary service, the banking system steers the monetary market. Monetary stability is entirely grounded on the relationship between banking reserves and the credit/discount rate that, in Del Vecchio's view, replaces the traditional stability mechanism based on the relationship between stock of money and level of prices. This mechanism makes money totally endogenous to the economic system.[4]

To clarify what will be presented below, we may synthesize Del Vecchio's reasoning on the role of the discount rate and credit as follows. Given an excess of money supply with respect to demand, $M^s > M^d$, it conditions the expectations of those real variables on which the expected prices are based. Changes in expected prices drive the demand for credit, which, in its turn, determines the trend of the discount rate. Certainly, the interrelationship between expected prices and the discount rate is one of the more interesting and intriguing parts of Del Vecchio's circulation theory, and it warrants careful examination. But it should be examined taking into account the banks' capacity to decide the amount of credit itself. In other words, the elasticity of credit to demand for loans for investments is crucial.

Del Vecchio devoted to credit in particular a series of writings published between 1913 and 1914, which include the long essay (practically a book), 'The Theory of Discount Rate'. First to be pointed out is that Del Vecchio's attitude towards the stock of money gradually changed. The amount of money, he argued, could be the result of multiple issue banks, with the involvement of the entire banking system. Hence, through credit and the discount rate, the banking system acted as a sort of 'supervisor' that guaranteed the match between the demand for and the supply of circulation instruments (money and credit) by adjusting the discount rate. Put briefly, it ensured that the supply of circulating instruments was adjusted to the demand for them.[5] To be stressed is that this concerned the banking system as a whole, not necessarily a hypothetical central bank. However, Del Vecchio was perfectly aware, as he admitted,[6] that the same conclusions could be drawn on assuming a single central issue bank.

Chapter 3 widely discussed the role of the selling group in defining the stock of circulating money, and it did so by considering more the demand than the supply side. Implicitly, the selling group is the actor able to decide the supply of monetary stock circulating in the economy. Although not envisaged by Del

Vecchio, the role of the selling group could well fit the banking sector, which was born as an intermediary, but can ultimately decide on the amount of monetary stock. As we shall see, when the banking system decides the ratio between reserves and credit, in reality it also decides the entirety of circulating money plus credit. Briefly, the banking system decides the amount of both circulating paper money and credit, i.e. it controls the circulation in the economy.

Although not defined as such, the discount rate analysis set out by Del Vecchio in his 1914 essay is a short-term analysis partially at odds with Del Vecchio as a structuralist mainly interested in the long-run behaviour of economic variables. As Alberto Zanni stated when reviewing the debate between Arthur Marget and Del Vecchio:

> Del Vecchio wrote an introduction to his collection of Italian monetary writings[7] ... in which he again confirmed his structuralist point of view ... yet Del Vecchio had original points of view on the short-run monetary theory as well.[8]

For Del Vecchio, short- and long-term features were permanently interwoven. What actually emerges here is the relationship between the discount rate decided by commercial banks and the long-term interest rate decided by the market.

The next section deals with the place occupied by credit in Del Vecchio's theory. This topic is then developed in analytical terms in the following section, which is entirely devoted to Del Vecchio's theory of the discount rate and the monetary market. The chapter continues by examining the possibility of a pure (logical) theory of credit, including the factors that determine credit, its relationships with expected and current prices and real variables. Finally, the chapter considers the interrelations among discount rate and some real variables, concluding with some notes on Del Vecchio's view on monetary policy.

From here on, we shall study the economic relationships 'at work' through time, i.e. how they operate in Del Vecchio's understanding of changing economic phenomena.

A 'Pure' Theory of Credit?

If 'pure' means logical, or at any rate not subordinate to psychological features, is a pure theory of credit possible? In his 'The Theory of Discount Rate', perhaps his most demanding but also most strictly economic work, Del Vecchio tried to give an answer to this question that will be summarized in following pages.

Generally speaking, and according to Del Vecchio, the role of money cannot be considered independently from production: Money first makes the circulation of goods and services possible. This induces consideration of money as a *technology of exchanges* and treatment of the theory of circulation separately from the theory of production. However, although money can be theoretically treated on its own, in truth it cannot be separated from production processes.[9]

On the other hand, money is also directly involved in production processes when it is considered as the basis for the deposits and reserves that enable banks to issue credit. Following Francesco Ferrara,[10] a nineteenth-century Italian economist, and recognizing the seminal contribution of Knut Wicksell,[11] Del Vecchio claimed that credit plays a crucial role in sustaining production and growth, even when it is kept distinct from the role performed by money.

In effect, Del Vecchio seemed to adhere to Francesco Ferrara's view that the contribution made by money and credit to production processes differs according to the time dimension considered.[12] Del Vecchio embraced Ferrara's idea that credit can shorten productive processes and sustain demand.[13] Again anchoring his reasoning to Ferrara's, Del Vecchio maintained that credit may substitute capital as a production factor besides land and labour. By increasing production, credit enlarges capital, i.e., it adds new value to capital goods: we may say that credit generates capital. Inevitably, on shifting to economic dynamics, credit increasingly appears an instrument for capitalization or production, not for current consumption or ordinary payments. This seemingly distances credit from money, both of which are, as frequently pointed out by Del Vecchio, overlapping assets. We find in Del Vecchio the same thought as later expressed by Ralph George Hawtrey]:

> It is true that we are accustomed to think of bank credits as money. But this is only because for the practical purposes of every day the distinction between bank credits and money is rarely of any importance.[14]

Del Vecchio wrote that the typical banking transaction is that of transforming short-term deposits into long-term loans. At first sight, banks do not create capital: rather, they provide a service, which, however, involves the anticipation of capital: 'Banking credit saves part of capital from monetary use'.[15] However, from his early writings onwards, Del Vecchio admitted that deposits can mismatch loans, a feature confirming that banks play a more complex role than the strictly intermediary one.

He explicitly stated: 'Summing up, banking activities are those where short term deposits are exchanged with more or less long term loans ... Thus, the banks can sell *monetary services* also *without money*'.[16]

That is to say, contrary to the idea of the neutral nature of credit, banks *create* credit, and thus capital. Del Vecchio stressed that credit can substitute money in transactions for both consumption and production. That is, it can be used for both routine payments and investments. Examples of money replacement are provided when credit entitlements are accepted as means of payment, or when transactions are followed by a credit clearance.[17] Evidently, credit cannot replace money as a measure of value, but it is certainly a means for payments and a reserve of value. Paradoxically, exchanges may take place by means of credit instead of money. In some sense, the weight given to credit induced Del Vecchio to challenge the rather obvious idea of the *monetization of exchanges*. From another viewpoint, Del Vecchio evoked the idea of the '*creditization*' *of exchanges*: that is, the use of credit as an intermediary in exchanges.

Finally, credit inevitably depends on trust, that is, on opinion and emotion. This causes oscillations in the stock of credit and then in prices. It is a matter of fact that when trust is growing, the economic cycle is expanding and prices are expected to increase, credit may exceed the level of deposits, assigning to banks a role different from that of intermediation. Although Del Vecchio repeatedly stated that the causal relation runs from prices to credit, on admitting a state of euphoria, he recognized the existence of a circular relationship between prices and credit. In these conditions, credit is actually a substitute for money.

Del Vecchio's ambition to build a pure theory of credit induces one to wonder whether he was a follower of the banking school, and therefore on this point at odds with Ricardo whom he admired. Pragmatically, Del Vecchio answered 'neither of those schools'.[18] Certainly, he believed that banks can supply credit as an instrument of circulation with no limit except the awareness that increased credit may favour a corresponding growth of prices, which in its turn requires new credit: 'Is the use of credit, as opposed to that of money, determined by economic calculus or habits? Or, better, how do calculus and habits individually concur to set up a system of credit?'[19]

In 1917, he added:

> We agree with the banking school when it affirms that the mass of credit that banks grant is independent from their will and thus independent from any economic calculus. It depends on the price dynamics. Forecasts on future prices determine the demand for credit.[20]

Thus, as well as the quantity of credit provided by a bank, the distribution of *clientele* becomes an important extra-economic factor influencing banking variables. This is a crucial point in Del Vecchio's theory: by influencing credit, a change in the clientele distribution may have economic consequences like a change in monetary variables (gold, money).[21]

Because it is difficult to anchor a bank's credit activity to its metallic reserves, Del Vecchio seemed aware that credit activity is regulated by the amount of deposits and, ultimately, by the banks themselves. But he treated credit separately from deposits, and this pushed him, in a certain sense, beyond the banking school because he considered credit to be an activity *per se*, as a technology of exchange. In this theoretical construct, one might expect the discount rate to be central: but in fact credit is central. Finally, to stress Del Vecchio's indifference to the above-mentioned debate between the metallic and banking schools, his interest in the velocity of circulation transformed into effectiveness did not find correspondence in either the currency or the banking schools, both of which were little interested in this matter.[22]

Del Vecchio later returned to the debate between the currency and banking schools, supposedly placing himself between the two, although the following quotation on credit positions him close to the banking school: 'Both the schools were right and wrong. If it is true that notes take the place of metal, it is truer that notes are replaced by deposits'.[23]

Finally, Del Vecchio remained an overtly nonaligned follower of the classical views to distance himself from any heterodoxy, for he was by nature a heterodox.

Discount Rate as a Monetary or Capital Variable?

I have already pointed out the monetary nature of the discount rate. However, the discount rate is also associated with capital/investments, the result being that relationships between monetary circulation and capital circulation are established. Obviously, the differences between monetary and capital loans can be identified only by considering their purpose, certainly not their form. Monetary credit is requested by firms for periodic payments when they reach their maturity. Monetary credit is also credit for consumption. Differently, credit for capital pertains to investments. Hence the discount rate matters.[24]

Therefore, there are two markets connected with the discount rate in the sense that they can influence or be conditioned by it. It is true that both markets generate a monetary demand for credit, but the purpose of such credit is evidently different: monetary payments on the one hand; investments on the other. However, Del Vecchio recognized that analysis of the interrelationship between the two markets – credit for payments; credit for capital – with the discount rate is extremely demanding, mainly because its purpose is to establish which of the two markets ultimately determines the short-term rate. But, as we shall see, this did not prevent Del Vecchio from claiming that in each moment the market with the higher value of the discount rate prevails.[25]

However, it must be noted that the demand for monetary loans occurs at constant prices; while the loans for investments are provided in the condition of rising expected prices.

Summing up, the discount rate results from the comparison between two values: the one emerging from the match between the demand for and supply of circulation instruments, and the one resulting from the demand for and supply of capital. If the demand for monetary loans prevails, the discount rate will be determined in the monetary market. In this case, payments play a crucial role, as Frank Knight would stress in his famous 1921 *Risk, Uncertainty, and Profit*.[26]

On the other hand, if rising expected prices boost the credit for investments, the discount rate will be determined on the capital market. Obviously, the supply of capital goods will play an essential role in determining the price of short-term capital, that is, the discount rate. This must be distinguished from the price of long-term capital – the rate of interest – although Del Vecchio stated that, according to a conception of monetary equilibrium, the discount rate would converge towards the long-term rate of interest, thus confirming the virtual relationship between the discount rate and the long-term rate of interest. But, on assuming the independence of the discount rate from the psychological one, is it possible to establish a hierarchical order between the two markets – monetary and capital – that determines the discount rate.

It was the long and detailed empirical analysis of discount rate trends conducted in his 1913 article, 'The Periodic Changes of the Discount Rate', that enabled Del Vecchio to reach some initial conclusions concerning the periodic variations of that monetary variable.[27] He stated that the normal level of the discount rate is due to the capital market, while *oscillations* in the discount rate are ascribable to the money market.[28]

The nature of the division into periods can be largely traced back to customs concerning payments by means of banks: monthly, quarterly, half-yearly and yearly. Some movements are determined by technology and the dynamics of production and circulation (harvest seasonality and industrial cycles). All these movements have monetary consequences, meaning that the periodic concentration of payments determines changes in the discount rate and the value of money.

Del Vecchio observed that the value of the discount rate changes in correspondence to payments because credit is requested for ordinary payments (in this case not to purchase capital). This shows that credit is fully a circulating instrument. Del Vecchio carefully compared different circulation systems – those of England, Prussia, the United States, Canada, Italy and other countries – pointing out the relationships between monthly or seasonal payments and discount rates. According to the characteristics of each monetary system, Del Vecchio listed its strengths and weaknesses, reaching a conclusion with regard to the issue of paper money, an aspect, however, which he did not treat extensively:

> A system with the free issue of paper money can resolve its circulation problem more easily than a system where the issue is regulated ... In the former case, the banker can face the monetary demand more efficiently, because he follows his rules and not the financial or political ones.[29]

According to Del Vecchio, this was the case of Canada. Concluding his analysis, it appeared clear that 'divided, regular payments with elastic end-terms are those that produce the least strain on the elasticity of circulation'.[30]

Fortunately, Del Vecchio noted, payments also occurred by means of instruments like bills and cheques, which eased the pressure on money. In effect, a wide elasticity of credit reduces the changes in money that cause the discount rate to vary. If payments are mainly of a monetary type, their periodicity or concentration at a given time alters the discount rate. By contrast, if payments are fed by loans and credit entitlements, which react promptly to changing demand, the discount rate remains stable. Hence, positing an elasticity of the short-term credit market made possible by the banks' access to reserves, the same banks decide to peg the discount rate on the basis of the demand for liquidity.[31]

In this way, the elasticity of credit absorbs the pressures on money and thus on prices. Also for this reason, Del Vecchio reiterated that prices change because of other factors, and only to a limited extent because of the non-perfect elasticity of the circulation instruments. In a non-elastic system based solely on monetary payments, strong oscillations of the discount rate arise in correspondence to periodic payments. The demand for monetary payments then conditions the discount rate. By contrast, 'the credit elasticity is very high, if not perfect'.[32]

Here, an old assumption by Del Vecchio crops up again: the smaller the payments, the fewer the circulation instruments (Cantillon's scheme payments). The more frequent the payments, the greater the probability that irregular payments will off-set each other. Irregular smaller payments are less important than big ones. Finally, the elasticity of maturities favours the reduction of exchange instruments. Elasticity of deadline and elasticity of credit may off-set each other.

'The demand for money is represented by the amount that the public holds at each moment; it depends on its habits'.[33] The demand for liquidity, however, depends on current and future exchanges. Del Vecchio could consequently claim that the demand for money is not elastic to changes in the discount rate. As in the case of periodic payments, the discount rate follows the demand for money more than steering it.

If the demand for money is rigid in relation to changes in the discount rate, it is necessary to investigate the relationship between the discount rate and the money supply. Del Vecchio's first and exhaustive treatment of the money supply was conducted only in 1914. He wrote that, given the inelasticity of demand, a change in the money supply is not matched by the demand, with a consequent change in the discount rate. But Del Vecchio was persuaded of the difficulty of plotting the demand and supply of money schedules, with the result that what was finally observable was the excess of the demand for or supply of money. Banks observe the supply of money, its excess or shortage, adapting it or letting the unbalance determine the discount rate.

A first important conclusion concerns the discount rate, which is ultimately decided by the banking system according to the demand for monetary loans coming from the market. Certainly, the demand for loans is steered by expectations on prices, but to be verified is the extent to which changing demand modifies the discount rate. This depends on the behaviour of banks in regard to credit.

Hence, having stated that the discount rate is essentially a monetary variable, in the sense that it is conditioned by the monetary market, it is possible to single out two paths leading to discount rate changes. The first starts from the money stock and arrives at the discount rate via the banking system, and it will be examined in the following section. The second has the same origin but reaches the short-term interest rate via prices, and will be discussed in the subsequent sections.

Banking Reserves, Credit and Discount Rate

In 1914, in his 'The Theory of Discount Rate', Del Vecchio worked out a theory of banks' behaviour. Observing banks as regards reserves, he drew the first elements for his theoretical construct. More than as percentages of the deposits and the mass of money that they held, banks decided their reserves on the basis of *expectations* about future scarcity. These were not the expectations of firms or consumers, but those of the banks themselves, with their interest in the economic cycle. Put briefly, banks decide their reserves on the basis of their expectations about the economic conjuncture. Far from being simple intermediaries, in 1914 Del Vecchio described banks as agents actively influencing the economic system's operations.

Although banking reserves can be considered as sufficiently stable since they are not conditioned by changes in people's mood, at the same time they are presented as functions of forecasts about panics and crises. Put briefly, in 1914 Del Vecchio stressed the psychological and subjective causes of the demand for money caused by bank runs. The observation that panic gives rise to a never-ending money demand which cannot be controlled by means of ordinary reserves remained in the background. A negative conjuncture or crisis was treated as a factor potentially determining a shortage of liquidity and, implicitly, as a factor determining the demand for money: 'The quantity of money that banks demand to prevent panic represents the banking demand for money'.[34]

It is evident that the larger the banking reserves, the less important become fluctuations in the public demand for money. Therefore, banks fix the amount of money that they hold as reserves, putting all the rest back into the market. The basic idea was that if banks hedge their deposits against panic, panic itself does not occur. From another viewpoint, it is the cycle that steers the liquidity decisions taken by banks, not the monetary market equilibrium alone.

These introductory points confirm that banking reserves, and consequently the corresponding part of the money stock, are decided on the basis of forecasted economic fluctuations. This also means that the reserves of money are decided by the banking sector as if it were the *selling group*, i.e. the group that guarantees money to other productive subjects.

According to Del Vecchio, this was the general strategy of banks, which considered their monetary reserves to be an important stabilizing instrument. This was a first sign of how bank activity was associated with balance objectives. The condition was that banks must not be in a state of illiquidity.

It is striking that Del Vecchio extended the practice of forecasting, which implicitly involves expectations, also to institutions like banks. And this was in 1914, and therefore before he clearly argued for the importance of individual expectations about prices, as he did in his 1917 article.

This observation prompts another point: in Del Vecchio's mid-1910s' theoretical apparatus, the short-term monetary interest rate is not decided by a central bank or something similar to it, but it is fixed by the banking system as a whole or, better, by *competition* among commercial banks. Consequently, Del Vecchio's view was totally different from the first theories of central banking.[35] In effect, by concentrating his analysis on the entire English banking system,[36] he extracted a theory of the discount rate that could be applied to both issue systems, those provided by the central bank and those characterized by multiple issues.

This also explains why Del Vecchio devoted so many pages to *variations* in the discount rate, whether they derive from *monetary* or *capitalistic* causes, rather than to the *origin* of the discount rate itself. The discount rate is a mere result of the banks' credit activity. Certainly, the issue banks can vary the stock of money impacting on credit, but the banks decide the extent of this impact alone. Incidentally, this explains the lack of a theory on the discount rate as an explicitly monetary policy instrument in Del Vecchio's work. The following aspects are crucial for grasping the behaviour of the discount rate.

Del Vecchio tried to keep credit separate from money, but he eventually admitted that a growing demand for credit is a demand for money, or for reserves of money, which has a direct effect on the level of the discount rate. Both the level and the trend of the banking reserves influence the discount rate, which tends to fall when the reserves are high, or also when they tend to rise.[37] This link is a typical phenomenon of circulation, as Del Vecchio sought to argue on the basis of statistical data on the English banking system.

Banking Reserves

The change of the monetary ratio is expressed by the changes in bank money reserves that, consequently, influence the discount rate: 'Changes in banking reserves exactly express the change of the ratio between demand and supply ... Moreover, they also express the diverse effectiveness of different types of money'.[38]

Intuitively, an excess of supply on the demand for money will be followed by an increase in banking reserves. Banks absorb the excess of liquidity and provide it when it is missing. Thus, a change in the monetary reserves stored by banks is an index of the monetary equilibrium. But, at the same time, an increase in demand for money may induce banks to increase their reserves so as to protect themselves against any risk of illiquidity. From another viewpoint, the liquidity not held by agents with a view to future exchanges is deposited in banks. This obviously causes problems for banks that undergo a change in their reserves/credit ratio. This statement can also be interpreted in the sense that Del Vecchio did not believe that the demand for money regulated its supply, as maintained by Wicksell in 1907, when he hypothesized a market alongside the pure credit one.[39] In Del Vecchio's system, it was the supply of credit, also independently from deposits, which balanced the monetary market.

What can be done is to resort to an index of the changes in the match between money demand and supply: this index is banking reserves. Del Vecchio believed that, whatever the factors determining the circulating money, changes in banking reserves guarantee the match between the demand for and supply of money. They constitute a sort of safety valve which balances the stock of money resulting from periodic payments and circulation (deposits and issue) with the demand for loans and credit (for both production and consumption). Assuming *ceteris paribus* conditions, Del Vecchio was persuaded that changes in reserves are the least inexact measure of the ratio's modifications.

Having stated this, the point is to establish how banks guarantee the balance of the monetary market: that is, how they ensure that the supply is equal to the demand for money. Here, the role attributed to the discount rate comes to the fore, also admitting, as Del Vecchio did, that the demand for money is not particularly sensitive to discount rate changes. However, given competition among banks, changes in the monetary reserves held by banks determine variations in the short-term interest rate: 'Banks must increase the discount rate when the reserves are low, in order to limit the loans to their loyal clients, while the discount rate must be lowered when the reserves are large, in order to maintain the clientele'.[40]

Therefore, an excess of money supply determines a diminished discount rate; a lack of money causes it to increase. Proof of this correspondence is provided by the discount rate itself, in that, during economic crises, it assumes high values as a result of the lack of liquidity or money. Money is hoarded privately, provoking a general lack of deposits and liquidity. But how elastic the discount rate must be to cope with a rigid demand for money Del Vecchio did not say.

If reserves can be assumed as the money supply of the whole system, it follows that the power to issue new money gives the bank system, or at least a part of it, the faculty to change the stock of money circulating in the system or stocked in the reserves.

However, these notes show the monetary nature of the discount rate determined by the banks' management of monetary reserves. Its character appears to be in contrast with the psychological nature of the long-run interest rate determined by the perceived utility of goods/capital. As said, Del Vecchio distinguished between the short-term interest rate, which is also the outcome of the *bank-rate policy*, and the 'psychic' or psychological one, which is a subjective or firm interest rate, reflecting individual inter-temporal preferences, and which changes according to agents (mainly firms). In 1914, Del Vecchio hypothesized that the disequilibrium between the discount and psychological rates may influence the level of the discount rate, but he treated it as 'a secondary effect'.[41] What happens in the world of firm self-financing by means of savings only indirectly conditions the trend of the discount rate, even when the latter is determined by the demand for credit by the same firms for investments. This is a crucial point because it concerns the *normal* condition of the system: the discount rate is lower than the psychological rate of interest.[42] However, the condition for a stable market is elastic credit capital. In this way, the monetary market will influence only partial changes in the discount rate.

The Monetary Paradox

In this examination of the relationships between banks and the discount rate, here we may insert what Del Vecchio called the *monetary paradox*. Having stated the monetary nature of the discount rate, Del Vecchio turned his attention to the monetary market, providing an interesting representation of it.

In his 1913 *Statistical Inductions for the Theory of Circulation* (*Induzioni statistiche per la teoria della circolazione*) Del Vecchio set out a monetary *paradox* that became a point of anchorage for his theory of circulation. He did not believe that quantity theory could offer a reliable explanation of the influence of the stock of money on the level of prices, although he did not deny the possibility of direct relationships among the monetary factors.

Del Vecchio[43] argued that the level of prices at a given time depends on various monetary variables, including past prices and expected (forecasted) ones. As we shall see, this double time reference to the past and the future is the basis for Del Vecchio's entire dynamic argument developed in his monetary theory.

Del Vecchio first examined the upward phase of the economic cycle, when the levels of prices, credit and the discount rate grow while the monetary reserves held by banks decrease. He then considered the downward phase, when the movement is in the opposite direction. Assuming the ratio between supply and demand for money as exemplifying the trend of the reserves, Del Vecchio's theorem stated that: '*When the money supply grows, the ratio between banking reserves of money and the credit built on them tends to decrease; on the contrary, when the supply of money diminishes, the same ratio tends to go up*'.[44]

The paradoxical character of this theorem is evident, because it leads to different conclusions when compared with the common belief linking the stock of money and credit trends. In fact, a growing money supply should lead to an increase in money reserves, which increases the ratio. A reduction of the reserves signals an excess of demand for money over the supply. However, the opposite outcome may occur when the growing stock of money involves a more than proportional increase in the demand for credit. That is to say, the denominator of the reserves/credit ratio increases more than the numerator. But why should credit increase proportionally more than money? The answer lies in the role played by expectations about prices.[45]

Del Vecchio termed *frictions* all the past factors influencing current decisions. And in accordance with the then common view, he called *speculation* the expected features conditioning the current variable. Thus, current prices will be determined according to the current variables, but taking into account the pressures exerted by speculation (or expectation) *opposed* to resistances due to frictions (habits).

This distinction matters solely in order to distinguish between the short-term and long-term effects of a monetary circulation. However, although Del Vecchio considered that time operates in both directions, he gave more emphasis to the influences deriving from the expected future values:

> The expectations of rising prices determine a growth of current ones larger than those necessary to offset the existing frictions and also beyond the level of the current stock of money. Such expectations, by increasing the demand for credit, increase the pressure on the banks, which consequently, reduce the ratio between reserves and credit. An opposite outcome is brought about by expectations of decreasing prices.[46]

Del Vecchio hypothesized a sort of overshooting effect characterizing price behaviour: once the frictions are overcome – that is, prices start to adjust themselves to expected values – the effect is to increase the demand for credit more than the increase in monetary reserves.[47] Put briefly, in 1913 Del Vecchio argued that a monetary increase will generate expectations of rising prices that heighten the demand for credit used for transactions. As credit takes the place of money, monetary reserves may not decrease. But precisely the fact that prices grow more than money determines a more than proportional increase of credit compared with reserves, with the result that the ratio between the two – reserves and credit – diminishes.

This is the paradox that Del Vecchio verified on analysing trends in the discount rate and monetary aggregates in the early twentieth-century London monetary market. Del Vecchio softened the paradox by stating that the outcome is undetermined because, given rising prices, the reduction of monetary reserves may be mitigated by an increase in deposits strengthening paper money reserves. In this case, the reserves may decrease less than was previously forecasted. 'In any case, it may occur that deposits, which are the basis of circulating money with low reserves, tend to replace paper money, with the result that reserves do not decrease because of expecting prices'.[48]

On the basis of statistical series, Del Vecchio argued that changes in credit can anticipate the expected variations in the money supply, maintaining the ratio between reserves and credit constant. The latter became the banking *tie*. Here I shall attempt to explain why.

First, growing prices are followed by a credit expansion. But, Del Vecchio argued, a theory of money cannot ignore the effects of a stock of money change, particularly if it coincides with a growth of the gold stock. The point is that any increase in the monetary stock generates changes in expected prices, credit and banking reserves. The outcome is undetermined. At that point, the effect of a monetary change on the discount rate is undetermined as well.

Summing up, the abundance of reserves caused by the increase in the money supply may reduce the short-term interest rate applied to deposits. In this way, the ratio between the reserves and loans remains constant. Conversely, by means of expected prices, an increase in the monetary stock may *raise* and not *reduce* the discount rate.

Money, Prices and Discount Rate

The other path linking the stock of money to the discount rate is the one mediated by prices. First, it should be pointed out that the notion of normal equilibrium prices only incidentally makes its appearance in this analysis, where the main dynamic relation is between the stock of money and expected prices. Therefore, the stationary condition envisaging price equilibrium and a stable discount rate was of little interest to Del Vecchio. Moreover, there is nothing to suggest that Del Vecchio likened the expected prices to the normal or long-term ones. Normal values are not really considered in this view polarized between past and future.

The link between the monetary stock and the discount rate can be represented as the sum of two other links: that between the monetary stock and prices; and that between prices and the discount rate. Del Vecchio sketched the first link and concentrated on the second. The intriguing feature of Del Vecchio's relation between money stock and prices is that he substituted the simple relation involving absolute levels of prices, as then stated by the quantitative theory, with a relationship between money change and *expected* prices. Specifically, his theory of expectations was cutting edge in 1914, since he exactly distinguished the effects on expected and current prices according to whether the increase in money was temporary or permanent.

Differently, the second link between prices and discount rate here assumes the same important role as assigned to it by many theories of that time and previously. In this regard, Marget wrote:

> No one familiar with the discussion of the effect of variations in bank-rate upon the amount of bank borrowing, from [Henry] Thornton and Ricardo through the Currency and Banking School controversy down to Marshall, could have argued that emphasis upon these variations as the crucial step in the mechanism of price-change should be regarded as a novelty.[49]

From Stock of Money to Discount Rate

Del Vecchio stated that the relation between prices and the discount rate concerns not only absolute values but also changing and forecasted values. Given an excess of the supply of money over the demand for it, $M^s > M^d$, it can yield different outcomes according to the nature of the monetary change, that is, (i) the excess of monetary supply is temporary; and (ii) the excess is permanent.

Del Vecchio[50] wrote that in case (i) the temporary increase of the monetary stock does not influence investments and consequently expected prices, the latter depending on productivity (see Chapter 2). As the banks see their reserves being increased as a result of monetary expansion, they issue credit that favours short-term payments in order to maintain the ratio between reserves and credit constant. The nominal discount rate diminishes, but the expected prices remain the same, with the result that the real monetary discount rate changes (diminishes).

In case (ii), with a permanent excess of monetary supply, changes concern future prices. Del Vecchio argued that the expectations of changing prices do not guarantee monetary equilibrium. The permanent enlargement of credit determines a shift of investments from short-term production processes to long-term more productive ones. Thus, investments change, favouring longer processes over shorter ones. At that point, future goods are preferred to current ones, with an expected price growth. The movement towards longer production increases the psychological rate of interest and boosts the demand for credit. Recall that on increasing P^e, it follows that $\frac{U_A - U_B}{U_B} > d$, which induces people to borrow money, increasing d, also because the real monetary interest rate diminishes. Gradually, the discount rate rises, thus restoring the previous equilibrium.

Moreover, expected growing prices increase the demand of credit not only for investments, but also for payments.[51] Therefore, permanent changes in the stock of money modify expectations about prices, and consequently the demand for credit, with impacts on the discount rate.

In general, rising expected prices are followed by an increase in the discount rate, while decreasing expected prices have a low or nil effect on the discount rate. Price equilibrium means that prices are always perfectly forecasted, and the demand and supply of money are those of equilibrium through time.[52] Instead, given monetary imbalance and expected price fluctuations, the discount rate will also tend to change. A rising discount rate pushed up by expected prices may, in the long run, tend to converge on the long-run interest rate, the 'psychic' interest rate. Thus:

> When the expected prices are growing, the rising discount rate will be determined by the monetary market. When the expected prices decrease, the discount rate remains low at the point that it tends to be established by the market of capitals.[53]

But an increasing discount rate reduces the profitability of new longer investments, thus restoring equilibrium.

To define a role for the discount rate, we must return to the monetary market. While there is no doubt that change in the monetary mass – that is, disequilibrium between the demand for and supply of money – can cause a change in the discount rate, the changed discount rate, in its turn, will condition prices, with the result of re-establishing the monetary equilibrium. The first immediate effect of this finding is that the theory of the discount rate is a component of monetary theory. Del Vecchio went further: 'it is an essential part of that theory'.[54] This is one of the few logical sequences that Del Vecchio recognized as such.

This important point can be concluded by considering what may happen if banks provide elastic credit, that is, if they respond to the demand for more capital credit by keeping the level of monetary interest rate low and stable. Since the discount rate is a factor influencing monetary payments, its stabilization avoids an increasing of costs on the monetary side, with positive effects on prices. Therefore, the banking system could be interested in stabilizing the level of the discount rate, which is determined on the side of credit for investments, in order to maintain a stable the monetary market. Incidentally, a lower or stable discount rate favours investment in longer, more productive production processes.

Credit as the Intermediary between Prices and Discount Rate

Therefore, a key role must be attributed to credit as an intermediary instrument. Variations in expected prices change the demand for credit, with the result that increasing prices oblige banks to deal with growing requests for loans. The entire re-equilibrating mechanism therefore works on the conditions that credit is elastic to the money supply and that there is no competition among banks: 'Banks may set a higher or lower discount rate because the supply of and demand for money are less elastic than the supply of and demand for credit'.[55]

If the credit is not elastic, then the discount rate may change in response to the growing demand, taking the competition among banks into account.

As shown, Del Vecchio's economy was similar to Wicksell's pure credit economy, but, despite his interest in the Swedish economist's theory, the prime source of Del Vecchio's credit analysis was undoubtedly Ferrara's theory. From Francesco Ferrara Del Vecchio drew the idea of competition among banks that is at the basis of his process of discount rate behaviour.[56] Lastly, discussion of the discount rate gave Del Vecchio the opportunity to debate a hypothetical *theory of credit*. In 1917, summing up what he had argued in his previous articles, Del Vecchio wrote:

> The quantity of credit that banks furnish to favour circulation is not determined by statistical-economic criteria: it results from the fact that credit is not a function of the discount rate paid to banks, that is, the circulating mass of credit is inelastic with regard to the discount rate's movements. According to this, an economic theory of credit is not possible. The determination of the mass of credit supplied by banks depends on psychological and dynamic assessments, the latter aimed at preventing sudden and too rapid price increases from generating dramatic changes of trust and panic.[57]

Affirming that an economic theory of credit is logically not possible means that the movement of the discount rate is deliberately restricted to both the level and the trend.

In 1931, Del Vecchio returned to the role of credit in an entry for the *Italian Encyclopaedia*. This entry is of interest because in it Del Vecchio clearly stated the centrality of credit for a monetary economy. Certainly, it is an instrument favouring circulation: for example, by saving some of the cost of monetary transactions. Del Vecchio added: 'Credit could substitute money, if not eliminate it'[58] when credit is accepted as title for payments and when the clearance of credit is allowed. Thus: 'Credit could replace money as medium of exchange; even if it cannot play the role of unit of value ... It is also a tool allowing accumulation'.[59]

Although one credit can guarantee another credit, the issue of a monetary basis for all types of credit arises. Del Vecchio called this 'the chain of credit', although he was unclear as to the ratio between the amount of credit and the 'reserve' of money. In 1927, he wrote that credit elasticity must be secured by metallic reserves.[60]

Del Vecchio was interested in clearing practice or the clearing house. The idea was that circulation could be made more efficient by favouring the clearing of credits and debts among banks. In this way, monetary, or better, credit, circulation could occur without an instrument actually circulating, on the condition that the public maintained its trust in the banking system.

But as may happen with money, trust in banks and thus in credit may oscillate, altering the price trend. This explains why a policy of credit stabilization is required for credit as well as for money.

However, what emerges is that a substantial elasticity of credit allows stabilization of the discount rate and, finally, the stability of the whole economic system. Changing expected price may not affect the discount rate, provided that the credit is sufficiently elastic to absorb the changing demand for loans.

Del Vecchio reached this conclusion by shifting his attention from the discount rate to credit elasticity. A first consequence of this was that the discount rate was permanently lower than the long-term rate of interest.

From Discount Rate to Prices

Del Vecchio pointed out that the discount rate theory is the missing link between the stock of money and prices that completes the quantity theory. However, there is nothing mechanical in the relation between the discount rate and prices. Del Vecchio stressed that:

> *a*) the discount rate exerts a different pressure on prices according to the characteristics of products that may be security, wholesale goods, retail goods; *b*) prices reach their equilibrium through time; *c*) the value of money is grounded on the value change of its services (i.e. discount rate).[61]

Therefore, in regard to point *a*), the statement seems to be of logical type, although psychological factors play a crucial role in the relation between the discount rate and prices. However, it is true that discount rate changes will induce variations in those goods whose period of production is short, more than in goods requiring more time, because the latter are influenced mainly by the interest rate. Moreover, short-term bills will profit from the reduction. Similarly, shares issued by stock exchanges will react to change in the short-term rate.

Therefore, a diminishing or low discount rate, by reducing the cost of the short production process, makes goods requiring short production cheaper than goods that are the result of long production. The latter involves longer debt than the shorter process, so that it can only partially profit from the diminished discount rate because, Del Vecchio argued, all debts involving fixed instalments for longer production processes will not be affected by the discount rate change. The gap in the trend between the two types of goods entails that the long production process will be more costly than the short one, with an inevitable increase in expected future prices.

Obviously, increasing discount rate yields opposite effects, penalizing current short-term production. For this reason, any strategy intended to maintain the discount rate stable may favour the stabilization of the whole economy.

According to point *b*), the discount rate makes it easier to restore the price equilibrium starting from disequilibrium due to the monetary unbalance. However, Del Vecchio assumed a slow process of re-equilibrium, not an instantaneous one. The transition from one point of equilibrium to the next is slowed down by the existence of *frictions* (legacies of the past) that make it more difficult to reach price equilibrium.

Finally, as to the third feature, *c*), the value of money will depend on the real or nominal character of the discount rate change. It should be noted that, in 1914, Del Vecchio combined the analysis of prices with that of money value, although he conceived the latter mostly as the use value of money. Hence the discount rate became the cost of the use of money.

To conclude this section on the discount rate and prices, it should be pointed out that Del Vecchio substituted the direct relation between the stock of money and prices envisaged by the quantity principle with two indirect relationships in which the monetary stimuli are transmitted through credit, on the one hand, and through expected prices on the other. The first relationship found explanation in the fact that Del Vecchio clearly believed that the credit sector is more elastic to monetary stock changes than money itself. The banking system is more reactive to mass money changes than the market itself, and this is because banks immediately adapt credit to the new condition. The second relationship is grounded on the mechanisms driving expectations on prices and that Del Vecchio considered similar to those occurring into speculation.[62] Speculation, in the broad sense, and expectations can be considered as synonyms in regard to their effects on monetary variables. Both can influence the expected prices, and this influence can be transmitted to the discount rate by means of credit demand.

Discount Rate and Real Variables

If expected prices built on real variables may influence the discount rate, when does the discount rate condition real economic variables? To begin with the causal relation between the discount rate and other variables, Del Vecchio was sceptical about the influence of the discount rate on other real economic variables. First, he believed that the distribution of monetary income into savings and consumption is not influenced by the discount rate, which does not condition entrepreneurs' choices about investments. Thus, the discount rate does not have significant effects on the supply of capital, i.e. savings, nor on the demand by entrepreneurs. Del Vecchio then dealt with the consequences of the discount rate on the demand for and supply of money. He admitted that monetary exchanges are influenced by the discount rate, but – he continued – the latter exert the main effects on prices.

The above considerations are the only ones that Del Vecchio treated as logical or *a priori* as regards the relation between the discount rate and the other economic variables. By contrast, almost complete uncertainty surrounds the psychological relations between the discount rate and economic variables, where psychological relations involve a vague notion of time and different outcomes depending on whether they are forecasted or unexpected. But this makes the distinction between the discount rate and the long-term interest rate less definite, also because Del Vecchio's interest rate was entirely psychological. We can expect that the overlap between the discount and interest rates to be easier at times of crisis. But it was precisely this indeterminacy of the discount rate's psychological features that induced Del Vecchio to keep the discount rate as far as possible separate from the long-term interest rate, assigning logical aspects to the discount rate and psychological ones to the interest rate. In short, what is logical concerns the discount rate; what is psychological concerns the interest rate. The point is that Del Vecchio treated accumulation and capitalization as psychological facts, not as logical ones, with the result that the discount rate only partially influences the real economic variables.

Discount Rate and Exchange Rates

In 1913, Del Vecchio wrote a concise article entitled 'Problems of Treasury and of Circulation' ('Problemi del Tesoro e della Circolazione') in which he analysed the action of the then Italian Treasury Minister in relation to circulation problems. First he inveighed against the idea that an exchange rate normally corresponds to the point of gold. The exchange rate could be lower than that point because of trade among individuals and capital. This was a further proof of his impatience with once-and-for-all economic dogmas.

If international circulation is at stake, a crucial feature linking domestic to international relationships is the convertibility of paper money into precious metal. In order to maintain this relationship, the issue bank must restrict the circulating instruments even at the cost of refusing to satisfy all requests for credit. If the international reserves tend to diminish, the bank has to limit the emission of new paper money. This restrains the devaluation of the exchange rate unavoidable when the stock of unconvertible money grows. A high (de-evaluated) exchange rate is an index of wider circulation, but, Del Vecchio stressed,[63] it helps the recovery of exports and re-equilibrium of the current account. At a time of a declining gold standard, Del Vecchio treated the variability of the exchange rates as an important means with which to achieve balance of payments equilibrium.

But, here the focus is on the link between circulating money and exchange rates: that is, on how the national administration can condition the external equilibrium. Del Vecchio specified:

> Nobody claims that abundant circulating money determines an increase [depreciation] of the exchange rates without any intermediate facts. But, one can certainly state that the relationships between one country and all the others involve high exchange rates when the domestic circulating money is redundant.[64]

Even if the excess of monetary stock does not directly condition the level of exchange rates, it hinders the spontaneous re-establishment of equilibrium by means of market forces. However, what is surprising in De Vecchio's analysis is the weight that he gave to expectations: 'Some oscillations [of the exchange rates] find explanation in facts that, although not even existing, are currently discounted or anticipated'.[65]

This also explains why Del Vecchio considered as positive the speculative activity that, in his opinion, consolidated the importance of anticipating future events.[66] This emphasis on expected values enables us to focus on the set of variables that Del Vecchio considered crucial for any monetary analysis: prices, discount rate and exchange rates analysed in their current and expected values. Some years later, Del Vecchio would write: 'In these concrete phenomena [relationships among prices, discount rate and exchange rates] the purity of individual economic movements encounters the limits of monetary economic theory'.[67]

The point had also been considered in 1914, when Del Vecchio discussed the role of prices in relation to the discount rate, exchange rates, and international payments, drawing inspiration from Keynes's *Indian Currency and Finance*. The main point is the following: an unbalanced current account may produce (1) a domestic deflationary effect that re-establishes the equilibrium; and (2) a movement of short-term capital that delays current account restoration by balancing it with financial movements. The point that Del Vecchio highlighted was the one concerning prices, whose movement he considered to be only virtual. In fact, the current account deficit leads to exchange rate depreciation, a step necessary to restore equilibrium. There is no price movement unless we consider the long-term effect of export re-launching:[68]

> All things considered ... the current account equilibrium ... is yielded by the unbalances themselves between exportation and importation. The re-establishing of equilibrium is accelerated by the movement of exchange rates out of the gold points. Moreover, monetary perturbations are partially avoided by the short-term capital movements induced by the differences between discount rates.[69]

Del Vecchio assumed that price changes result from real variations in business relationships among countries, and not from monetary outcomes. This was consistent with his views on expected domestic prices. In his 1914 article, 'Contribution to Circulation Doctrines' ('Contributi alle dottrine della circolazione'), he sought to demonstrate this point by analysing the case of India. The main factors influencing Indian prices were harvests and economic crises, which modified the current account with consequences on the discount rate and exchange rates.

In regard to point (2), Del Vecchio treated this topic in his 'Theory of Capital Exportation' ('Teoria dell'esportazione del capitale'), a long essay of 1910, then completed by the 1911 'The Disposal Capital and its Circulation' ('Il capitale disponibile e la circolazione del capitale'). Capital, here, means financial capital. Exchanges of capital between two countries develop when the rates of interest are different because of different lengths of production processes, types of economy, business and banking organization, transport costs, among other factors. Del Vecchio distinguished long-term movements, which mainly depend on the interest rate, from the short-term movements linked to the discount rate. While the former type can be analysed by assuming a real perspective, short-term movements necessarily require a strictly monetary view.

Citing John E. Cairnes, the 'last' of the great Ricardians, Del Vecchio attempted to give a precise representation of the international distribution of capital which included the relationships among prices, interest rate, discount rate and exchange rate. The following are the main steps in Del Vecchio's attempt – conducted, as Pareto recommended, through 'subsequent approximations' – to build a model of the international circulation of (financial) capital.[70]

First step: a preliminary theory of exchange rates must be set up by including the distribution of precious metals among countries; analysis of international circulation on the basis of unique conditions of credit, and same interest and discount rates. Second step: the credit conditions are assumed to be different in the two national economies. Third step: the discount rate is left free to change, stimulating the trade in short-term capital. Fourth and final step: interest rates are assumed to fluctuate according to the conditions of countries with surpluses or deficits in their balances of payments, although in the absence of precious metal movements.

Setting the discount rate temporarily aside, the quantity theory stated that imbalances between the current accounts of different countries are off-set by flows of precious metal until the international equalization of prices reduces the disequilibrium. According to the then specie-flow mechanism, it will be the price changes that re-establish the balance between countries. Once the discount rate is reintroduced, it involves an action that makes this process more gradual. Effectively, by reintroducing the discount rate, the flows of metal and price changes are partially limited or removed because of arbitrage on the discount rate. The deficit countries show an increase in both the exchange rates and the discount rate, while the surplus countries experience diminishing exchange rates and discount rate. The simplest explanation of the differences between discount rates lies in the fact that the importing country has at its disposal a relatively high proportion of current goods vis-à-vis future ones.

To understand this point, recall that the country with longer production processes is necessarily also the country with the lower discount rate, for the simple reason that otherwise it could not develop capital-intensive production. Accordingly, Del Vecchio provided this definition of export/import capital:

> We have a supply of capital when an agent buys a stock of future goods supplying current ones; on the other hand, an agent demands capital when he buys current goods offering future goods. Credit is crucial in enabling these transactions to take place without modifying their nature. According to this view, a country exports capital when it sells current goods buying future goods; whilst a country imports capital when it sells future goods buying current ones.[71]

However, the outflow of precious metal increases the discount rate. Thus, the difference between discount rates feeds the movements of deposits to the countries with the higher discount rates. In this way, the discount rate's action makes the change of prices more gradual and less abrupt.[72] The effect of the discount rate will be greater as long as frictions preventing a sudden recovery of equilibrium by means of prices exist.

Del Vecchio added that the same increase in the discount rate provokes an economic depression that reduces the level of prices, thus favouring the recovery of exports. But, if an immediate effect is obtained, it involves payments that, because of the increase in the discount rate, will be delayed, with a positive effect on the balance of payments. To sum up, the change of the discount rate following the current account disequilibrium helps restore the equilibrium by reducing the out- or inflow of money. The capital flows reduce the movement of the exchange rates, the latter oscillating only between the gold points.

According to Del Vecchio, a monetary paradox also characterizes international monetary relationships. It consists in the fact that 'money tends to abandon countries with high interest rates and to accumulate in countries with low interest rates'.[73] The reason is apparently simple. The ratio between utility of money and its cost is smaller where money is abundant – that is, the discount rate is low – compared with those countries where money is scarce. Moreover, Del Vecchio said, money is also more useful in countries where the rate is lower because it can be employed more easily. This may entail that money abandons countries with high interest rates and accumulates in countries with lower rates. But this is no more than a theoretical provocation in Del Vecchio's style.

The international economic relations emerging from this representation anchored to the role of the discount rate show fewer discontinuities than the classic gold standard picture based on precious metal flows and the re-equilibrating action of prices. Del Vecchio wrote that a concept of the monetary market as 'changing continuously and in its parts' thus took shape.

The Banking Equilibrium in Symbols

The key role that Del Vecchio attributed to banks' monetary reserves enables us to reinterpret the idea of monetary equilibrium by abstracting from the traditional conception of a single central bank and adopting the proposal of multiple issues that effectively assign the money issue function to the entire banking system.

In light of the above, we can assume that all banking reserves immediately convertible into loans, and therefore circulating money, represent the monetary supply in a given economy.

$$M^S = M^R + CU \qquad 4.1$$

where M^S is the money supply, M^R are the banking reserves and CU the current circulating money in the economy. Positing that CU is employed for goods and services transactions only, and assuming it as constant, the monetary supply change corresponds to banking reserves change. Consequently, as noted above, the banking system may assume a role similar to that of a 'selling group'. If we hypothesize that the amount of circulating money remains constant, $CU = K$, the stock of money is decided by the banking system, and its changes are expressed by changes in the banking reserves. Given a multiple issues system, the monetary reserves M^R can be considered equal to the money supply M^S, so that 4.1 can be rewritten as:

$$\Delta M^S = \Delta M^R \qquad 4.2$$

We know that the relationship between monetary reserves and credit CR, $\frac{M^R}{CR}$ is an indicator of monetary stability and that banks tend to maintain it constant. Consequently, an increase in monetary reserves is followed by an increase in credit, CR, with the result that:

$$\Delta M^S = \Delta M^R = \Delta CR \qquad 4.3$$

And consequently:

$$\Delta M^S = \Delta CR \qquad 4.4$$

At least in the short term, the demand for money is determined by the expected prices, which condition both the demand for loans directed to short-term investments and demand monetary credit directed to payments. We know that the discount rate has a monetary cause, i.e. it is determined by payments that depend on production but also by the structure of payments, here expressed by the effectiveness of money. If the ratio between expected national production, QP^e, and the effectiveness of money, E, represents this monetary demand for loans, we can write the change of demand for money in the short term as follows:

$$\Delta M^D = \frac{Q\Delta P^e}{E} \qquad 4.5$$

Finally, positing a monetary equilibrium:

$$\Delta M^S = \Delta M^D$$

And recalling the 4.4 we have:

$$\Delta CR = \frac{Q\Delta P^e}{E} \qquad 4.6$$

Finally, we know that it may happen (monetary paradox) that $\Delta CR \geq \Delta M^R$ and $\Delta d > 0$.

That is the condition envisaged by Del Vecchio: a permanent growth of monetary supply, by means of expected prices, pushes up the demand for money provoking a reaction of the banking system. The latter supplies more credit and may increase the discount rate. In this way the monetary equilibrium can be restored. The discount rate is used by banks to assure the above banking condition of stability.

A concluding remark concerns E. The effectiveness does not change in the short term, but it is sensitive to any change of habit concerning payments or the structure of economy. We can hypothesize that, during crises, the effectiveness consistently decreases, pushing up the demand for money and reserves. And, as noted above, when the banking system is unable to maintain the elasticity of credit, the result is that the discount rate is pushed up.

5 MAKING MONETARY WEALTH CIRCULATE

Together with money and the discount rate, the long-term interest rate represents the third variable to which Del Vecchio anchored his theory of circulation: he treated it with the same marginal approach as applied to the other two[1] but eventually worked out a rather eclectic theory. This supposed originality did not diminish the crucial role played by the interest rate in Del Vecchio's monetary equilibrium, as expressed by the fact that the interest rate precedes the value of money without the latter influencing it. This means that a theory of money implies an existing theory of interest, not the contrary. In this regard, Del Vecchio was in good company: the already-mentioned Böhm-Bawerk, Wicksell, Fisher, Adolphe Landry, among others.[2]

Already in the first paragraphs of his long essay 'General Outlines of the Interest Theory' ('Lineamenti generali della teoria dell'interesse') focused on this topic, Del Vecchio spoke of a *subjective* long-term interest rate presented as the ratio between the utility of current goods and the utility of future ones, where, evidently, changes in the utilities signify interest rate changes. This simple definition immediately recalls Böhm-Bawerk's theory that interest is an *agio* between current and future goods. In effect, Del Vecchio started from Böhm-Bawerk's future premium to arrive at Fisher's more subjective conception of the interest rate, but conceiving the latter as a *relationship* between current and future value, not as revenue from a specific production factor, as stated in Böhm-Bawerk.

From this perspective, the measure of the interest rate did not matter, as proved by the fact that the interest rate was not assumed to be a factor conditioning savings. What mattered was the subjective conceptualization of a relationship between current values and future ones. Briefly, in order to understand Del Vecchio's swings between subjectivism and objectivism, it must be borne in mind that he postulated two long-run rates of interest: first, the subjective one expressing more a relationship between current and future value than a measurable variable. But, given this perspective, it was obvious that a second, more objective, interest rate gradually came to the fore. This was the interest rate determined by the length of production processes and representing the *normal* rate of interest. When the conditions of production change, this normal long-term rate of interest may change, determining a new relationship between current and future goods.

A measurable rate of interest must exist; and in this regard, Del Vecchio preferred to return to Böhm-Bawerk instead of fully adhering to Fisher's definition of interest as the average between impatience and anticipation. It seemed that the subjective rate of interest should converge on the normal one, but, finally, Del Vecchio framed each of them in a specific perspective: normal interest in a static perspective; subjective interest in a dynamic one.

Both are necessary in this theory, because while the objective or normal interest rate, by conditioning capitalization, influences production and circulation processes, finally conditioning the value of money, the subjective interest rate is a bridge between existing production and individual expectations concerning investments and accumulation. The subjective interest rate synthesizes the many features, not all of an economic nature, influencing individual choices about future economic acts: consumption, investments, and so on. These early remarks highlight how time and cognitive or psychological aspects matter, all the more so if we consider that many decisions are taken by agents in view of the changing economy, which is neither necessarily a growing nor a stable one.

To conclude these preliminary statements, consideration must be made of the relation between the interest rate and saving. As will be shown, no interest rate, whether short- or long-term, subjective or objective, determines the level of saving, whose amount is determined by other factors. Saving is obviously important for fuelling banking deposits and, consequently, capitalization, but it is never strictly associated with the interest rate. Thus, it is better to speak of a non-relationship between saving and interest.

These few points are sufficient to understand that everything that concerns accumulation is only marginally conditioned by monetary features, or not at all. Here, psychological or mental variables play a pivotal role, i.e. investments are mainly decided according to ambitions or other psychological determinants. To be noted is that Del Vecchio attributed a *psychological* characterization to the interest rate – *psychic* (*psichico*) in his vocabulary. Money plays no role, while it is crucial in conditioning ordinary transactions and payments.

In those years, a German scholar, Theo Suranyi-Unger, described Del Vecchio's theory of interest thus:

> [Del Vecchio] works especially on the extra-economic, the social and psychological relations of interest and tries to prove that a satisfactory solution of this problem can be achieved only by constantly considering these aspects. Del Vecchio attributes a decisive role to custom in the origins of savings and consequently in the formation of capital and in the fixing of the interest rate and considers that its importance in economics is too often underrated.[3]

On glancing at the then theoretical panorama, one can say that it included economic and non-economic theories of interest, and economic and non-economic theories of accumulation. This double distinction is particularly plain in Del Vecchio, who remained loyal to the dogma that analytical tools precede historical ones, although he also believed that both are necessary in the large majority of cases. This methodological sequence was set out in his 1914 article on economic crises, which treated the topic analysed here, and where an economic theory of the interest rate overlapped with a non-economic theory of accumulation. The exact determination of what is related to interest – that is, what is economic – and what concerns accumulation was the subject of his long 1915 essay 'General Outlines of the Interest Theory', a treatment presenting a broad examination of the role played by saving.

The following sections deal with the intertwining among the interest rate, savings and accumulation. Once these points have been examined, the focus will move to economic crises, phenomena that Del Vecchio crucially linked with accumulation. The discourse on crises then continues with contextualization of Del Vecchio's insights in theoretical developments by Italian economists.

Subjective and Objective Rates of Interest

On describing Del Vecchio's theory of interest involving both subjective and objective features, first to be pointed out is that he distanced himself from Böhm-Bawerk's subordination of subjectivism to objectivism[4] and shifted towards Fisher's viewpoint, which affirmed the dependence of capital, and thus accumulation, on the determination of the subjective interest rate. Del Vecchio followed Fisher[5] in his attempt to bring the subjective interest rate back to the theory of circulation, after Böhm-Bawerk had consigned it to an objective theory of production. But he decided to treat the theories of interest rate and accumulation separately.

Böhm-Bawerk included the length of production processes among the factors determining the interest rate, whereas, by contrast, Fisher believed that the subjective preference for current consumptions as opposed to future ones was the sole basis for the theory of interest: put briefly, Böhm-Bawerk's capital marginal productivity was opposed to Fisher's 'impatience'.[6] On considering the theoretical conflict, Del Vecchio certainly sided with Fisher, writing that: 'Given a subjective economics, as in both Böhm-Bawerk and Fisher, objective facts cannot be put on the same level as subjective ones, but the former are subordinate to the latter, as stated by Fisher in opposition to Böhm-Bawerk'.[7]

But he also added that his theory differed from both of them.[8] Del Vecchio agreed with Fisher on the subjective theory of interest, but this did not mean that such a theory had to ignore the production process.[9] Del Vecchio was persuaded that a complete theory of interest must also be a theory of production and distribution, as well as of circulation, thus evoking 'a theory of economic equilibrium in the widest sense of that expression'.[10]

Del Vecchio cemented the link between the interest rate and the dynamic sphere of accumulation, where the latter depends mainly on extra-economic factors. Neither of the two theories – interest and accumulation – are independent of each other, as in Böhm-Bawerk's thought, nor are the two blended, as Fisher stated. Certainly, as Fisher had widely argued, the theory of interest must be moved from production to accumulation, with the clear assumption of a dynamic perspective. Although decisions on accumulation do not depend on the rate of interest, it was clear, Del Vecchio stated, that the stock of capital is linked to the interest rate: 'The estimation of capital stock is not possible without establishing the rate of interest ... and the value of the capital stock depends on that rate'.[11]

Briefly, the existing capital, and consequently the length of production processes, defines an objective rate of interest that in Del Vecchio is the *normal* one.

The normal objective rate of interest, developed on Wicksellian insights, is easily understandable. It is an average value depending on past decisions about production processes and their length and their effects on prices.[12] Consequently, it is obvious that the *other* rates of interest, the subjective ones, but also what Del Vecchio called the *current* value of the interest rate, tend to the *normal* one. In other words, the interest rate has a *current* level which tends towards a *normal* level.

Summing up, on seeking an autonomous conceptualization of the interest rate on which accumulation might be grounded, Del Vecchio spoke of a *subjective* interest rate when considering consumer's choices between current and future goods; the reasoning of savers and speculators on financial investments; and entrepreneur's investment decisions. But he finally admitted that such individual psychological rates might tend towards a *normal* level, whose existence reflected the weight of production processes on this variable determination.[13] Given that the normal interest rate is determined by the length of the production process, production and accumulation meet when the synthesis between the normal and psychological interest rates has been accomplished.[14]

Static and Dynamic Interest Rate

Writing in 1915, Del Vecchio could not evade the problem raised by Schumpeter[15] concerning the existence of a single *static* interest rate. Del Vecchio pointed out that the interest rate can be part of a static representation of the economic system's operation, and that the normal interest rate is fully consistent with a static representation of the economic system.

In a static perspective, the interest rate is represented by the marginal productivity of capital, to which the individual demand for capital must be adapted. It is true that the interest also exists in a stationary economy, but the conditions for obtaining a constant interest rate are stringent: the constancy of a country's rates of population and capital growth and of its national wealth. But, as Del Vecchio pointed out, those are not working hypotheses, but simply 'statements without basis or aim'.[16]

But it was only on setting the interest rate in a dynamic environment that the subjective characteristics of the interest rate come to the fore.[17] The point is to conceive the interest rate not as a *thing*, as a certain stock of goods, but as a *relationship* or a *ratio* between elements of an economic system,[18] and precisely between current and future ones.

The known utilities $\frac{U_A - U_B}{U_B} = i$ can be related to production groups, with the result that the interest rate is no longer a subjective variable, but a variable expressing attitudes and relationships within and between groups. Here the normal rate can emerge from the main selling group, attracting the other subjective rates of interest.

The problem is that dynamic features involve non-economic besides economic aspects. An economic theory of interest does not suffice because it ignores certain basic features: 'The choice between static [stationary] and dynamic analysis is not an arbitrary question. Certain facts require a dynamic theory. Then, if also the dynamic economic perspective is not sufficient, it must go beyond economic frontiers'.[19]

The conceptualization of a dynamic view of the interest rate allowed Del Vecchio to move towards accumulation. Accumulation is a matter of individual expectations about the future, and this can aid understanding of the psychological interest rate expressing choices between current and future consumption. But the interest rate cannot contribute to explaining decisions about accumulation, since these are grounded on entirely different motivations, for example ambition. The psychological rate of interest does not explain, but in some sense it expresses ambition and attitude to invest. Briefly, it represents an individual or group propensity to invest or to lengthen economic processes.

Interest Rate and Saving

Having stated that the interest rate has primarily a subjective characterization, Del Vecchio analysed the theories of Jevons, Fisher, Thomas N. Carver and Landry in order to determine the weight of psychological features in the distribution of consumption over time: 'An increasing rate of interest appears as a cause of future consumption increase, with a consequent reduction of its final utility, penalizing current consumption, whose marginal utility increases'.[20]

Thus, when the interest rate guarantees some gain, it induces the postponement of consumption. By contrast, the interest rate may also favour the anticipation of future consumption by means of loans. This switch of consumption calls attention to saving, although Del Vecchio did not believe that saving is determined by the interest rate.

The fact that saving is not simply a function of the interest rate does not mean that it is totally independent from interest. In effect, capitalization is the result of previous savings, and the distribution of disposable means of production finally defines the normal interest rate towards which the psychological rates of interest converge.[21] It is true that in certain cases individual saving has an economic explanation because it is intended to be the basis of a future pension, but: 'Most of the saving of which our societies have need is yielded independently from any economic or hedonistic calculus and thus independently from any interest-rate value'.[22]

But, the fact itself of conceiving the psychological interest rate as a relationship, instead of an income, distances interest from the idea that it can determine saving between the present and future.

Del Vecchio treated the theory of accumulation as exogenous to economic theory, 'because an economic theory of accumulation is not possible'.[23] While the interest rate can receive an economic explanation (see the normal rate of interest), this is apparently not possible for accumulation. This point can be understood only by analysing saving. The proof that accumulation explained on economic bases was not possible consists in the impossibility itself of an economic theory of saving, whose demonstration became Del Vecchio's prime concern.

What did saving mean? 'Saving involves the choice of a set of future remote consumptions instead of a closer set'.[24] Starting from the known aspect, Del Vecchio thought that accumulation concerns a small part of current saving.

On seeking to determine the relationships between savings and accumulation, Del Vecchio considered the link between income and saving. If income explains saving, it is clear that some reasons for an economic interpretation of accumulation can be maintained. To affirm that saving is a function of income and/or wealth is to state that saving grows when income or wealth increases. Del Vecchio did not believe that affluent classes have on average a greater propensity to save than poorer ones. In 1915, Del Vecchio wrote that the correlation between income concentration and saving had still to be demonstrated. When income increases also saving grows, but this was simply an observable fact.

Just as a quantitative relation between saving and income cannot be established with certainty, so the economic rate between the two variables cannot be maintained. However, this does not mean that there is no link between them. For example, Del Vecchio admitted that saving is certainly the outcome of habits characterizing the middle class. In this case, saving must be considered a bourgeois virtue. However, it is clear that Del Vecchio related saving not only to the level of income but, as we shall see, also to its origin.

Del Vecchio thus distanced himself from the then prevailing attitude stating an economic link between the levels of income and saving, and he disagreed with those who argued that saving is an increasing function of income.[25] Saving grows more than proportionally to income when the marginal utility of saving is explained by features such as ambition. But, in arguing thus, Del Vecchio took the theory of saving outside the economic domain.

Del Vecchio stated that saving is determined by the individual ambition to ascend the social ladder, more than by the economic calculus conceived as gain; and this makes it difficult to demonstrate any relation between saving and class or economic group. If, however, it is true that behaviour changes according to the economic group or category, it is likewise true that the relationship between saving and income is understandable in light of the kind of income more than its level. Profits yield more savings than rents. Consequently, saving is not a problem of the income level, but of the type of income.

Profits, which are not constant over time, and not rents, which by contrast involve constant levels of consumption, may be the source of new savings: 'Because profits are less regular gains, they do not induce habits, or to a lesser extent than rents, which on the contrary are commonly stable through time'.[26]

Thus, saving occurs when income exceeds its normal value, when profits determine an uncommon increase in income. This is a source of saving. Essentially, Del Vecchio was interested in saving when it derives from occasional disposable income (profit) or income saved because of a desire to climb the social ladder.

Static and Dynamic Saving

According to Del Vecchio,

> The distinction is between *static* saving and *dynamic* saving, where only the latter matters for social accumulation. Dynamic saving comes from those incomes presenting a large dispersion around the average income of the social class considered, which are not stable.[27]

Thus, the majority of the population have only static savings, which contribute little to accumulation. This occurs because the aim of these savings is to acquire the security that the worker wishes to guarantee for themselves and their family. In 1915 Del Vecchio supposed that consumption could be determined by looking at the life cycle of workers: '[Static] saving is spent to deal with diseases or during old age ... The savings of workers must reach a very high level before they change from being static to dynamic'.[28]

In general, the savings of those people who can enable their children to improve their lives are extraneous to any accumulation process. These are not dynamic savings.

The aggregate analysis of saving cannot be of *ceteris paribus* type because a particular factor behaves differently depending on whether the other factors are assumed to be constant or changing:

> The supply of saving is dynamic, because it is basically caused by the turnover of social classes, the economic cycle, political upheavals, monetary transformation; technological changes, and by many other elements. Thus, it is a typically dynamic fact, which cannot be represented by means of static analysis.[29]

At that time, economic dynamics were frequently the subject of theories in which economic calculation was not the *explicans* – as in this case, where subjective and psychological features play a crucial role. In effect, Del Vecchio stated,[30] both *habit* and *ambition* are psychological factors orienting the distribution of wealth over time. Both have a subjective and psychological nature that induces formulation of a pseudo-economic theory of interest. Del Vecchio investigated the two factors. He started with habit, a 'mental' variable at that time frequently associated with dynamic behaviours.[31] Here habit concerns saving, since the source of the latter must be sought in those gains and incomes exceeding the amount necessary to satisfy normal needs. It is necessary to consider the high incomes deriving from extraordinary gains to find the origin of dynamic savings: 'The absence of high consumption habits ... is the condition allowing the making of much saving'.[32]

However, while habits establish the condition for acquiring static savings, the second factor, ambition, drives accumulation: 'Savers do not aim to increase pleasure: by contrast, an important general objective is achievable by means of accumulation, i.e. to ascend the social hierarchy'.[33]

The economists who had studied economic accumulation – Del Vecchio was convinced – had paid insufficient attention to trivial motives explaining the saving and consumption of the upper classes. Habit and passion for work induced the newly rich to continue their business, industrial and financial activities, even if their consumption habits prevented them from consuming all their incomes. It was ambition that pushed them towards new accumulation. Therefore, habits and ambition operate together to determine social accumulation.

The rise (by means of new incomes) of some individuals above their original social station, and above the average level of wealth, is therefore a condition for accumulation. However, because the increase in wealth is confined to a small part of the population, such an increase will be discontinuous rather than gradual, irregular rather than steady. On extending the psychological view on saving behaviour, the latter appears to be the result of the contrast between the pleasures expected to derive from the possession of wealth and the effort of foregoing immediate enjoyment. The theory of accumulation can be based on such an effort, so that it assumes a qualitative more than quantitative character. In effect, it is not possible to measure effort and enjoyment using an economic calculus. Del Vecchio's accumulation theory is a psychological one.

However, some comments are in order. For low-income earners, saving is an expensive act, which is necessarily avoided unless the possession of savings is of greatest importance. As income grows, so the cost of saving decreases, inducing individuals to accumulate more. Del Vecchio stressed that it is ambition, fuelled by the satisfaction derived from the possession of savings, that induces people to save more than proportionally to increased income. According to Del Vecchio, this is also the reason why wealth tends to concentrate among a few individuals, bringing to the fore the relationship between accumulation and concentration or distribution. The following passage clarifies his thought:

> The fundamental distinction between static and dynamic saving avoids any confusion between the following two statements: first, accumulation is independent from any *state* of wealth distribution; second, accumulation depends on a distribution that is *different* from a *previous one*. For example: the award of a million to an individual favours accumulation not because there is one *more* millionaire in the country, but because there is a *new* millionaire.[34]

Del Vecchio was persuaded that accumulation is influenced by the *change* in the distribution of wealth and incomes: different individuals have different ambitions. Dynamic saving is the main source of accumulation, which is fed by the circulation of wealth.

Accumulation and Distribution of Wealth and Income

At this point, Del Vecchio was ready to single out the relationships among interest rate, accumulation, and aspects such as the distribution of wealth and incomes, social dynamics, economic progress, social change, political constitution and economic cycle. These are the main, but certainly not the only, factors influencing and influenced by accumulation.

We may start with the first: the distribution of wealth and income. Del Vecchio noted that neither the Pareto income distribution curve[35] nor the Rodolfo Benini property distribution[36] provides an explanation for this (unequal) distribution. Even the statistical observation that the concentration of income and property grows as income increases says nothing about the causes. Yet it would be useful to know whether income concentration depends on that of property or whether, conversely, the former determines the latter:

> If, as is more probable, the income curve and the wealth or property curve are interdependent of each other, then savings, which are the means by which the interdependence takes shape, should be considered as related to income and property. Consequently, the fact that property is more concentrated than incomes is a proof that savings mainly derive from higher incomes.[37]

Thus, the distribution of incomes contributes to explaining the distribution of wealth or property, the two being connected by savings. But this does not make it possible to add something more about accumulation.

However, Del Vecchio returned to general factors explaining part or some aspects of the problem. He emphasized the role of the Paretian circulation of elites. Every great change or revolution had produced a new elite that immediately became hereditary in order to maintain the power acquired. For this purpose, one of the tools available to aspirants to power is saving: '[Saving] does not pertain to the wealthy, but to those people that aspire to ascend the social hierarchy by means of it'.[38]

However, the notion of social hierarchy requires clarification. It is determined by the distribution of wealth. According to Del Vecchio, only wealth matters in defining the social hierarchy. Consequently important are the transmission of wealth among generations, its distribution, and the way in which new wealth comes about, and so on. The accumulation process is not continuous and uniform but proceeds by leaps, thus exhibiting discontinuity. Finally, although new wealth increases on average, it tends to concentrate into a few hands, thereby augmenting the level of inequality.

The social hierarchy is strictly connected with political power. Suffice it to point out that, in the course of history, the accumulation of large quantities of wealth has been preceded by the establishment of a particular political and military apparatus. Wealthy individuals, wrote Del Vecchio,[39] exist before large quantities of wealth are accumulated. Moreover, the urge to accumulate sometimes arises because individuals seek to reach the power positions held by other individuals by means of economic wealth:

> Periods during which it is possible freely to accumulate private wealth are short, and they lead to a single outcome: wealth and power tend to concentrate in the same hands, either because power involves wealth or because wealth leads directly or indirectly to political power.[40]

Del Vecchio believed that, at that time, the latter process was decidedly more frequent than the former.

Del Vecchio was persuaded that a complete explanation of accumulation required investigation of the objective sources and the historical and social conditions of saving. History had shown that the *great accumulations* had been due less to special psychological qualities of individuals than to the objective conditions creating the environment that fostered otherwise latent individual aptitudes.

In 1915, Del Vecchio wrote that those objective conditions included general aspects concerning the law, such as individual safety, the protection of property rights, and a certain international and domestic political order.[41] All these favour accumulation as well as economic progress. Social and political changes and economic oscillations contribute to creating the environment in which psychological factors can act. It is clear that accumulation was not associated with a stable and harmonious economic environment. On the contrary, Del Vecchio saw in what we can generally call 'economic and social change' the condition propitious to economic accumulation. This conception drew largely on Pantaleoni's theory of economic dynamics.

On building his theory of accumulation, Del Vecchio distanced himself from both the Austrian and the mathematical views. He preferred a view close to classical political economy, which presented economic facts as concrete phenomena which dominated other social aspects: 'In this way, economic development is anchored to historical and then social schemas ... Political economy is transformed into philosophy of history'.[42]

Apparent here is the influence of Antonio Labriola, Del Vecchio's acknowledged master. It can be added that Del Vecchio himself cited Friedrich List, Marx, Achille Loria, Werner Sombart, among others. In effect, as regards the causes of accumulation, Del Vecchio seemed to fluctuate between different approaches. He appeared resolute in his intent to remove human action from the sterile calculus of individual interests and to deduce it immediately from social factors operating as objective ones. He did not renounce his empirical method, but he combined it with a view in which history is not a constantly changing flow, but rather a process anchored in certain fundamental movements. Put briefly, he embedded his view of accumulation based on individual and psychological features in a historical process.

To conclude these sections on the non-relationship between rates of interest and saving, it should be pointed out once again that Del Vecchio's subjectivity was confined within the boundaries of individual expectations, here referred to potential changes in the social hierarchy. Individual ambition, and not individual profit, is the engine of economic and social change. Accordingly, the individual equilibrium assumes the appearance of the changing equilibrium, and the interest rate becomes the relationship connecting current and future time. While the discount rate is clearly a monetary variable, the subjective interest rate is conceived as a mental or psychological variable expressing the attitude of an individual towards the future, which *may* coincide with the objective *normal* interest rate.

Del Vecchio's Thought in Symbols

Reformulation of Del Vecchio's above concepts in symbolic terms may be of help in understanding them.

As Del Vecchio wrote in 1909: 'The monetary theory should be built as an application of the theory of interest',[43] meaning that there is a relationship between the value of money and the interest rate. Del Vecchio thus accelerated his transition from a static monetary theory to a dynamic one by integrating the monetary function of medium of exchange with that of *store of value* for future payments.

In this regard, ever since the *Principii*, and all the more so in his subsequent essays, Del Vecchio sought to anchor the value of money to the interest rate.[44] It should be stressed that Del Vecchio did not consider the interest rate to be a monetary variable clearing savings and investments; by contrast, he regarded it as a psychological variable converging towards a *normal* interest rate. Although the 'terms of interest must all be subjective',[45] Del Vecchio maintained that the many subjective rates of interest can be treated as economic variables only if they are distributed around an average or normal value. However, the subjective interest rate does not lose importance, because it is the mental variable conditioning choices about accumulation.

But to focus on the current or normal level, individuals exchange on the basis of comparisons between the marginal utilities of goods, and the interest rate springs from a subjective comparison between utilities of goods. We know that Del Vecchio defines the interest rate, *i*, for that individual as:[46]

$$i = \frac{U_A - U_B}{U_B} ,$$

but, finally, assuming that it also represents the *normal* interest rate. In deciding to hold money, individuals compare the utility of money with the utility of the goods whose purchase is delayed:

> *Each individual holds money in such a quantity and for some time till he obtains from the last quantity of money held and for the last period of time during which he detains money an increment of utility equal to the decrease in the utility of the goods he will purchase.*[47]

Del Vecchio implicitly stated that changes in the interest rate, by influencing decisions about goods, *cause* changes in the value of money. There thus gradually emerges a theory of circulation where money rides on the interest rate: the higher (lower) the interest rate, the smaller (larger) the amount of goods purchased and, thus, the smaller (larger) the demand for money.

In dynamic conditions, given that the interest rate influences the composition of liquidity, it also affects the circulation of money, which cannot be postulated, in line with the interpretations of the quantity theory predominant in Del Vecchio's time.[48] If the interest rate is conceived as the cost of money:

> by determining the cost of money, the interest rate regulates purchases ... if it decreases, the amount of transactions grows and, consequently, the value of money increases; conversely, if the interest rate increases the opposite occurs.[49]

The obvious conclusion is that variations in the value of money (inversely) follow changes in the interest rate:

$$V_M = f(\underset{-}{i}) . \qquad 5.1$$

On treating the value of money as a function of the interest rate, the former loses part of the objective character expressed above and acquires a subjective dimension.

Finally, taking developments involving future prices into account, the current value of money is grounded on 'predicted future conditions' influenced by psychological perturbations.[50] Dynamic facts associated with uncertainty are here represented by the parameter z. We may thus rewrite the previous equation 5.1 as follows:

$$V_M = f(\underset{-}{i}, \underset{+}{z}). \qquad 5.2$$

And, taking account of equation 3.12, we have:

$$V_M = f(\underset{+}{Q}, \underset{-}{M}, \underset{-}{E}, \underset{-}{i}, \underset{+}{z}) \qquad 5.3$$

According to the early Del Vecchio, we may state that the value of money is simultaneously determined by the demand for, and the supply of, money, where demand mostly depends on *psychological* factors (habits, preferences), while supply is affected by banks' decisions about reserves.[51] Del Vecchio's analysis of the role of the interest rate sometimes seems to place his theory closer to the theory put forward by Marshall in *Money, Credit and Commerce* than to Walras's theory. Marshall wrote that 'the "value of money" ... at any time is the rate of discount, or the rate of interest for short period loans charged in it'.[52] At first sight, Del Vecchio replaced the objective meaning of the value of money with a more subjective concept.

Contrary to neoclassical thought, as we shall see, also savings are mainly determined by social and psychological factors, such as individual ambitions, and only partially by economic factors such as wages, profits and wealth.[53] Finally, the interest rate does not matter, because it never equalizes savings and investments. Clearly, organizational aspects crop up again and again.

Given that a time gap exists between the selling and the buying of goods, Del Vecchio stressed the need to pay general attention to the uncertainty surrounding every decision on the cash to be held for consumption. Time, and therefore uncertainty, became important factors in defining the value of money in Del Vecchio's theory. Since the interest rate is treated as the variable that gives expression to time in that theory, subjective elements consequently increase their influence on monetary circulation.

Considering that the demand for money depends on the consumption of goods, the interest rate, *i*, indirectly affects the circulating money (and therefore the value of money). The greater the interest rate, the more delayed the consumption will be, and the smaller the demand for money.

Differently from the short term, in the long term there are changes in both expected prices and production. Moreover, changes in production, ΔQ, may also determine change in the economic organization, i.e. in the money effectiveness ΔE.

Thus, the monetary equilibrium now involves possible changes in all the variables expressing demand. Equation 3.9 must be rewritten as follows:

$$M = f(\underset{+}{Q^e}, \underset{+}{P^e}, \underset{-}{E}) \qquad 5.4$$

Where ΔM can be determined by ΔQ^e, ΔP^e and also ΔE.

Accumulation and Crisis

Del Vecchio did not conceive accumulation as growth. To accumulate did not have an intrinsically positive meaning: more simply, it was an aspect of economic life that Del Vecchio treated more from the viewpoint of distribution than of growth. Del Vecchio was not particularly interested in factors favouring economic expansion. The ordinary real operation of the economy attracted him – also because it was always a dynamic, and therefore unstable, process. Proof of this was Del Vecchio's refusal to consider the equality between savings and investments as illustrative of a stable condition. As we have seen, investments are determined by factors entirely different from savings.

The theory of crisis proposed by Del Vecchio in 1914 provides us with a view of how the phenomenon was then conceived by an economist who attempted to give classical anchorage to new ideas. Understanding economic crises requires establishing relationships among causes, facts and symptoms. Del Vecchio was persuaded that 'economic progress and economic crises' are phenomena too deeply-rooted in the modern economy for them to coincide accidentally.

Put briefly, he judged a crisis to be a phenomenon typical of a 'modern or capitalistic regime'.[54] Believing that a cycle theory could not ignore what 'comes before' ('the flow of progress or economic development'), Del Vecchio sought to develop 'an economics of crises': that is, a broad approach able to explain the various movements and dynamic phenomena characterizing capitalism, to which – as stressed by Sombart in 1904[55] – economic crises are linked. While the theory was not able to explain why cyclical fluctuations conditioned the trend, according to Del Vecchio it was clear that long-term economic progress influences crises, which he depicted as necessary periodic market reorganizations leading to the expulsion of less competitive firms. Del Vecchio affirmed that 'crises are secondary but necessary events of a dynamic and progressive economy':[56] progress feeds on crises.[57]

A comprehensive theory of crisis was more than a simple description of these events. This endeavour induced Del Vecchio first to apply a causal method to define the features of such a theory. The specification of symptoms, occasional impulses and causes made Del Vecchio's approach original compared with contemporary treatments: for example, the analysis grounded mainly in psychology proposed by Pareto in the second volume of the *Cours*. More widely, Del Vecchio sought to integrate statistics and theory in a homogeneous interpretation of this phenomenon. This explains why his 1914 article comprises both an 'analytical approach' stressing the variety of the causal aspects and their mutual relationships and a 'historical approach' taking account of the specific contexts examined.

Del Vecchio wrote that economic interdependence makes it more difficult to understand crisis phenomena, and that examining non-economic facts does not generate sufficient data to explain crises entirely. He inferred that, because crises are events of the modern or capitalist regime, historical elements must be examined as well. Nonetheless, as said, he eschewed historicism.[58] His theory appears to be a theory of the capitalist economy, but in which history is based on scientific concepts. His theory was not linked to temporal, spatial, or national aspects. Del Vecchio treated crises as dynamic phenomena depending on the progressive movement called 'capitalism'. In other words, capitalism was depicted as Spiethoff's 'economic style', and the crisis was a symptom of this inexorable movement. From this viewpoint, crisis, and not capitalism, is the historical 'fact' that requires theoretical and historical methodologies for its analysis.

Del Vecchio maintained that complementarities between pure-economic categories and historical-concrete ones are meaningful not only for the explanation of crises but also for all economic theories. Pure-economic categories pertain to the *conception* (*concezione*) of economic phenomena or their contents; historical-concrete categories pertain to the *explanation* (*spiegazione*) of economic phenomena or their logic. Del Vecchio gave explanation a less universal characterization than conception, because it involves further historical specifications and topics different from those of pure economics. In fact, topics which are valid in their conception are correct but insufficient in their explanation.[59] While crisis phenomenology requires pure economic instruments alone, its rationalization needs an explanatory scheme which treats crises as historical events intrinsically bound up with capitalism.

As previously stated, to give expression to this complementarity between theory and history, Del Vecchio singled out the following five 'research orders' of crises: first, the description of facts attesting to the crisis, i.e. employment, prices; second, the specification of concrete historical contexts, in particular the 'modern' forms of production, trade and distribution that lead to crisis; third, the formulation of theory, that is, the definition of a 'simple scheme' showing the reasons for 'prosperity' and 'decline'. He gave a theoretical function to the third level alone, which included aspects such as the differing elasticity of supply and demand, the lag among economic phenomena during the cycle and the dependence of the cycle on economic progress.[60] The third level was that of thought experiments. This was because Del Vecchio argued that crisis theory does not deal with causes, or symptoms, or various facts concerning crises; rather, it starts from these elements and shows their interconnections. The theory focuses on the relationships among objects, facts and other features. It may include pure economic arguments alone, or it may also consider concrete-historical, technical or legal aspects.

If economic-logic analyses prevail, then what will result is an economic theory of crisis; otherwise, one may have a psychological-social theory of crisis. In this regard, Del Vecchio stated that the English classical economists had already built an incomplete theory of crisis hinging on the equilibrium between fixed and circulating capital, without explaining the genesis of crises. The upsetting of this equilibrium meant the occurrence of the crisis, even if that theory was unable to explain *why* the crisis occurred in that exact moment.[61] The fourth order concerned the description of symptoms characterizing that specific crisis. The fifth one involved the specification of the 'initial' cause that had given origin to the phenomenon.[62] Investigation of such a cause must not be confused with the theory of crisis, because it is an error to search for the cause in one of the previous research orders.

On analysing Albert Aftalion's book, *Les crises périodiques de superproduction* (1913),[63] Del Vecchio reiterated his disagreement with those theories of crisis based on over- or under-production, and over- or under-saving. Rather, he was interested in the study of periodic changes in costs and productivity, and in their combination with wage trends. He stressed that from this analysis: 'We derive the important consequence that changes in monetary wages follow the corresponding changes in prices with a lag and less intensity'.[64]

The theoretical problem of crises was that of determining the causes of economic oscillations. Besides psychological factors, are there also monetary ones? The distinctiveness of Del Vecchio's analysis consists in its emphasis on the importance of relationships among factors, instead of on factors themselves. Crises occur because of the kinds of relationships connecting economic to non-economic factors. In other words, theory must go ahead on a pure economics basis as long as it is possible to progress, and then it must move to historical analysis.

Among the causes of crises Del Vecchio singled out the following. First: 'expected increasing prices due to a new ratio between circulating money and goods'. Also in this case, the focus is on expected prices, not current ones. This is also a classical monetary cause of crises that, according to Del Vecchio, 'have also a monetary origin'.[65] He added: 'most crises exhibit long periods of increasing prices caused by change in the ratio between the demand and supply of money'.[66] However, Del Vecchio conceived the monetary causes of crises as possible but secondary ones, i.e. crises have other non-monetary determinants – for example, production determinants, to which monetary disequilibrium and expectations on prices must be added.

The fact that crises do not have a single monetary origin derives from the fact that monetary equilibrium is not crucial in Del Vecchio's theory. Rejection of the quantitative principle entails denial that monetary changes can provoke the price variations that cause crises. Monetary disequilibrium may coexist with equilibrium in the capital or production sectors without the onset of any crisis. However, to conclude this crucial point, Del Vecchio was convinced that the crisis was a much more profound phenomenon than a simple change in prices, even if it manifests itself in a price change.

The second cause involves immediately distributive issues: 'increasing profits due to the more rapid growth of prices compared with wages'. Increasing prices favour profits and penalize fixed income as wages, thus causing difficulties for workers. In Del Vecchio, economic crises always have a distributive dimension, whatever their origin.

Del Vecchio then singled out other causes of crisis. Third: 'the incomplete exploitation of production forces due to the tendency of firms to favour incomplete competition and monopolistic positions. Fourth: 'a conflict in the use of raw materials between the production of final goods and equipment'. He concluded with a point that would prove crucial more than twenty years later with publication of Keynes's *General Theory*. In effect, Del Vecchio pointed out a fifth cause of crises: downward wage rigidity if compared with downward price flexibility.[67] However, a crisis is a much more profound phenomenon than a simple price change. The latter is a manifestation of crisis, but not its cause, which must be sought in disequilibria concerning production and capital.

Crises occur because an economy based on capital transformation is intrinsically unstable; this is the meaning of the third theoretical level. Reversal of the conjuncture always has a cause in production, or better, 'an excess of fixed capital production'.[68] This means that it is the third level of research that needs further close examination. Del Vecchio expressly referred to the works of Aftalion, Mikhail Tugan-Baranovsky, Spiethoff and Jean Lescure, all of whom sought to identify the causes of economic crises in the mechanisms of production. Taking a classical view, Del Vecchio narrowed the range of causes to disequilibrium between different production sectors when the economy goes through an expansion. According to him, the disequilibrium does not only concern the relationship between production and consumption; it may also concern different production sectors. A crisis derives from imbalances among sectors, principally those producing equipment and final goods.

In particular, the imbalance among production sectors is linked to the growth phase of the economy. Growth contains the seeds of economic crisis. Del Vecchio considered the over-production of fixed capital to be intrinsic to capitalism, stating that the entrepreneurial choices made when an economy grows are more susceptible to errors in defining the rate between fixed and circulating capital. The link between the growing economy and imbalances in capitalization is the final point in our historic-theoretical reconstruction.[69] The theory of industrial transformations as the theory of crisis or of economic fluctuations can be built upon it. However, Del Vecchio was not precise on this important aspect. It is well known that imbalances may be produced by investments and disinvestments. These changes may be favoured by the availability of monetary capital. However, only a growing economy may reduce the amount of free capital, so that change of production becomes very difficult.

Monetary phenomena, like the discount rate and stock exchange panic, are only signals of the imminent crisis, which does not originate in one sector alone. The entire production system is at the basis of a crisis. Del Vecchio spoke of: 'an inevitable tendency to exceed the correct ratio between the production of short- and long-term goods'.[70] When this disequilibrium occurs, changes like the rise in the interest rate are not sufficient to prevent crisis. The interest rate still remains below the level necessary to re-establish equilibrium between current wages and expected future prices.[71]

In a 1932 article on the world crisis,[72] Del Vecchio considered capital transformation as a key cause of that crisis. He argued that the relationship between fixed capital in different sectors must be formulated in a more precise and thorough manner by taking account of the changes occurring in production assets. He repeated that 'this transformation is at the basis of a theory of crisis' more than any hypothesis concerning excess production.[73]

Del Vecchio's analysis of the causes of crises requires us to consider the composition of production factors, and not just their amount. This allows investigation of one of the theoretical foundations of industrial fluctuations, which are thus explained by endogenous and not external or accidental causation.

Capital Transferability and Mobility

Del Vecchio's theory on economic crises fits perfectly in the Italian tradition that, in the late nineteenth and early twentieth century, proposed a dynamic approach to organizational changes in the production system. The economists embracing this view theorized that development processes are disrupted by more or less periodic shocks and by sudden 'heavy' events in monetary and financial markets. They insisted on searching for a theory that treated the crisis as an event linked to the development of the capitalist economy, which could not be traced back to a single symmetrically repeatable fact. Besides Del Vecchio, this group of economists included Camillo Supino, who wrote on economic crisis at the beginning of the twentieth century, later followed by Bruno Foà, Guglielmo Masci, Manlio Resta, Giuseppe Papi and Marco Fanno, who tried to refine the theory of crisis as a theory of capital transformation. This persisting reference to capital as the pivotal feature of economic transformations anchored these economists to the classical nineteenth-century theory.

The economy was viewed as a dynamic and changing reality, not as a stationary fact; and this induced the above-mentioned authors to investigate mainly imbalances in production as an important cause of economic crisis. In this representation stressing continuous change, the problem of 'capital liquidity' existed, and it was developed from a viewpoint interested in the economic and physical transformation of tools and instruments. Therefore, discussing the problem of 'capital transformation' meant analysing the problem of how to convert existing equipment for different or new production purposes. If this 'liquidity' or 'mobility' is not attained, crisis and depression may ensue. In this regard, the vision analysed here was a 'classical' one.

In the Italian economic literature, the first assertion that capitalization causes crisis was made by Francesco Ferrara, who in 1864 wrote that 'the excessive conversion of circulating capital into fixed capital' may generate economic crisis. The origin of this theory must be sought in Ricardo, but also in economic events such as the English crisis of 1847, when 'excessive investment in railways gave rise to economic depression'.[74]

Ferrara carefully analysed the excess of fixed capitalization as the source of crisis. He reached the conclusion that errors in investing, and not capitalization in itself, may cause economic imbalance. This occurs when the amount of fixed capital does not correspond to the demand for final goods. Hypothesizing a market in which each good is exchanged with a good of equivalent value – that is, following the *law of markets* – Ferrara did not believe that capital may easily absorb existing wealth without yielding further wealth. If this happens, the damage is due to choice errors, not to capitalization:

> The damage must not be sought in the conversion of circulating capital into fixed capital, but in the specific utility of such a venture. If we observe the failure of the operation, we may deplore the choice of capitalization, not as conversion as such, but because it has represented sterile consumption.[75]

Therefore, crises are the outcome of wrong investments, not of investment *tout court*: 'If the crisis makes its appearance, it derives from wrong investment in the production of goods that are not demanded and traded in the market'.[76] In this case, Ferrara concluded, crisis is caused by the excess of credit enabling these investments, and never by capitalization.[77]

The topic was subsequently taken up and developed by Camillo Supino, who, in 1891, wrote a short book, *Theory of Capital Change* (*Teoria della trasformazione dei capitali*), which anticipated some of the themes developed by Mikhail Tugan-Baranovsky in those years on the transformation of fixed capital as a source of economic crisis. On analysing the conversion of fixed into circulating capital, Supino called attention to the temporal dimension of this conversion, particularly in economies with a high density of capital. During the monetization of fixed capital, forecasting errors may occur and cause a change in the ratio between the use-value of capital (a sort of return rate) and its cost-value (the interest paid). This change may result in economic crisis.[78]

In his following and better-known *Economic Crises* (*Le crisi economiche*) (1907),[79] Supino denied that crisis phenomena can be explained by ignoring monetary circulation. Because circulating money influences the level of nominal prices, it determines the choices made concerning capital transformation. Indeed, precisely because the transformation of fixed capital into final goods requires time, the economic system may be incapable of transforming fixed capital into money and then money into other production processes. This is the case in which instrumental goods have decreasing prices that make their sale difficult. Supino conceived 'liquidity' with the meaning that would become most common later: that is, of 'monetization'. However, if equipment loses its value because of technological innovations, it is clear that the consequent price reduction makes the monetization and transformation of equipment into other more innovative instruments difficult.

The link connecting industrial transformations with economic crises was thoroughly investigated by Guglielmo Masci in 1934. In a long essay entitled 'Some Current Aspects of Industrial Organization and Changes' ('Alcuni aspetti odierni dell'organizzazione e delle trasformazioni industriali'),[80] Masci sought to disentangle the question of the movement between the production of consumption goods and capital goods.

Masci introduced his reasoning – here only sketched – by supposing a single industry composed of three sectors: the first devoted to the production of capital goods employed by all three sectors; the second producing equipment used by the other two; and the third yielding final or consumption goods. An interesting hypothesis is that the physical capital employed by the three sectors can be moved from one to another sector without its monetization. In this way, the transformation of capital assumes the meaning of capital 'mobility'.

Masci stressed that, with growing production sustained by credit and savings, the expansion of the most indirect sector invariably occurs: that is, the first sector producing capital goods expands. Attracted by increasing profits, the other sectors converge towards the first one, which causes a diminishing supply of goods supplied by the second and third sectors. As a consequence, prices increase in these two sectors, draining producers from the first one, which in the meantime has experienced decreasing prices. Thus, industrial production shows the movement of firms among different sectors.

Problems do not arise if it is possible to finance this movement with unemployed monetary capital. The situation becomes more complicated when the passage from one to another sector involves the disintegration (disinvestment) of the former and the integration (investment) of the latter. 'Theories cannot abstain from considering as a feature of the economic crisis the fiction contrasting the monetization of fixed capital and its re-employment as payment means which can be transformed into consumption goods'.[81]

The transfer of specific capital goods presupposes that the 'previous reduction to consumption goods involves a disinvestment process and the subsequent investment process, whose duration represents an inverse measure of the capital liquidity'.[82]

Interpretation of the economic cycle could not ignore this two-way process of enhancement and demobilization taking place among the production sectors with alternating phases. Economic development is characterized by a continuous transformation of capital, which raises the problem of capital 'liquidity': that is, its 'transferability' from one use to another. According to Masci, this feature directly conditions production structures. In effect, the organization of firms into coalitions could be an answer to the need to make all the production sectors more 'liquid'.[83]

The degree of expansion of a given economy depends on what Masci termed the *rate of reproductiveness* of the sector producing capital goods. This rate measures the ratio between the amount of equipment produced by the sector and the amount of capital employed for such production. The need to increase the rate of reproductiveness during the expansion of the economy means that 'Industrial growth implemented by means of new monetary capital may be obtained only by partial and temporary movements of existing equipment to the sector considered. These movements are bound to end in a short or less short time'.[84]

In that perfect capital mobility between sectors does not exist, the growth of the economy will be characterized by frictions and rigidities that, according to Masci, emphasize the oscillatory progress of the economy.

Some years after Masci's contribution, Manlio Resta[85] pointed out that an Italian position on the problem of capital transformation had been progressively consolidating. This national interest was partially explained by the importance given by Pareto to the 'non-variability' of the production coefficients, a feature that limited the transferability of equipment and capital. Pareto's point had implicitly raised the problem of the mobility of capital.[86] Consequently, Resta started with a terminological clarification of concepts such as 'mobility' and 'liquidity'.

The first aspect of the theory of capital transformation (or transferability) hitherto inadequately treated was the source of the transformations themselves. These transformations, it was said, were driven by technological innovation or by changes in demand, but they were always mediated by the entrepreneur's expectations. The entrepreneur was required to interpret the demand for capital goods according to the expected demand for consumption goods.[87] On this basis, he decided to move or to change the capital. As argued by Marco Fanno, this decision was not immune from errors concerning time and quantities. This is a fundamental step in our reconstruction: the reinterpretation of the classical theory of capitalization as a cause of economic crises involves uncertainty enveloping the entrepreneur. However, we shall return to this topic later.

To remain with Resta, he proposed a Böhm-Bawerkian analysis of a production system organized into stages that begin with capital goods and end with final or consumption goods (a sort of vertical integration of the production process). The first stages produce goods used by the subsequent ones.[88] This leads to the idea that fixed capital and circulating capital do not remain in that condition forever.[89] Capital is fixed or circulating according to its use at a given stage of the production process. Moreover, this distinction depends on the temporal perspective assumed: the shorter this perspective, the more the fixed capital employed; the longer the perspective, the more circulating capital.

Given these aspects, Resta assumed a *medium* time and tried to measure its mobility. If 'liquidity' defines the level of transferability of capital in the vertical production process, the notion of 'mobility' shows that capital can be transferred from one use to another 'horizontally', that is, among different production processes.[90] While the liquidation of capital leads to its monetization, the mobility of capital involves its transfer to another use without monetary mediation. This is the case of integration or merger between firms whereby capital previously employed in one production process is now used for a different one: 'Liquidity necessarily implies the transformation of capital goods into final goods, while mobility is a change in capital goods when they pass from one process to another'.[91]

Resta studied industrial transformations by concentrating on the 'concrete possibility to transfer equipment'[92] without monetary mediation. However, aside from monetary aspects, the issue was the possibility of re-employing the same capital for different production. If this is possible, the fixed capital may be transferred. Obviously, it is necessary that there be demand for the existing capital, meaning that the transferability must be of an economic type and not only physical. Thus, imbalances and crises may affect those production sectors with a limited mobility of fixed capital, where it is unlikely that equipment can be re-employed in other production processes.

Consequently, both low capital liquidity and mobility may be the cause of imbalances, according to Resta, and of crises, according to Del Vecchio. If fixed capital is maintained in the original production process, capital or consumption goods may over-produced with consequent price decreases and a decline in profits. By contrast, if this capital is abandoned before its complete 'liquidation' in consumption goods, the costs due to its lack of use will increase. Therefore, when an entrepreneur chooses to capitalize, he should compare the cost of 'abandonment' with the cost of 'transformation'. Excessive capital 'immobilization' therefore means the condition in which fixed capital has scant transferability, which is different from an inadequate proportion between fixed and circulating capital.

In this way, the economic crisis problem is brought back to the problem of the *organization* of the production, as Resta (and others) seemed to believe: 'Generally ... the difficult transfer of fixed capital from one production to another is explained by the size and organization of the firm'.[93]

Concluding Remarks

Del Vecchio, as stressed by Caffè,[94] adhered to a 'unitary' view of economic phenomenon, meaning that his analysis did not omit any of the components of the system itself, because it is the 'game' among the parts that makes it possible to grasp the system's overall evolution, which in its turn influences each component part. This 'unity' of economic science consists of a horizontal synthesis between production and distribution, which includes institutions and exogenous relationships, and a vertical synthesis between cycle and trend and between crisis and capital accumulation.

This view is perfectly consistent with the more 'subjective' than 'sociological' insights that Del Vecchio introduced, as we have seen, in his theory of accumulation. In particular, he singled out 'ambition' and 'spirit of emulation' as the factors inducing individuals to modify their habits and to invest. All this occurs in a socially fragmented environment marked by class differences, in which saving is an instrument of social mobility. However, it derives from profits or borrowing: saving is a means of individual progress because it helps a person 'to climb the social ladder'.[95] Therefore, saving does not pertain to only the most affluent or leisured classes; rather, it is held by the 'most dynamic groups', those that 'are anxious to achieve social improvement'.[96]

Accumulation is thus anchored to psychological factors like 'ambition', which also determines the distribution of wealth in the economy. This interpretation is plausible only on admitting an economy crowded with individuals who are not ordinary but able to distinguish themselves from the others: without differentiation there is no stimulus for economic action.[97] Social dynamism – that is, turnover among the social classes – influences the supply of savings, being also conditioned by the 'economic cycle', 'political reversals', 'monetary changes' and 'technological changes'.

One may say that, precisely because of the amplitude of the treated phenomena, this theory of accumulation seems to lack a clear relationship between savings and investments. In effect, instead of an economic theory of savings, Del Vecchio propounded a sociological interpretation of the role played by savings in favouring the turnover of individuals among social classes. But it would be erroneous to dismiss this theory of savings because of its sociological bias. As Del Vecchio wrote, the subject of his 'sociological' theory is *economic processes*, and these too are determined by non-economic causes. 'Social ambition' is a factor with economic consequences: it determines investments, connecting them to savings also through intermediation by the banking system. Investments are driven less by profit than by social and psychological motives like ambition. However, it is precisely this process that constantly fuels dynamism in an economy.

6 DEALING WITH IRREDUCIBLE RISK

This chapter describes the specific entrepreneurial archetype that appeared at the margins of the neoclassical line of inquiry during the 1920s and 1930s. Del Vecchio did not deal much with this topic, but, almost paradoxically, the two short articles that he wrote during the 1910s and published in 1928 in a German collected work edited by Hans Mayer, Frank A. Fetter, and Richard Reisch brought him international acknowledgment from Frank Knight as a forerunner of radical uncertainty analysis. As seen in the previous chapters, uncertainty permeates Del Vecchio's monetary analysis in its entirety, but he never stated it so clearly as when he treated the risk experienced by entrepreneurs.

When Del Vecchio examined saving and accumulation, it was already clear, even if not yet definitively so, that his economics was a theory grounded on the role played by profits. It is these that drive the system, albeit at the cost of constant instability.

But in the Italian academic environment of the time, Del Vecchio was not the only scholar to investigate entrepreneurial choices. On the contrary, many contemporaneous economists wrote on the topic and created a sort of Italian view on the entrepreneurial role. For this reason, the following treatment begins with the Italian theoretical environment, the description of which should clarify the original aspects of Del Vecchio's theory or, better, the radical tone of his interpretation. The next two sections present the main analyses of the figure of entrepreneur proposed by Italian economists in the early decades of the twentieth century. The subsequent section returns to Del Vecchio, and the role played in his theory by the radical uncertainty surrounding entrepreneurial choices. Finally, his view of an entire economic system dominated by instability makes it definitive appearance.

The Evolution of the Entrepreneur's Archetype in Italy

In order to provide a detailed description of the debate on the entrepreneur in Italy in those decades, there follows a rapid survey of the main economists who wrote on the topic at that time. The treatment starts with the theories of Costantino Bresciani-Turroni, Giuseppe Ugo Papi and Marco Fanno, three Italian economists who, as regards the role of the entrepreneur, did not accept the neoclassical dogma that economic agents adapt to incidental circumstances. By contrast, they affirmed the importance of the entrepreneur's initiative as the result of a specific view of the functioning of the economic process. The entrepreneur was the prime mover of this process. He constantly looked for external or internal events in the economic system that could increase his chances of profit.

The specific attention towards this topic was not the outcome of influences by Mises,[1] on the one hand, and Pigou,[2] on the other, who wrote important pages on this topic. In addition, Italian economists traditionally attributed 'a very central position' to the entrepreneur in the economy.[3]

At first sight, it seems that the above-mentioned Italian economists only sought to integrate Schumpeter's theory of novelties into the neoclassical framework. However, in Bresciani-Turroni's and, generally, in Papi's and Fanno's works, the entrepreneur is a more complex and multi-functional actor than the Schumpeterian 'positive eponym'[4] to whom the progress of the economic system is due. According to their analyses, the entrepreneur was also an 'opportunistic' agent able to turn events and circumstances to his advantage. Because this approach was, on the one hand, inconsistent with the theory of innovations and the neoclassical idea of entrepreneurship and, on the other, consistent with analyses anticipated by historical economists (Sombart),[5] it demonstrates that a new *archetype* of the entrepreneur was slowly taking shape.

This transformation began in around 1910, when the entrepreneur was still mainly regarded as the guarantor of economic equilibrium who periodically *innovates*, and it emerged clearly in the 1930s, when the figure of a generic promoter of initiatives more alert to market opportunities than to innovation was implicitly if not explicitly included in economic analyses.

The evolution of the entrepreneur also involved a change in the theory explaining his remuneration. Profit progressively appeared to be a gain associated, not with a specific function, nor with innovation or a risky production initiative, but with the malfunctioning of markets, as all the above-mentioned economists suggested. The priority was given to profit in *itself*, or to a payment disconnected from the production of 'civilization' or 'well-being' as contrarily asserted by Schumpeter and by most of the nineteenth-century writers.

The above figurative and functional evolution raises at least one methodological issue. In fact, all the above-mentioned Italian economists adopted a dynamic and disequilibrium perspective – in other words, a method that enabled them to represent 'speculative' and 'opportunistic' entrepreneurial behaviour. This was consistent with the branch of the neoclassical theory which, from J.B. Clark[6] onwards, worked out a dynamic view of *profits*, *expected profits* and *extra-profits*. Thus, the evolution of the entrepreneur's archetype in economic theory came about through the development of a dynamic analysis.

Costantino Bresciani-Turroni: From the 'Innovative' to the 'Speculative' Entrepreneur

Costantino Bresciani-Turroni's works are a valuable basis on which to gain thorough understanding of the change that took place in entrepreneur analysis during the first four decades of the twentieth century. In fact, they show how the entrepreneur's role was detached from innovative initiative and progressively connected to several functions, all of them rather indefinite. These functions have a common purpose: the search for profits deriving not only from innovations, but also from speculation or opportunities resulting from market imbalances. In other words, the entrepreneur was increasingly linked not to a specific function, but to the search for profits, even when the latter were unconnected with a production activity.

Bresciani-Turroni drew his theoretical pattern by unifying the 'innovator' with the 'speculator'. In his early writings, he associated the investment boom with the appearance 'of new factors increasing the productivity of industry',[7] such as technical discoveries, new markets and new firms. His conception of economic innovation was similar to Schumpeter's.[8] Obviously, profit expectations were at the centre of this perspective. Indeed, increased profits 'in certain industries enlarges business, expands the demand for monetary loans, increases the discount rate and prices'. Then 'the growth of prices in its turn causes an increase in profits in the remaining industries'.[9]

In this regard, although Bresciani-Turroni agreed with Irving Fisher and with those authors who affirmed that there was a correspondence among prices, interest, and the discount rate, he remained faithful to the classical account that profits influence the discount rate, and not the reverse. In his early works, profits were invariably associated with a specific function: innovation.

In Bresciani-Turroni's subsequent writings, as he progressively developed a more 'complex' and 'manifold' vision of economic reality, the significance attributed to innovation weakened. By stating that 'both expansion and depression are due to many causes',[10] Bresciani-Turroni widened his concept of entrepreneurial activity.

Furthermore, on assuming that profitability was connected with dynamic economic phenomena,[11] he argued that profits may arise as a consequence of unexpected changes which move the economic system away from the condition in which prices balance costs, i.e. the stationary state. In other words, profits are linked to changes and to uncertainty. For this reason, profits may be conjunctural revenues and not solely the result of innovations. On this broader conception, the entrepreneur is no longer the positive hero who unremittingly transforms the economy; he may also be the agent able to transform 'rents' or occasional 'revenues' into 'profits'. The latter are mainly *temporary* revenues produced by the entrepreneur's capacity to anticipate future events, such as an increase in demand, or exogenous events, such as wars or other events producing a growth in prices. Indeed, because 'unexpected events usually damage the majority of people', they determine 'chances for earning in which the entrepreneur has no merit'.[12]

Bresciani-Turroni gave a lucid portrait of this new archetype when he described the inflation of the German economy. He stated that this inflation had generated a 'new class of brokers, dealers, modest stock gamblers, mean profiteers from monetary depreciation'[13] (who, together with the traditional entrepreneurs, had sought to take advantage of the movements of wealth associated with the increase in prices). The taxonomy of subjects who grew rich as a result of First World War inflation is illustrative of this new archetype: 'Hoarders of stocks, of firms, of buildings, of commodities, of goods, those people who bet with foreign currencies or loans'.[14] Bresciani-Turroni pointed out that these activities were not exclusive to speculators; they also concerned 'industrial companies' specialized in 'every kind of operation'.[15] Put briefly, Bresciani-Turroni identified the source of 'conjuncture profits' with all types of speculative activity that increase both inflation and price uncertainty.

Finally, it must be pointed out that Bresciani-Turroni's statements shifted entrepreneurial activity away from technical factors and the production process in the direction of the market. The evolution of the entrepreneur's figure was guided by the emergence of the market as an 'autonomous' source of profits, independently of any production or transformation activity. This view was a first step in the direction of considering profits to be 'unimputable income', as Knight outlined in those years,[16] or, better, imbalance revenues.

Giuseppe Papi's Theory of Errors

Compared with Bresciani-Turroni's empirical or factual interpretation of the entrepreneur's archetype, Giuseppe U. Papi's was more theoretical. Papi postulated that the entrepreneur acts by trial and error 'taking advantage' of short-term fluctuations that he himself contributes to causing. According to Pigou,[17] Papi developed a 'theory of errors' in which an excess of 'optimism' or 'pessimism' alternatively characterizes entrepreneurs' forecasts[18]. The entrepreneur tries to grasp market signals in order to make profits, but in doing so, he commits errors. Contrary to neoclassical theory, Papi emphasized behavioural aspects inasmuch as they contributed to explaining the entrepreneur's choices.

The recurrence of errors is the result of an economic climate in which fluctuations influence the entrepreneur's behaviour, even when they are exogenously determined: 'When an external event abruptly alters the economic equilibrium, the chances of profits increase, so that any entrepreneur tries to expand his production, even if the prices of production factors grow'.[19] At the beginning of the cycle, the entrepreneur is unable exactly to quantify the cost of the entire production process and may consequently purchase an excessive amount of production factors.[20] Failure to stabilize the production flow is symptomatic of an excess of production capacity vis-à-vis market demand.

Errors may also occur if variable expenditures are classified as constant expenditures. Moreover, the computation of costs may be erroneously low: 'When the entrepreneur observes a margin of gain between prices and costs, he is induced to expand his supply. Yet an increase in production determines a rise in costs that he is unable to compute. Such excessive costs may generate a deficit in the balance sheet'.[21] For Papi, the upward phase of cycle is a tumultuous increase in the supply that takes place because all production shifts towards the more profitable sectors.

The higher the production of consumption goods, i.e. the gap between supply and demand is filled, the greater the production surplus of instrumental goods. 'In such a situation the unitary cost grows more rapidly than the unitary price'.[22]

Papi worked out a 'phenomenology' of economic movements rather than a rigorous theory of the cycle. By setting movements on a behavioural basis, he disproved any mechanical or logical cause of the cycle. Profit is a 'goal' that induces entrepreneurs to increase investments excessively to the highest point of the crisis, at which the cycle reverses. Analogously, entrepreneurs commit errors in reducing both the supply and the unitary cost during the downward phase. Once the contraction of production has started, it continues until the level of costs is so low as to allow new savings. This is possible because costs decrease more rapidly than prices as a consequence of errors of excess in the dismantling of production. The length and the intensity of the downward movement will depend on the decisions of entrepreneurs. The greater the error in reducing production, the shorter the depression period will be.[23]

In Papi's opinion, the economic upswing was linked to propitious events, such as a surplus of labour, technical innovation or inflation, which may occur during the downturn phase. According to the traditional analysis, these events favoured investments, which moved the trend line upwards. Yet Papi also envisaged that the trend could move downwards. If disinvestments continue for an extended period, the trend decreases. Papi maintained that downward trends 'are not mysterious or exceptional' but 'common in the history of human civilization'.[24] Moreover, long-term movements and short-term cycles may exhibit the opposite tendency: this happens when exogenous events maintain their positive influence on the economic system beyond one cycle despite disinvestments.[25]

Finally, the trend may also be influenced by errors committed by entrepreneurs when they are unable to recognize either the *intensity* or the *duration* of the events influencing production.[26] In short, when entrepreneurs evaluate exogenous events, they commit errors that affect structural movements like short-term ones. Clearly, Papi's economic theory fully reflected the uncertainty enveloping the industrialized economies during the 1930s.

We must ask why Papi's entrepreneur was not rational and why he was unable to learn from previous errors. Firstly, Papi explicitly accepted the entrepreneur's 'irrationality' expressed by his inability to understand market signals correctly. Papi's economic actor was a historical individual who sought to act in the market, but he was unable to understand the market perfectly. Secondly, the dynamic perspective implicitly weakens the postulates of rationality. Erroneous choices are caused by fluctuations and concur in generating them.

Moreover, as Papi stated some years later, his notions on entrepreneurs' errors and the links between entrepreneurial activities and trends definitively distanced him from neoclassical thought. For a long period, he judged as useless both the 'classical schemes of general equilibrium' and the 'analysis of the dynamic equilibrium, preferring to consider the trend as a historical movement characterized by real events influencing fluctuations'.[27]

The entrepreneur's behaviour was the fulcrum of Papi's economic scheme. Both short-term and long-term economic movements depend on entrepreneurs' choices and on their ability to interpret the information from markets. Papi shifted from analysis of innovations to the more complex question of the entrepreneur's behaviour hinged on the market.

Whilst Bresciani-Turroni modified the entrepreneurial archetype along historical lines, Papi changed it on logical bases. He adopted a theory of errors, and since errors cannot be analysed in static terms, he took a dynamic perspective that comprised cycles and trends.

The trials and errors mentioned above recall speculative actions and all initiatives based on future change in economic variables. It is now clearer that, during the 1930s, the notion of 'entrepreneurial initiative' comprised a wide range of behaviours both innovative and speculative.

Marco Fanno's Theory of Economic Fluctuations

The theory of errors played a crucial role also in Fanno's business fluctuations theory. In fact, errors of *measure*, of *quality*, of *cost* and, above all, of *time* concur in generating fluctuations. Yet, unlike Papi, Fanno did not believe that they were the sole causes of economic movement.

At first sight, there was no reason to ask whether entrepreneurial error gave the first impetus to movement, because Fanno's economic system did not involve stationary equilibrium or steady growth: instead, his system perpetually moved.[28] At most, the early impulse to movement may be an error of time: in other words, the inability of producers to foresee changes in consumer tastes or their propensity to save in such a way that supply corresponds to demand.

This entrepreneurial inability originates from the time characterization of production, i.e. the gap between the decision concerning production and the availability of the final goods.[29]

If time errors represent a 'first impulse to fluctuations',[30] other types of errors may be committed during the economic movement: errors of quality concerning the unsuitability of goods to consumer tastes; errors of measure, when the amount of goods does not equal the demand or when investments exceed savings with a consequent increase in loans; errors of costs, when the evaluation of production costs does not correspond to the actual values.

In Fanno's opinion, all these errors together were at the basis of economic movement. Errors determine small oscillations which by adding to each other, as stated by Eugen Slutsky[31] and Udny Yule,[32] give rise to wider movements. By asserting that 'the economic system develops because of the simultaneous action of several factors that accidentally combine',[33] Fanno stressed a crucial point that distinguished his opinion from that of other economists theoretically close to him.[34] He stated that economic development does not have one single cause; rather, it is the result of the interrelation of several factors. Entrepreneurs come to the fore because the internal oscillations of the economic system are due to their initiative and errors, and once the economic movement has occurred due to advances or lags in production, it intertwines with external (exogenous) factors, primarily political ones and population growth.

It may now be clear why Fanno considered fluctuations to be variable phenomena and postulated disequilibrium as the normal condition of the economic system. He treated this unbalanced state as propitious to firms' initiatives.

Since Fanno did not envisage equilibrium as the rule, he distinguished the *trend of potential development* – similar to Henry Ludwell Moore's 'moving equilibrium'[35] – from the *trend of secular development* around which swing the oscillations that constitute the *trend of effective development*.

The path of secular development maintains itself at a constant distance from the path of potential development, and it represents the ideal line along which savings equalize investments, and on which the cycle is grounded. Yet the system does not remain on the secular path: it tends to move away from it. In fact, the savings/investments equality does not guarantee full employment of all the production factors. Consequently, along the trend of secular development there is an equilibrium of under-employment[36] which provides new opportunities for investments and profits. Once entrepreneurs have ascertained that there is a gap between potential development and secular development, they are induced to invest.[37]

This type of investment, which Fanno called *leading*, increases the demand, thus determining a further kind of investment, called *secondary*. All the investments draw the trend of effective development closer to the trend of potential development. It is clear that Fanno accepted Richard Kahn's theory of the multiplier.

Owing to leading and secondary investments, the system enlarges until it reaches the upward turning point at which the path of effective development intersects the trend of potential development. At this point, unemployment diminishes to zero. Nevertheless, although investments are such to guarantee employment of all the production resources, the system does not achieve stability. It should be borne in mind that Fanno envisaged an economic mechanism that constantly maintains the propensity to make new investments. In fact, at the upward turning point the full employment of production factors raises wages and prices, but the demand for capital goods ceases. Consequently, the sector of instrumental goods is constrained to reduce production, and then the number of employees. This has immediate repercussions on the demand for consumption goods. Which means that the cycle enters the downturn phase.[38]

The point of full employment does not constitute a 'stable attractor' or a 'fixed point' because it reduces expectations of profit. The latter exist as long as markets record underemployment or offer opportunities for new investments. Because the full employment condition reduces profit expectations and triggers disinvestments in capital production, it is rather unstable.

Once the downward trend has begun, monetary income decreases more than the flow of goods. The consequent over-supply of goods reduces prices, and consequently profits, whose rate is now lower than the interest rate. The lessening of investments proceeds even beyond the secular trend, where disinvestments equalize dissaving. This situation persists until the government intervenes by giving subsidies to private individuals or applying an expansionary monetary policy. These measures halt the fall by enlarging demand and increasing consumption.[39] The point of greatest distance between effective development and potential development, or the downward turning point, is reached.[40]

Since the trend of wages lags behind prices, the new situation is propitious for new revenues. New expectations encourage entrepreneurs to make investments using the unemployed production structures and labour. The trend turns upwards until it reaches the path of secular development. New leading investments appear, followed by secondary ones.

To sum up, the initial conditions of the economic system include disequilibrium in one or more sectors due to errors committed by economic agents. Disequilibrium increases profit expectations and boosts entrepreneurial initiatives, which, as they converge towards the most prominent sector, produce an overproduction in that sector. Consequently, the system is subject to a downward movement which will be halted by exogenous intervention. Production and investments then re-start.

Unemployment serves as an investment engine because it heightens profit expectations. In effect, unemployment is possible because the labour market is unable automatically to reach an equilibrium point. We may suppose that the low level of wages also influences profit expectations. Moreover, technical innovations and changes in loans may influence the downward and upward turning points, but they do not change the nature of the theory based on profit expectations.

Fanno conducted a typical microeconomic analysis of prices and costs against a macroeconomic background in which unemployment plays an important role.[41] Consequently, unlike in Schumpeter, competitive advantages derive from the availability of labour or of other production factors, and not solely from the introduction of innovations. At the same time, the economic system does not appear to be 'self-ordering': In fact, public intervention is necessary to revive the economy, enlarge consumption, and promote growth.

Fanno set an upper limit on fluctuations determined by the supply of the production factors, including labour,[42] and a lower limit conditioned by public policies. By imposing these structural limits on the cycle, Fanno unified trend and cycle into one single scheme.[43] As pointed out by Giovanni Caravale[44] and Terenzio Cozzi,[45] the presence of these limits made the trend of secular development appear superfluous. Actually, although this path remains virtual, it is useful for showing the essential feature of the economic system: it follows a path that never cancels expectations of profit. This is a crucial postulate in Fanno's theory.

From a historiographical point of view, Fanno's analysis stands out for its inclusion of both endogenous factors acting on conjuncture, and traditional exogenous factors influencing the structure. Nevertheless, on analysing the endogenous factors – increase in consumption, the advanced renewal of capital, growth of productivity, the production of new goods, and change in the propensity to save and invest[46] – it is evident that internal movements are interwoven with the growth of the economic system.

Cycle and development are linked; and this confirms the existence of an at least partial endogenous causality. In other words, whilst a military conflict or another external factor may boost a stationary economy, the expansion of consumption subsequent to population growth, the renewal of capital, and the other above-mentioned endogenous factors can only produce positive effects if the economy is *already* developing. As a consequence, the question inevitably arises as to whether development should be assumed as a pre-condition for the appearance of such factors, or whether population growth and other factors should be treated as the main causes of the system's take-off.

The issue of the propulsive elements was a rather controversial point in Fanno's theory. He did not explain why the system moves away from the steady state, except in the case of time errors. Moreover, his theory admits a stationary state only at the lower level, in the absence of public expenditure or other exogenous factors. The lowest phase is the only state of the economic cycle in which profit expectations are subordinate to the appearance of exogenous events. It is true that Fanno made constant reference to the exogenous demographic trend, but population is too uncertain an element for the system's destiny to be attributed to it. In fact, it is an *ex post* variable that increases when development begins.

Nor did Fanno resolve the doubts concerning the impetus to development when, in 1956, he rejected the notion of *autonomous* investment formulated by the 'Anglo-American economists' and adopted that of *leading* investments.[47] It is not easy to distinguish the meaning of Fanno's 'leading investment' from that of Alvin H. Hansen's 'autonomous investment'.[48]

To sum up, the distinctive feature of the theory examined here is the permanent existence of a gap between effective and potential development in the presence of both autonomous investments and exogenous factors. This gap is postulated and indeed logically explained. If it is denied, profits will disappear and investments will decrease. Fanno's system cannot remain in equilibrium. According to his analysis of fluctuations, the economic system can develop only in disequilibrium. The reason seems tautological. Only in disequilibrium does the most important incentive to economic initiative emerge: namely profits. From this point of view, the dynamic theory is the study of profit dynamics.

Entrepreneurial Initiative and Disequilibrium

Two main categories exemplify the Bresciani-Turroni, Papi and Fanno line of inquiry: *entrepreneurial initiative* and *disequilibrium*.[49]

The category of *entrepreneurial initiative* is a crucial notion in this perspective since it involves detachment from the traditional *homo œconomicus*. Unlike in neoclassical theory, here 'rationality' implies that the entrepreneur is a prime mover who determines changes and does not undergo them. This suggests the abandonment of the 'equilibrium of pure competition' and adoption of an approach grounded on economic change.

The neoclassical tradition also admits change, but it does so in the form of exogenous or external change. All the above-mentioned economists maintained that external factors are decisive for economic movement, but at the same time they put forward economic dynamism as a consequence of initiatives originating in the economic system.[50] One might speak of endogenous dynamics, but this notion involves a mathematical characterization not particularly manifest in the theories analysed here.[51] According to Fanno, it is better to talk of concurrent impulses generated by both endogenous and exogenous factors.

The entrepreneur is certainly the *maker* who acts on the economic variables according to the trend of endogenous factors. He is described in various, more or less positive, terms. The innovator/speculator depicted by Bresciani-Turroni is certainly the most realistic, and maybe the least positive, figure. The models proposed by Fanno and Papi are more theoretical and hence more controversial. They resembled the model formulated by Luigi Lugli, who enlarged Schumpeter's archetype by arguing that the entrepreneur is the 'active force' that transforms final goods into capital goods by employing free factors.[52] Economic development is usually due to both structural forces and short-term impulses.

The above-mentioned theories contrasted with the Schumpeterian tradition because they envisaged a type of 'initiative' more extensive than Schumpeter's notion. Moreover, the entrepreneur's activity was not identifiable with a specific function but involved generic activities centred on the search for profits. Admitting the importance of a large set of initiatives raised the issue of the *motives* inspiring the entrepreneur; motives that had always been ignored by the theories of general economic equilibrium. The fulcrum of entrepreneurial activity thus shifted from decisions concerning production to speculative or profit motives. The dissemination of functions entailed understanding the motives implied by each of them; but this meant adopting at least a behavioural, if not psychological, approach to entrepreneurial activity. Even though in only historical terms, Bresciani-Turroni also shifted to this kind of conceptualization.

Furthermore, the previous separation between the figure of the capitalist and that of the entrepreneur required an autonomous theory of profit, or of entrepreneurial revenue, that was not explained by the static neoclassical theory. Described above was the twofold dispute on the dynamic character of a theory of profits and the historical or institutional quality of the profit category. Although not explicitly, Papi's and Fanno's theories were efforts to give a dynamic interpretation to profit formation closer to the institutionalist or historical approaches than to the neoclassical one.

Entrepreneurial initiative distinguished a branch of the neoclassical theory that was dynamically grounded and was anomalous *vis-à-vis* the equilibrium framework. In fact, it was based on the idea that profits are the result of disequilibrium. All three economists implicitly or explicitly admitted disequilibrium as the market condition in which the entrepreneur acts, and from which new opportunities for profits spring. Bresciani-Turroni ascribed the imbalance to the dynamic feature of modern economies characterized by continuous change in consumer tastes and technical innovations. According to Papi, disequilibrium sprang from errors. Finally, Fanno saw the disequilibrium of one or more sectors as the source of economic investments.

This was the outcome of a profound transformation of the entrepreneurial function. The latter was changed into manifold functions including both speculative actions and production innovations. This was a theory in which profit might take the form of either retribution for a specific function or rent. This multiplicity of functions makes it impossible to pinpoint one single entrepreneurial role and, consequently, one single notion of profit. Finally, enlargement of the entrepreneur's function implies that the explanation of profit should be sought in market relations rather than in production mechanisms alone.

The Entrepreneur and Irreducible Risk

The above long digression on the conceptions of capitalist dynamics and entrepreneurial choices in the Italian economic literature of the time allows better contextualization to be given to the last Del Vecchio topic treated here: profit associated with entrepreneurial risk. This is perhaps the least known of them, but, as said, it received the most authoritative acknowledgement. It was the subject of *Investigations on the Theory of Entrepreneurial Profit* (*Untersuchungen zur Theorie des Unternehmergewinnes*), the 1928 article published in German which Knight cited in 1959 as one of the first in which the irreducible risk that entrepreneurs undergo was presented as a source of profit. This was in accordance with the views of Schumpeter and Erik Lundberg. The following quotation from Knight testifies that Del Vecchio had developed an economic theory involving irreducible uncertainty:

> Among European economists, the importance of the element of risk bearing was recognized by Hans von Mangoldt and later by Theodor Mithoff and Karl Diehl among others; more recently a theory of uninsurable risk has been developed by Del Vecchio.[53]

That article followed the essays that Del Vecchio wrote on insurance from 1912 onwards; and in certain respects it completed his analysis of the irreducible or radical uncertainty characterizing the economic sphere.[54]

His study proceeded from acknowledgement that, given a modern dynamic economy, profit is the most characteristic income, and that it requires a *positive* theory, not a *residual* one. 'The simple premises on which Walras grounded his views on profit must be substituted with others allowing a positive and not negative theory of profit'.[55]

Those premises should be replaced by the following:

1) The costs of the production factors are not the same for all entrepreneurs. In other words, the market of production factors is not perfectly competitive, and if the entrepreneur suffering the highest costs has zero profit, the others enjoy a positive profit that can be determined in analogy with the differential rent. This rent originates from the entrepreneur's 'specific attitudes to organizing production'.[56]
2) Organizational features are associated with the entrepreneur's willingness to assume risk. It can be said that organization plus risk generates a sort of monopolistic income, i.e., profit. But Del Vecchio stated that the

profit deriving from risk does not remain in the entrepreneur's hands in its entirety because some of it flows to other entrepreneurs as rent. The combination of the following features – capital availability, flair for management, and propensity for risk – are so rare that the few entrepreneurs possessing them enjoy a sort of monopolistic gain.

3) The assumption of risk must be paid for, even if it is difficult to warrant this remuneration in a context of perfect competition. Since the marginal disutility incurred by the risk-taking entrepreneur is higher than the marginal utility of his profit in the case of success, his profit must be increased in order to balance the marginal utility with the marginal disutility.

4) But profit is a dynamic category. It occurs because only in a dynamic perspective can it result from the difference between production, given a static approach, and production in dynamic conditions requiring the entrepreneur's contribution. Contrary to Marx's view, the entrepreneur gains possession of only a part of the whole that he brings about.[57]

Finally, profit is not just a part of the current product; it is also a discounted remuneration for future product:

In a dynamic and progressive economy, the outcome of economic activity is *something more* than the product itself.[58]

The main remaining questions are the following: from which flow of income does profit derive? Why does competition among entrepreneurs not transform profit into remuneration for other production factors? Is non-insurable risk the source of profit? Given dynamic conditions, the product is not the sum of the contributions of the production factors: this was a static truth, said Del Vecchio.[59] Risk is a dynamic category yielding profit because it allows the anticipation of future income.

Consequently, profit is not an income deriving from exploitation, nor is it a residual income. Its *raison d'etre* consists in the set of differences between *expectations* and *reality*. The positive theory of profit argued by Del Vecchio finds its ultimate expression in this statement, which presents several points worthy of development. First, profit is not the outcome of wrong expectations, but rather of the entrepreneur's ability to achieve a result that was *not expected*. Second, the dynamic economy is the *form* which allows profit, not its cause, which consists in the above divergences. Therefore: '[P]rofit is the compensation for the psychological [psychic] cost deriving from risk'.[60]

Third, expectations are the crucial component enabling the economic system to function. Without expectations, profits are not possible, and the entire economy is doomed to failure.

It is indeed difficult to establish whether profits are always bigger during the upward phase of the cycle compared with the downward one. Del Vecchio concealed himself behind the absolute difficulty of providing an answer once and for all. Certainly, his arguments on the fact that, during the downward phase, the more competitive firms may have an advantage over the less competitive ones confirm that he conceived profit as an opportunity emerging during recessions as well. In fact, it may arise when expectations are different from current circumstances. Following Pantaleoni, Del Vecchio believed that the downward phase is useful for *selecting* entrepreneurs themselves, so as to make the economy more dynamic, and that profits are an expression of the dynamic character of a given economy.

To conclude the summary of Del Vecchio's thought on this crucial point,[61] he drew up a list of points defining the phenomenon of profit. In our opinion, this is a list that well represents Del Vecchio's view on economics, which combined loyalty to classical economics, respect for neoclassical dogma, but also an endeavour to subvert some well-established laws.

1) The level of profits is a function of the rapidity of social dynamics. Dynamic phenomena like monetary crises and cycles, given their intrinsic dynamic nature, exert large influence on expectations and play a role in determining profit.
2) The level of profits cannot be determined, not even roughly, on assuming a static perspective that might suffice to determine other incomes.
3) Profit is not a further cost that must be summed. It 'organizes' other costs and for this reason, it might be useful to *multiply* such cost for the other ones.
4) Not only does risk differ among entrepreneurs, but so does the psychological pressure on the latter, also because they have different amounts of wealth.
5) The monopolistic factor may influence risk-taking and then profit-making.
6) The subjective cost ascribable to risk tends to diminish with firm enlargement. Both vertical and horizontal integration reduce the objective risk arising in the determination of prices and quantities, but also the unitary subjective cost linked to individual irreducible risk.
7) Insurance and profit are competitive responses available to the entrepreneur. The only way to distinguish insurable from non-insurable risk is to distinguish between premium and profit. Profit appears only when the risk cannot be insured against.
8) Economic speculation is one type of insurance. Stock exchange and speculation *lato sensu* may reduce both objective and subjective risk, but they also move the economy away from competition: 'Removing risk means reducing price changes, that is, erasing the continuous adaptation of prices to competition that occurs when prices are not guaranteed'.[62] The

persistence of risk, both objective and subjective, generates this continuous change accompanying production processes.

9) To sum up:

> 'There are two theoretical systems contrasting each other. The first proposes the economic theory as equilibrium theory, where dynamics represent a perturbing factor. The second admits that economic theory is a dynamic theory, and that equilibrium troubles are special cases. The analysis of profit is consistent with this second viewpoint, and it can complete the results obtained in consequence of the impressive development of the first viewpoint'.[63]

Many years later, in his 1961 *General Economics*, Del Vecchio reiterated his view on profit by stating that *organization* and *profit* cannot be adequately analysed without taking a dynamic perspective.[64] Organization is a dynamic category because 'to organize means to establish production processes according to specific forecasts'.[65] Innovation and the risk associated with it are the sources of profit, which appears when changes and innovations allow a reduction of costs not forecasted.

From Individual Irreducible Risk to Systemic Instability

It has been said that Del Vecchio treated as the *normal* condition of a capitalist economic system neither the steady state nor steady growth, but rather abnormal change. He wrote in 1933:

> The solution that appears as obvious to the problem [of establishing the normal condition of economic relationships] – that is, considering an economic stationary state as normal – must be discarded for the simple reason that if there is something normal in the current economic system, it is precisely the fact that it is continuously changing.[66]

Del Vecchio theorized continuous change as intrinsic to capitalist production because it is capitalism itself that 'yields changes',[67] which in their turn give rise to continuous, i.e. irreducible, uncertainty. Change is not just a possibility; it is the necessary condition for the economic system's development. By contrast, given a stationary state, 'capitalism would be doomed to die'.[68] Change does not necessarily lead to growth. What Del Vecchio stressed is that change is a normal condition of the capitalist system, even when it involves the economy's redistribution and reorganization without any growth. The stationary state is the specific case. At the analytical level, this entails a shift from the equilibrium paradigm to the change paradigm. In this regard, Del Vecchio wrote: 'Abandoning the hypothesis that there exists a trend towards economic equilibrium, study of that economy shapes the discipline called *economic dynamics*: this discipline is currently largely incomplete'.[69]

It can be argued that the new paradigm was that of 'resilience', since it was essential to study the system's behaviour in response to continuous stimulus and change, also of remarkable magnitude. By contrast, the paradigm of stability, grounded on the system's capacity to regain equilibrium after any temporary perturbation, was dismissed. Del Vecchio thus stressed the central importance of economic change for the economic system's survival.

On referring to the 'philosophers of time', such as Henri-Louis Bergson and Alfred North Whitehead, Giovanni Demaria, Del Vecchio's most outstanding pupil, introduced both the subjective and objective notions of time to argue that individuals perceive only a fraction of the economic changes which occur, while the other part is not registered. From this feature derives the importance of recognizing both the exogenous and endogenous character of economic movement. Developing Del Vecchio's insights, in his *On the Concept of Time* (*Sul concetto di tempo*) Demaria gave a precise meaning to the notion of 'time as change'.[70]

According to this approach, although it may appear rather contradictory, the system's instability is more probable in the presence of a stationary state than economic change: 'If the economic mechanism tends to rigidify, capitalism is doomed to collapse'.[71]

The implosion of the economic system due to the absence of any change is a phenomenon different from an economic crisis, which is a self-organizing fact rooted in capitalism itself. Del Vecchio hypothesized that one or more actors acting individually move the system away from its equilibrium position towards a new equilibrium different from the previous one. The second position is not necessarily more advanced from an economic viewpoint than the previous one: it suffices that it be different. Del Vecchio wrote: 'The capitalist system is the result of an infinitive series of actions and reactions involving population, wealth, general organization, and economic organization which interact with each other'.[72]

What emerges is an approach to economic dynamics grounded on investigation of economic relationships that assume the role of the 'internal engine' of economic movement, in evident contrast with those analyses which assumed that the cycle is determined by a single factor in isolation from the trend: it is not possible to understand the movement of one part of the system ignoring the evolution of the remaining parts. Accordingly, Del Vecchio developed his analytical tools – 'research orders' and 'infinitesimal orders' – associated with the idea that it must be understood how a factor contributes to the overall outcome.

In conclusion, it should be mentioned that in 1925 Del Vecchio applied his 'systemic' view to the international economy as well. He theorized that the stability of the world economy was grounded on the plurality of national capitalisms:

> The plurality of the capitalist economies is the main strength of the capitalist regime. This occurs because competition among economies pushes them in the direction of economic progress and rules out the possibility that any perturbation can destroy the whole system.[73]

It may appear curious that this view on the strength of capitalism induced Del Vecchio to write as follows in 1925:

> Also admitting that capitalism has ended in Russia, we cannot believe that it will end in Great Britain as well. On the contrary, we can suppose that capitalism will eventually return in Russia, for the simple reason that international competition does not permit a country to maintain a condition of backwardness when it comes into contact with developed economies.[74]

Such is the strength of economic relationships!

EPILOGUE

We started with two dichotomies – the subjective/objective and the individual/aggregate – to investigate the monetary and circulation analyses proposed by Del Vecchio. Eventually the conclusion was reached that those dichotomies were less marked than appeared at first sight, especially if considered through the lens of a dynamic or time perspective. Subjective and objective views necessarily mix in valuing money and analysing the interest rate. Individuals and aggregates do not constitute a dichotomy because they need different interpretative instruments: they follow different logics that make them different actors. In this case, Del Vecchio enriched the panorama by stressing the key role of intermediate figures, i.e. groups.

However, almost paradoxically, as these dichotomies faded, so a further decisive one gradually made its appearance, although it was never explicitly named by Del Vecchio. It was a more economic one, in the sense that, more than method or perspective, it concerned the theoretical content. In certain respects, this emerging dichotomy evoked the distinction between the monetary discount rate and the psychological interest rate, but in fact it did not coincide with it. This was also because equality between the two rates was, from time to time, described by Del Vecchio as the condition for general monetary equilibrium.

We can reconstruct this dichotomy by outlining its two sides. The first concerns the area of the monetary relationships governed by money, credit and the discount rate. It includes everything to do with monetary distribution, relationships between monetary stocks and prices, and monetary payments. Here money is treated as an important factor enabling the better organization of economic transactions.

It emerges that money is an asset or has value, not because it yields returns, but because it allows transactions to be conducted and improves economic relationships. Money can be considered an economic organizer, and the measure of monetary organization is given precisely by the effectiveness of money, *E*, which changes when the structure of payments, the relationships between production groups and the level of competition are modified. The effectiveness of money is an index of economic organization that provides information about the use of money.

The other side of the dichotomy concerns accumulation. It is not strictly monetary, although money is necessarily involved. This is the area of the psychological interest rate, of individual ambitions and entrepreneurial initiatives, of profit and uncertainty. The resources for investments come from individual savings, but also from banks. Put briefly, economic accumulation is in the hands of individuals and their ambitions. Psychological motives exceed any monetary factor in attempting to improve social conditions. Certainly, money is a cost for the entrepreneur in search of profits, but individual expectations are more important than the monetary rate of interest.

A number of variables connect the two areas. The first of them is the interest rate. It is true that the interest rate is conditioned by accumulation without influencing it, but it conditions the value of money without being biased. It reflects individual views, but it necessarily stands in relation to the monetary discount rate. Because it is a measure of accumulation, it plays a role, albeit a minor one, in investment decisions.

Finally, if investments and accumulation are facts inevitably linked to the future, the psychological interest rate tells us something about how individuals view the future. Proof of this is provided by the banking system, which seeks to keep credit elastic in order to stabilize the discount rate. In this way, not only is uncertainty reduced, but the entire monetary market is stabilized. Hence the banking system seems partially able to condition decisions on long-term investments, even though the latter depend mainly on psychological attitudes and individual ambitions.

Credit is another variable common to the two areas. Del Vecchio did not propose a dual economic system or something similar. Maintaining a unitary view of the economic system's workings, he recognized that any improvements in monetary and credit circulation would enhance economic performance. These improvements work in two main directions.

In the short term, the monetary equilibrium is ensured by credit:

$$\Delta CR = f(\underset{+}{Q}, \Delta \underset{+}{P},^{e} \underset{-}{E})$$

If a change in expected prices modifies the equilibrium between the supply of and demand for money, the new equilibrium may be re-established by changing credit.

In the long term, the monetary equilibrium has a structural dimension:

$$\Delta M = f(\Delta \underset{+}{Q}, \Delta \underset{+}{P},^{e} \Delta \underset{-}{E})$$

However, apart from the constraint due to the disposable reserves, there is nothing to prevent the banking system from stabilizing the economy by keeping the discount rate low and providing the requested credit for longer investments as well:

$$\Delta CR = f(\underset{+}{\Delta Q}, \underset{+}{\Delta P^e}, \underset{-}{\Delta E})$$

In this case, economic stability is guaranteed by credit, while the discount rate may not converge towards the interest rate.

The third variable is the effectiveness of money. I suggest that, like the interest rate, this is a linkage between the monetary and accumulation areas. In effect, a change in effectiveness is symptomatic of a change in the structure of payments or in the way in which monetary (and credit) circulation is organized. It is a long-run phenomenon, not just a conjunctural one.

Effectiveness is a distinctive component of Del Vecchio's theory, in regard to either its weaknesses or novelties. The weaknesses concern its measurement. It will be recalled that monetary effectiveness originates in the relationship between overall production and that of the main selling group, where the definition of the latter appears to be more difficult as the economic system evolves. But there is no doubt that the way in which money circulates matters, and that an index condensing aspects like monetary distribution and the market regime is crucial for understanding the monetary market.

Besides interest rate, credit, effectiveness, there is another aspect – more than a variable – that traverses the two areas: uncertainty. On considering Del Vecchio's monetary theory as a whole, what stands out is not the attempt to reduce uncertainty through inclusion of expected prices or the subordination of accumulation to psychological or mental variables. Uncertainty is an irreducible feature of the economic system. Radical uncertainty is necessary to guarantee the profits that stimulate entrepreneurial activity. Uncertainty means that errors are possible and that entrepreneurs can fail. But this is part of this evolutionary system grounded on the circulation of economic and political elites or, more simply, positions.

Uncertainty originates from expectations. Expectations on prices establish the 'encaisse désirée' of Del Vecchio's agents (firms and consumers), and they decide the hoarded money that may be subsequently employed in exchanges. Similarly, the banks decide the money reserves (hoarded money) according to their forecasts about the economic or financial cycle. This is more than a precaution; it is a specific demand for money shaped by expectations. We may term it 'uncertainty', meaning that in a dynamic or changing economic world, such as the one depicted by Del Vecchio, forming expectations is a *normal* practice, not an exceptional one. Certainly, far from being 'rational' in the modern sense, these expectations fuel irreducible uncertainty, which is the condition for profit-making.

However, these contrasting trends towards stability, on the one hand, and uncertainty determining instability on the other, characterize Del Vecchio's view on economic change, which he never represented as regular growth. Obviously, economic crises are natural outcomes of this dynamic relationship.

To conclude this theoretical excursus, brief discussion is required on where Del Vecchio can be located in the history of monetary theories. The world that we have investigated is a world of relative magnitudes, where dogmas are absent and the few recurrent rules are built on observation more than on *a priori* principles. Suffice it to mention the role of credit, whose stabilization function Del Vecchio established by studying the English monetary and banking market. Del Vecchio's theoretical world was marked by thought experiments situated in the flow of events and history; he used theories instead of arguing for or against them. It is sufficient to mention his position on the quantity principle or individual maximization. Therefore, it is not easy to assign him to a definite school of thought; and this may be also a reason for his substantial marginalization in the history of economics.

His admiration of Ricardo and his interest in pre-classical theory seemingly anchored him to the nineteenth century. But this is a view immediately contradicted by his marginal approach and his interest in expectations. Finally, as evoked above, Del Vecchio was often likened to Schumpeter,[1] and perhaps the Schumpeterian evolutionary approach is the closest one to his analysis.

However his theory was free from theoretical dogmas and this enabled him to introduce innovative or less considered topics. We mention here one for all of them: the distribution of money. Perhaps what was lacking was a rigorous and – why not? – mathematical representation of such a theory.

'The distinctive trait of Del Vecchio's personality was that he was a completely free spirit'.[2] He instilled this feature not only in his method, to the point that he never wrote about method, but also in his articles and books. And he did so in his theory, which is pervaded by a sense of freedom: individuals are free to form their expectations; banks are free to decide the money supply and, mainly, credit, with stabilizing effects according to their forecasts. However, the aspect that most embodies this sense of freedom is accumulation, which is entirely due to individual attitudes, ambitions and hopes. The latter are the source of any economic change.

Finally, freedom does not mean anarchy. The market is not a supreme sovereign intolerant of other powers. The market has different levels of efficiency, to the point that society, which contains it, yields instruments with which to improve its working and organization. Traditionally money is one of these instruments, but it is also something more, in the sense that its use is a source of market efficiency.

NOTES

Introduction

1. See D. Giva, 'Gustavo Del Vecchio', in *Dizionario Biografico Italiano* (Rome: Istituto dell'Enciclopedia Italiana, 1990); F. Caffè, 'Vecchio, Gustavo Del', in J. Eatwell, M. Milgate and P. Newman (eds), *The New Palgrave. A Dictionary of Economics*, 4 vols (London: Macmillan, 1987), vol. 4, pp. 800–1.
2. On Giulio Salvatore Del Vecchio, see T. Bagiotti, 'Giulio Salvatore Del Vecchio teorico della causalità sociale', in *Studi di economia finanza e statistica in onore di Gustavo Del Vecchio* (Padua: Cedam, 1963), pp. 83–110. Also to be mentioned is Giorgio Del Vecchio, Giulio Salvatore's son, who was a respected jurist.
3. See L. Dal Pane, 'Commemorazione di Gustavo Del Vecchio', *Giornale degli Economisti e Annali di Economia*, 32:11–12 (1973), pp. 826–36.
4. T. Martello, *La moneta e gli errori che corrono intorno ad essa* (Florence: Le Monnier, 1883).
5. G. Antonelli, 'Gustavo Del Vecchio', in D. Mirri and S. Arieti, *La cattedra negate. Dal giuramento di fedeltà al fascismo alle leggi razziali nell'Università di Bologna* (Bologna: Cleub, 2002), pp. 177–83, on p. 178.
6. G. Del Vecchio, *La sintesi economica e la teoria del reddito* (Padua: Cedam, 1950), p. 397.
7. G. Del Vecchio, 'Risposta al questionario indirizzato agli economisti della Commissione parlamentare di inchiesta sulla disoccupazione', *Atti*, 4:4 (1953).
8. T. Suranyi-Unger, *Economics in the Twentieth Century: The History of its International Development* (New York: Norton, 1931), p. 200.
9. In his *Obituary*, Dal Pane, a pupil of Del Vecchio, wrote that, according to his teacher, economic phenomena should not be considered in their equilibrium state, but as continuous flows. Dal Pane, 'Commemorazione di Gustavo Del Vecchio', p. 831. Here 'economic flow' is translated as 'economic becoming'.
10. See R. Scazzieri, 'Del Vecchio, Gustavo', Treccani, online at http://www.treccani.it/enciclopedia/gustavo-del-vecchio_(Il_Contributo_italiano_alla_storia_del_Pensiero:_Economia)/ [accessed December 2013], p. 7.
11. See G. Tusset, *La teoria dinamica nel pensiero economico italiano. 1890–1940* (Florence: Polistampa, 2004), pp. 95ff.
12. See K. Dopfer, 'Evolutionary Economics: Framework for Analysis', in *Evolutionary Economics: Program and Scope* (Boston, MA, Dordrecht and London: Kluwer A. P., 2001), p. 4.
13. Keirstead wrote some years later: 'It is our contention ... that economic change is a complex phenomenon, that it has many causes, often inter-related, and that it must be

studied in terms of ... complex causal structures'. B. S. Keirstead, *The Theory of Economic Change* (Toronto: Macmillan, 1948), pp. 36–37.

14. See J.-G. Prévost, *A Total Science: Statistics in Liberal and Fascist Italy* (Paris: McGill Queens University Press, 2009).
15. As subsequently stressed by Henry Schultz, Rodolfo Benini was one of the first statisticians to derive the elasticity of the demand for one or more goods from time series (see *The Theory and Measurement of Demand* (Chicago, IL: University of Chicago Press, 1938), p. 64). And, as pointed out by George J. Stigler, he also had primogeniture of the use of multiple regressions ('The Early History of Empirical Studies of Consumer', *Journal of Political Economy*, 62 (1954), pp. 95–113, on p. 85 and R. Benini, 'Sull'uso delle formule empiriche nell'economia applicata' *Giornale degli Economisti*, 35 (1907), pp. 1053–63). Another important contemporaneous economist and statistician, Corrado Gini, made use in 1910 of a bivariate form to express the demanded quantity of a good as a function of both its price and that of a surrogate or complementary good (C. Gini, 'Prezzi e consumi', *Giornale degli Economisti e Rivista di Statistica*, 15 (1910), pp. 99–114; 235–49).
16. G. Del Vecchio, 'Le teorie economiche di Rodolfo Benini', *Giornale degli Economisti e Rivista di Statistica* (1929), pp. 957–66, on p. 958.
17. R. Benini, 'Una possibile creazione del metodo statistico "L'economia politica induttiva"', *Giornale degli Economisti* (1908), pp. 11–34.
18. Ibid., p. 17.
19. Ibid., p. 30.
20. C. Bresciani-Turroni, 'Alcuni effetti economici dei prestiti esteri in Germania negli anni 1924–1929', *Giornale degli Economisti e Rivista di Statistica* (1929), pp. 994–1067, on p. 994.
21. G. Mortara, 'Recensione a C. Bresciani-Turroni. Le vicende del marco tedesco', *Giornale degli Economisti e Rivista di Statistica* (1932), p. 286.
22. D. Cavalieri, 'L'analisi economica tra causalità e interdipendenza: elementi per una valutazione storico-critica', *Quaderni di Storia dell'Economia Politica*, 5–6 (1987–8), pp. 9–56, on p. 31.
23. Blaug wrote that 'scientific realists ultimately validate theories in terms of a match with observational data inferred from the world-out-there'. M. Blaug, 'Ugly Currents in Modern Economics', in U. Mäki, *Fact and Fiction in Economics. Models, Realism and Social Construction* (Cambridge: Cambridge University Press, 2002), pp. 35–56, on p. 49.
24. Differently, Zanni wrote that Pareto was acknowledged in Italy more for his contributions to pure economics than to sociology. A. Zanni, 'La "Nuova Collana di Economisti" di Bottai ed Arena', *Annali della Fondazione Luigi Einaudi*, 45 (2011), pp. 99–112, on p. 101.
25. G. Del Vecchio, 'Questioni fondamentali sul valore della moneta', *Giornale degli Economisti e Rivista di Statistica*, 55 (1917), pp. 117–74, on p. 118.
26. G. Del Vecchio, *Grundlinien der Geldtheorie* (Tübingen: Verlag, 1930).

1 Making Economic Relationships Dynamic

1. G. Del Vecchio, *Ricchezze immateriali e capitali immateriali* (Alessandria: Società poligrafica Alessandrina, 1908), p. 235.
2. G. Del Vecchio, *Introduzione alla finanza* (Padua: Cedam, 1954), p. 29.
3. Del Vecchio, *La sintesi economica e la teoria del reddito*, p. xi.

4. Ibid., p. xii.
5. F. B. W. von Hermann, *Staatswirtschaftliche Untersuchungen* (1870; München: Werber, 1932).
6. Del Vecchio, *Introduzione alla finanza*, p. 224.
7. G. Del Vecchio, *Vecchie e nuove teorie economiche*, 2nd edn (Turin: Utet, 1956), p. 105.
8. A. Labriola, *Saggi sul materialismo storico* (1925; Milan: Editori Riuniti, 2000), p. 241.
9. G. Del Vecchio, *Lezioni di economia applicata. Dinamica Economica*, 3rd lithographic edn (Padua: Cedam, 1930), p. 187.
10. G. Del Vecchio, 'Lineamenti generali della teoria dell'interesse', *Giornale degli Economisti e Rivista di Statistica*, 51 (1915), pp. 272–327, 367–408, on p. 304.
11. Del Vecchio, *Lezioni di economia applicata* (1930), p. 173.
12. G. Del Vecchio, *Lezioni di economia applicata. Dinamica economica* (1933), pp. 11ff.
13. A. Spiethoff, 'The "Historical" Character of Economic Theories', *Journal of Economic History*', 12 (1952), pp. 131–9, on p. 132.
14. E. Salin, *Politische Ökonomie. Geschichte der wirtschaftspolitischen Ideen von Platon bis zur Gegenwart* (Tübingen: Mohr, 1923).
15. K. Knies, *Geld und Kredit* (Berlin: Weidmann, 1873).
16. Spiethoff, 'The "Historical" Character of Economic Theories', p. 136.
17. G. Del Vecchio, 'La costruzione scientifica della dinamica economica', *Giornale degli economisti e Annali di economia*, 11:9–10 (1952), pp. 584–91, on p. 590.
18. Del Vecchio, *Lezioni di economia applicata. Dinamica economica* (1933), p. 150.
19. Ibid., p. 151.
20. In particular, Del Vecchio heeded Ferrara's advice to keep production and distribution in a single perspective that can be deepened by means of pure theory.
21. See G. Tusset, 'The Italian Contribution to Early Economic Dynamics', *European Journal of the History of Economic Thought*, 16:2 (2009), pp. 267–300.
22. See another Italian evolutionary economist, C. Supino, 'Scienza economica e realtà economica', *La Riforma Sociale*, 5 (1896), pp. 397–415.
23. Labriola, *Saggi sul materialismo storico*, p. 325.
24. See C. E. Russett, *The Concept of Equilibrium in American Social Thought* (New Haven, CT and London: Yale University Press, 1966).
25. Del Vecchio, *La sintesi economica e la teoria del reddito*, p. 3.
26. Del Vecchio, *Vecchie e nuove teorie economiche*, p. 240.
27. A. Loria, *Dinamica economica. Studio sulle leggi delle variazioni* (Turin: Bocca, 1935).
28. Faucci, *L'economia politica in Italia. Dal Cinquecento ai giorni nostri* (Turin: Utet, 2000), p. 293.
29. L. Walras, *Eléments d'économie politique pure, ou théorie de la richesse sociale*, 2 vols (Lausanne: Corbaz. 1926), translated in English as *Elements of Pure Economics* (Homewood: Irwin. 1954), p. 318.
30. V. Pareto, *Cours d'économie politique* (Genève: Droz, 1896–7), vols 1 and 2, new edn, ed. G. H. Bousquet and G. Busino (1964).
31. V. Pareto, *Manuale di economia politica con una introduzione alla scienza sociale* (Milan: Società Editrice Libraria, 1906; Rome, Edizioni Bizzari, 1965).
32. Ibid., p. 104.
33. Pareto, *Cours d'économie politique*, sec. 592.
34. Pareto, *Manuale di economia politica*, p. 105.
35. See, besides G. Del Vecchio, 'Sulla teoria economica delle crisi', *Giornale degli Economisti e Rivista di Statistica*, 48 (1914), pp. 425–52 and C. Supino, *Le crisi economiche* (Milan: Hoepli, 1907).

36. Boianovsky and Tarascio wrote that 'Wicksell is correct' when, interpreting Pareto's cycle's theory, affirmed that 'Pareto's business cycle does not admit the possibility of an "equilibrium" interpretation'. In effect, this represented a somewhat anomalous Pareto's viewpoint when inserted in his whole perspective. M. Boianovsky and V. J. Tarascio, 'Mechanical Inertia and Economic Dynamics: Pareto on Business Cycles', *Journal of the History of Economic Thought*, 20:1 (1998), pp. 5–23, on p. 13.
37. M. Pantaleoni, 'Di alcuni fenomeni di economica', in Pantaleoni, *Scritti vari di Economia. Erotemi* (Bari: Laterza, 1925), translated into English as 'Some Phenomena of Economic Dynamics', in A. T. Peacock, W. F. Stolper, R. Turvey and E. Henderson (eds), *International Economic Papers No.5.* (London and New York: Macmillan, 1955), pp. 26–57, on p. 27.
38. Ibid., pp. 27ff.
39. M. Pantaleoni, 'Caratteri delle posizioni iniziali e influenza che esercitano sulle terminali', *Giornale degli Economisti*, 23 (1901), pp. 333–55, on p. 342.
40. M. Pantaleoni, 'Una visione cinematografica del progresso della scienza economica' (1907), in Pantaleoni, *Scritti vari di Economia. Erotemi* (Bari: Laterza, 1925), pp. 211–22, on p. 216.
41. Ibid.
42. Ibid., p. 217.
43. To understand the theoretical climate in which the successive approaches to dynamic equilibrium and to disequilibrium developed, we must extend the discussion beyond Pareto's and Pantaleoni's fundamental contributions, at least to the statistical advances achieved at that time by Italians. As stated by Henry Shultz (*The Theory and Measurement of Demand* (Chicago, IL: University of Chicago Press, 1938), p. 64), Rodolfo Benini was one of the first statisticians to derive the elasticity of demand from time series, by using a method then employed by Henry L. Moore (1914) in his works on the empirical demand curve. Again, Benini ('Sull'uso delle formule empiriche nell'economia applicata') is considered the father of multiple regressions. Corrado Gini first introduced a bivariate form expressing the demand for a good as a function of both the price of that good and the price of an additional good. These methodological innovations were just as important, because many economists believed that statistics could offer important support for the development of dynamic studies. Statistical analysis was largely employed by Del Vecchio (Gini, 'Prezzi e consumi').
44. Labriola, *Saggi sul materialismo storico*, p. 225.
45. B. M. Anderson, *The Value of Money* (New York: Macmillan Company, 1917), p. 468.
46. G. Del Vecchio, *Prodotto netto e monopolio* (Bologna: Noè, 1905), p. 78.
47. G. Del Vecchio, *Ricerche sopra la teoria generale della moneta* (1932), 2nd edn (Padua: Cedam, 1967), p. 9.
48. F. Ferrara, *Esame storico-critico di economisti e dottrine economiche*, 2 vols (Turin: Utet, 1889–91).
49. F. Ferrara, *Opere complete*. Vol. 5: *Della moneta e dei suoi surrogati*, ed. B. R. Ragazzi and F. Caffè (1856; Rome: Associazione Bancaria Italiana, 1961), p. 3
50. F. Ferrara, 'Delle crisi economiche' (1864), in *Opere Complete*, vol. 4: *Prefazioni alla Biblioteca dell'Economista*, ed. B. Rossi Ragazzi (Rome: Istituto Grafico Tiberino, 1956), p. 198.
51. G. Del Vecchio, *Capitale e interesse* (Turin: Einaudi, 1956), p. 19. See also Scazzieri, 'Del Vecchio, Gustavo', p. 4.
52. Del Vecchio, *Prodotto netto e monopolio.*

53. The 1908 article on 'intangible' wealth and capital dealt with an argument recurrent during the second half of the nineteenth century, i.e. the extent of the class of economic goods. Recalling the classical distinction between productive and unproductive labour, Del Vecchio wrote that workers' skills should be treated as fixed capital (*Ricchezze immateriali e capitali immateriali*, p. 208), showing that factors traditionally excluded from the economic field have, on the contrary, economic weight. Hence, on the assumption that economic facts depend on many causes, Del Vecchio directed his theory towards the 'frontier area' of economics.
54. Del Vecchio, 'Introduzione' to G. Del Vecchio (ed.), *Economia pura. Nuova collana di economisti italiani e stranieri* (Turin: Unione Tipografico – Editrice Torinese, 1937), p. 8.
55. Von Hermann, *Staatswirtschaftliche Untersuchungen*.
56. Del Vecchio, *Ricchezze immateriali e capitali immateriali*, p. 231.
57. Del Vecchio, 'Introduzione' to Vecchio (ed.), *Economia pura*, pp. 7–31.
58. Del Vecchio, *Ricchezze immateriali e capitali immateriali*, pp. 233ff.
59. H. D. Macleod, *Principles of Economical Philosophy* (London: Longmans, 1872).
60. R. Faucci, 'La cultura economica fra le due guerre mondiali', in G. Becattini (ed.), *Il pensiero economico: temi, problemi e scuole* (Turin: Utet, 1990), p. 200.
61. E. von Böhm-Bawerk, *Rechte und Verhältnisse vom Standpunkte der volkswirthschaftlichen Güterlehre* (Innsbruck, 1881).
62. C. Menger, *Grundsätze des Volkswirtschaftslehre* (Wien: Holder-Pichler-Tempsky, 1923).
63. Del Vecchio, *Ricchezze immateriali e capitali immateriali*, pp. 230–1
64. Ibid., p. 255.
65. Ibid., p. 274.
66. Del Vecchio, 'Introduzione' to Vecchio (ed.), *Economia pura*, p. viii.
67. The reference to Marx was put forward by R. Faucci, *L'economia politica in Italia. Dal Cinquecento ai giorni nostri* (Turin: Utet, 2000), p. 295.
68. One finds this expression in Pareto (*Cours d'économie politique*).
69. Del Vecchio, *Ricchezze immateriali e capitali immateriali*, p. 269.
70. Ibid.
71. Ibid., p. 267.
72. C. Dietzel, *Das System der Staatsanleihen in Zusammenhang der Volkswirtsschaft betrachtet* (Heidelberg: Mohr, 1855).
73. F. H. Knight, *The Economic Organization* (New York: Kelley, 1967), p. 6.
74. Del Vecchio, *Ricchezze immateriali e capitali immateriali*, p. 268.
75. V. Gioia, 'Il contributo epistemologico di Gustavo del Vecchio', *Quaderni di Storia dell'Economia Politica*, 8 (1990), pp. 147–67.
76. Del Vecchio, *Ricchezze immateriali e capitali immateriali*, p. 253.
77. Del Vecchio, *Teoria del prodotto netto* (1905). Reprinted in Del Vecchio, *Scritti di teoria economica e statistica* (Milan: Giuffrè, 1966), p. 3.
78. F. Caffè, 'L'opera economica di Gustavo del Vecchio', *Studi di economia finanza e statistica in onore di Gustavo Del Vecchio*, 2 vols (Padua: Cedam, 1963).
79. A. De Pietri-Tonelli, *Corso di politica economica. Introduzione* (Padua: Cedam, 1931).
80. See Scazzieri, 'Del Vecchio, Gustavo'.
81. On this point see Gioia, 'Il contributo epistemologico di Gustavo del Vecchio', pp. 154ff.
82. Ibid., p. 155.

2 Valuing Individual Demand for Money

1. A. W. Marget, 'Léon Walras and the "Cash-Balance Approach' to the problem of the Value of Money', *Journal of Political Economy*, 39:5 (1931), pp. 569–600, on p. 593, n. 54.
2. Walras, *Elements of Pure Economics*.
3. G. Del Vecchio, 'I principii della teoria economica della moneta', *Giornale degli Economisti e Rivista di Statistica*, 39 (1909), pp. 255–72, 507–53, on p. 269.
4. Ibid.
5. P. Bridel, *Money and General Equilibrium Theory. From Walras to Pareto (1870–1923)* (Cheltenham: Elgar, 1997), p. 123.
6. G. Demaria, 'La moneta nell'equilibrio economico generale'. Preface to Del Vecchio, *Ricerche sopra la teoria generale della moneta*, pp. 17–29, on p. 28)
7. Walras, *Elements of Pure Economics*, p. 321.
8. See C. Rist, *History of the Monetary and Credit Theory: From John Law to the Present Day* (New York: Kelley, 1966), p. 349. Schumpeter regarded the Italian economist as one of the first to develop a monetary theory on Walrasian bases (J. A. Schumpeter, *History of Economic Analysis* (New York: Oxford University Press, 1954), p. 1326) and to deal with the notion of *encaisse désirée*, crucial in Walras's monetary theory.
9. G. Del Vecchio, 'Prefazione', to G. Demaria, *Le teorie monetarie e il ritorno all'oro* (Torino: Bocca, 1928), pp. v–xiii.
10. Del Vecchio, 'I principii della teoria economica della moneta'.
11. Ibid., p. 509.
12. Pascal Bridel first suggested this interpretation of Del Vecchio's conception of money as *technology of exchange*.
13. L. von Mises, *Theorie des Geldes und der Umlaufsmittel* (München, 1912), translated and reprinted as *The Theory of Money and Credit* (New York: Foundation of Economic Education, 1971), p. 29.
14. Appropriate for defining Del Vecchio's idea of money is what a German author, Karl Helfferich, wrote in 1903: 'the position of money in the general economic organism rests on its being a medium of economic intercourse between individuals' (K. Helfferich, *Das Geld* (1903), translated into English as *Money*, 2 vols (London: E. Benn Limited, 1927), vol. 1, p. 291). This minor author devised the same idea of economic relationship as advanced by Del Vecchio.
15. F. von Wieser, *Natural Value* (1893; New York: Kelley, 1971), pp. 33–4.
16. Ibid., p. 47.
17. Del Vecchio used the term *final* utility, meaning *marginal* utility.
18. Del Vecchio, 'Questioni fondamentali sul valore della moneta', p. 123.
19. Del Vecchio accorded the primacy of establishing a pure monetary theory to *Das Wesen und die Währungsfrage von Hochschule zu Hannover*, a book by W. Launhardt dated 1885 (G. Del Vecchio, 'La teoria della moneta secondo W. Launhardt', in *Economic Essays in Honour of Gustav Cassel* (London: Allen & Unwin, 1933), p. 666). He also aimed at establishing a 'pure theory of circulation' as stated in 1914: 'Our aim from the *Principles* onwards has been to give account of the institutions useful for circulation making use of the same tools used to explain consumption and production, that is, on economic bases' (G. Del Vecchio, 'Teorie dello sconto', *Giornale degli Economisti e Rivista di Statistica*, Supplement (1914), reprinted in Del Vecchio, *Capitale e interesse*, pp. 108–207, on p. 137).

20. The issue concerning the quantitative expression of the marginal utility of money was not resolved once and for all. More than twenty years later, in 1935, Hicks would write that: 'Now money is obviously capable of quantitative expression, and therefore the objection that money has no marginal utility must be wrong. People do choose to have money rather than other things, and therefore, in the relevant sense, money must have a marginal utility' (J. R. Hicks, 'A Suggestion for Simplifying the Theory of Money', *Economica*, 2:5 (1935), pp. 1–19, on p. 3).
21. Del Vecchio, 'I principii della teoria economica della moneta', pp. 509–10.
22. Ibid., p. 510.
23. Ibid., p. 513.
24. Ibid., p. 518.
25. Ibid., pp. 523–4, n. 1. The idea of aggregate as autonomous subject was already put forward in *Ricchezze immateriali e capitali immateriali*, sec. 25, 28.
26. Knies, *Geld und Kredit*.
27. Also mentioned in Anderson, *The Value of Money*, p. 12. Anderson added: 'Knies's value-theory ... is explicitly modelled on that of Marx, to whom he refers, the difference being that Knies takes an average of individual use-times, while Marx takes an average of individual labor-times, as the causal explanation'.
28. Anderson specified: 'The social mind is an organic whole, in which no factors exist 'pure', and in which there is constant give and take' (Anderson, *The Value of Money*, p. 34).
29. Ibid., p. 25.
30. J. B. Clark, *The Philosophy of the Wealth* (Boston, MA: Ginn & Co., 1907).
31. Del Vecchio, 'I principii della teoria economica della moneta', p. 270
32. Ibid., p. 513.
33. Ibid., p. 514.
34. Ibid., p. 515, n. 1.
35. Ibid., p. 517.
36. Ibid., p. 517–8, n. 1.
37. Del Vecchio, 'Questioni fondamentali sul valore della moneta', p. 159.
38. In this regard, Riccardo Realfonzo pointed out the absence in Del Vecchio's works of a clear theory of both direct and indirect utility of money. R. Realfonzo, 'Gustavo Del Vecchio: Critical Conscience of the Italian Neoclassical School', in W. J. Samuels (ed.), *European Economists of the Early 20th Century* (Cheltenham: Elgar, 2003), pp. 50–1.
39. We presume that Del Vecchio knew Helfferich's work on money, *Das Geld*, published in German in 1903, while Del Vecchio was in Germany. Helfferich wrote: 'the basis of a definition of money cannot be its substance or the form in which it appears, but only its functions' (Helfferich, *Das Geld*, vol. 1, p. 277). Helfferich was a student of Knapp, well known by Del Vecchio.
40. Del Vecchio, 'I principii della teoria economica della moneta', p. 256.
41. Ibid., p. 257.
42. Anderson, *The Value of Money*, p. 3.
43. To depict the climate in which Del Vecchio worked out his theory of money value, we can use a short quotation from Rist's well-known book on monetary theories: 'When attempting to formulate a general theory of the value of money, that is to say of variations in its purchasing power ... the majority of economists at the end of the nineteenth century are inevitably drawn to formulas which make the value of money depend primarily on its supply. By general consent this has been given the name of the "quantity" theory ... But it did not end here. In the early years of the twentieth century there are signs of a

tendency to insist more and more on the part played by the demand for money in determining its value. It was realized that the idea of velocity of circulation is but the converse of the idea of the demand for money, and that the latter is infinitely more significant' (Rist, *History of the Monetary and Credit Theory*, pp. 337–8).

44. M. Pantaleoni, *Pure Economics* (New York: Macmillan, 1898), p. 227.
45. Ibid., p. 227, n.1.
46. A. Marshall, *Money, Credit and Commerce* (1923; New York: Kelley, 1965), p. 14.
47. The idea of *need* for money is put forward by Menger in 'Geld' included in the *Handwoerterbuch der Staatswissenschaften*, III vgl, No. 24 (1892).
48. Del Vecchio, 'I principii della teoria economica della moneta', p. 513.
49. Von Mises, *The Theory of Money and Credit*, p. 35.
50. Del Vecchio, 'Questioni fondamentali sul valore della moneta', p. 167.
51. Ibid., p. 132.
52. Ibid., p. 159.
53. Ibid., p. 160.
54. Ibid., p. 167.
55. Ibid., p. 173.
56. Del Vecchio, 'Sulla teoria economica delle crisi'.
57. Del Vecchio, *Teoria dello sconto.*
58. Del Vecchio, 'Lineamenti generali della teoria dell'interesse'.
59. Del Vecchio, 'Questioni fondamentali sul valore della moneta', p. 159.
60. Del Vecchio, *Vecchie e nuove teorie economiche*, p. 248.
61. Del Vecchio, 'Questioni fondamentali sul valore della moneta', p. 132.
62. J. N. Keynes, *The General Theory of Employment Interest and Money* (London: Macmillan, 1936), p. 293.
63. G. Del Vecchio, 'Il problema storico del valore della moneta', *Archivio storico italiano* (1912). Reprinted in *Ricerche sopra la teoria generale della moneta*, pp. 171–7, on p. 173.
64. Although Del Vecchio met the Austrians more than once and discussed his theory with the Austrian school, he never admitted similarities between his thought and the theories of Menger and Mises, among others. He recognized the importance of the Austrian school, as well as the fact that at its beginnings it had been studied mainly in Italy and in the United States, but he was inclined to judge the proposals of Mises and others as too abstract, too far from economic reality: 'Excellent and precise their School, their theory appears less meaningful and useful when related to economic life' (G. Del Vecchio, 'Review of Mises L., Robbins L, and Conrad O'., in Del Vecchio, *Progressi della teoria economica* (Padua: Cedam, 1936), p. 152).
65. Von Mises, *The Theory of Money and Credit*, p. 97.
66. Ibid.
67. Ibid., p. 98.
68. Fisher considered the following factors as influencing the velocity of money circulation: '1. Habits of the individual. *a*) As to thrift and the hoarding; *b*) As to book credit; *c*) As to the use of checks. 2 Systems of payments in the community. *a*) As to frequency of receipts and of disbursement; *b*) As to regularity of receipts and disbursements; *c*) As to correspondence between times and amounts of receipts and disbursements. 3. General causes. *a*) Density of population; *b*) Rapidity of transportation'. (I. Fisher, *The Purchasing Power of Money* (New York: MacMillan, 1911), p. 79.) He assumed them as exogenous and institutional factors, differently from the behavioural, and thus in some cases endogenous, treatment developed by Del Vecchio.

69. Although Marshall was not the author that Del Vecchio cited most extensively in his work, his theory represented a sort of 'model' for Del Vecchio. Suffice it to mention his enthusiastic review of *Money, Credit and Commerce* (Del Vecchio 1923 in Del Vecchio, *Progressi della teoria economica* (Padua: Cedam, 1936)). With Maffeo Pantaleoni and, in a more problematic position, Vilfredo Pareto, Alfred Marshall represented true reference points for Del Vecchio's reasoning
70. Del Vecchio, 'Questioni fondamentali sul valore della moneta', p. 132.
71. Ibid., p. 133.
72. In regard to 'horizon', the term is borrowed from Shackle's study on time: '[Horizon] is usually taken to mean the length of future time from the present which the individual deems it worthwhile to take into account in forming his expectations and plans'. Horizon involves that 'For the individual human consciousness time is not a mathematician's space nor a historian's panorama but a moment. In this solitary moment all the consequences that the decision-maker seeks or accepts must necessarily be contained' (G. L. S. Shackle, *Time in Economics* (Amsterdam: North-Holland Publishing Co., 1967), p. 33).
73. Del Vecchio, 'Questioni fondamentali sul valore della moneta', p. 133.
74. M. Blaug, 'Why is the Quantity Theory of Money the Oldest Surviving Theory in Economics?', in M. Blaug (ed.), *The Quantity Theory of Money. From Locke to Keynes and Friedman* (Aldershot: Elgar, 1995). Blaug clarified thus: 'The "circularity" bogey is the idea that the value of money cannot be said to be determined by its marginal utility, as with ordinary commodities, because the utility of a given nominal quantity of money depends on its real value and this cannot be known until the price level is first determined; that is, to assume that the price level depends on the marginal utility of money is to argue in a circle' (pp. 45–6).
75. Del Vecchio, 'Questioni fondamentali sul valore della moneta', p. 132.
76. Del Vecchio, 'I principii della teoria economica della moneta', pp. 508–9.
77. Ibid., p. 519, fn. 1; Del Vecchio, 'Lineamenti generali della teoria dell'interesse', p. 327.
78. Del Vecchio used the term 'psychic' rate of interest in a sense analogous to that of the 'psychological' rate of interest, as subsequently defined by Maurice Allais in 1974 (M. Allais, 'The Psychological Rate of Interest', *Money, Credit and Banking*, 6:3 (1974), pp. 286–7); that is, the rate of interest 'used by the community to discount the future'.
79. Del Vecchio drew the idea of natural rate of interest from K. Wicksell, *Geldzins und Güterpreise* (Jena: Fischer, 1898), translated in English as *Interest and Prices* (London: Royal Economic Society, 1936), ch. 8). On Del Vecchio's distinction between the discount rate as monetary variable and the interest rate as financial variable, see Realfonzo, 'Gustavo Del Vecchio', p. 53).
80. Del Vecchio, 'Lineamenti generali della teoria dell'interesse', p. 395.
81. Del Vecchio, 'I principii della teoria economica della moneta', p. 535.
82. Del Vecchio, 'Teorie dello sconto', p. 134.
83. $d = i$ is one of the necessary conditions to have general economic equilibrium. Del Vecchio, *Vecchie e nuove teorie economiche*, p. 254.
84. Del Vecchio, 'I principii della teoria economica della moneta', pp. 539–40.
85. According to recent approaches, money reduces the transaction cost of exchanging goods. Del Vecchio stressed the costs of organization that the use of money reduces, but presenting itself as a cost. The point is that money allows a level of organization that a barter economy cannot reach. For the link between money and costs of transaction in a general equilibrium scheme, see R. M. Starr, *Why is there Money?: Walrasian General Equilibrium Foundations of Monetary Theory* (Chelthenam: Elgar, 2012).

86. A. C. Pigou, 'The Value of Money', *Quarterly Journal of Economics*, 32:1 (1917), pp. 38–65, on p. 40.
87. Del Vecchio, 'I principii della teoria economica della moneta', pp. 540ff.
88. Ibid., p. 544.
89. I. Fisher, *The Rate of Interest. Its Nature, Determination and Relation to Economic Phenomena* (New York: MacMillan, 1907), p. 86.
90. Del Vecchio, 'I principii della teoria economica della moneta', p. 545.
91. Del Vecchio, 'Questioni fondamentali sul valore della moneta', pp. 168ff.
92. Ibid., p. 168
93. However, examination of these analyses shows that Del Vecchio took account of the level of dependence of the effect on its cause, assuming the method that he called 'order of infinitesimals': (*ordine degli infinitesimi*). This infinitesimal order allowed the establishment of a hierarchy of dynamic variables or factors acting on the phenomenon, while also accounting for the reciprocal influences among all of them. The higher the infinitesimal attributed to a factor, the smaller its influence on the variable studied. This was a way to gauge the importance of each relationship and also to simplify the general equilibrium analysis. It was also a way to introduce a sort of 'partial analysis' into the general equilibrium, grounding the former on the weight of factors influencing the phenomenon being considered. The factors belonging to the higher orders are put aside in favour of the factors really carrying weight on the object. These weights are not constants through time and space, but they change with time and also with space. Del Vecchio was primarily interested in the changes through time, consistently with his attempt to build a monetary (but not only) dynamic theory. His ambition was to achieve a pure or abstract theory built by decomposing concrete features. This method allowed him to state that the change of the stock of money, which gives origin to a change in the monetary service, has an effect on production greater than the change of the discount rate, and this because the former has an order of infinitesimal smaller than the discount rate.
94. Del Vecchio, 'Questioni fondamentali sul valore della moneta', p. 169.
95. Ibid., p. 170.
96. Ibid.
97. Ibid., p. 171.
98. Ibid., p. 173.
99. Some decades later, Eraldo Fossati stated that the integration of money into a general economic equilibrium scheme needed a dynamic analysis. Money is a source of uncertainty that can be analyzed only by assuming a dynamic perspective. See E. Fossati, *The Theory of General Static Equilibrium* (Oxford: Basil Blackwell, 1957), ch. 11). On this point, see R. E. Kuenne, *The Theory of General Economic Equilibrium* (Princeton, NJ: Princeton University Press, 1963), pp. 301ff).
100. Demaria, 'La moneta nell'equilibrio economico generale', p. 18.
101. A. Zanni, 'La teoria monetaria di Walras: una polemica scientifica tra Marget e Del Vecchio', *Quaderni di storia dell'economia politica*, 7 (1989), pp. 135–45, on p. 143.
102. F. H. Knight, 'Profit' in *Encyclopaedia of the Social Sciences*, ed. E. R. A. Seligman and A. Johnson, 17 vols (New York: Macmillan, 1959), vol. 11, p. 483.
103. In 1892, Pantaleoni cited the essay by A. de Foville titled 'Essai de métérologie économique' published in the Bullettin de l'Institut International de Statistique in 1888 (M. Pantaleoni, 'Osservazioni sulla semiologia economica', *Revue d'Economie Politique* (1892), reprinted in *Scritti varii di economia* (Milan: Sandron, 1904), pp. 423–75, on p. 437). Nevertheless, in those years Pareto wrote: 'The distinguishing character of experi-

mental sciences consists of making use of premises drawn from experience'. (Pareto *Cours d'économie politique*, sec. 629 note 1) and here we stress once again that Del Vecchio admired more Pareto, the statistician of the *Cours*, than Pareto, the scholar of pure economics.

3 Distributing the Stock of Money

1. Del Vecchio, 'Teorie dello sconto', pp. 124–5.
2. G. Del Vecchio, 'Un capitolo di teoria monetaria', *Rivista bancaria* (1925), reprinted in Del Vecchio, *Ricerche sopra la teoria generale della moneta*, p. 317.
3. According to Rist, we can assume Cannan's 1921 article as symbolic of a time in which 'the concept of the demand for money really came into its own in monetary theory' (Rist, *History of the Monetary and Credit Theory*, p. 350. This does not mean that before those years the demand for money was ignored. The works of Wicksell, Menger, Walras, Marshall testify to the contrary. It did not represent the 'core' of the monetary theory.
4. Francesco Ferrara was a strenuous supporter of multiple banks of issue.
5. G. Del Vecchio, 'La teoria economica del credito. A proposito del libro del Prof. Fanno sul mercato monetario', *Giornale degli Economisti e Rivista di Statistica*, 46 (1913), pp. 200–13, on p. 202.
6. Del Vecchio, 'La teoria economica del credito. A proposito del libro del Prof. Fanno sul mercato monetario', p. 203.
7. In 1954, Del Vecchio definitively recognized that the 'modern economic theories are probabilistic and not categorical ones' meaning that 'they do not aim to exactly forecast what will occur ... but to establish the greater or lesser probability of certain phenomena'. See Del Vecchio, *Introduzione alla finanza*, p. 225.
8. Del Vecchio, 'I principii della teoria economica della moneta', p. 266.
9. Ibid., p. 258.
10. Ibid., p. 263.
11. Del Vecchio, 'Un capitolo di teoria monetaria', p. 314.
12. Del Vecchio, 'I principii della teoria economica della moneta', p. 263.
13. Fisher, *The Purchasing Power of Money*.
14. Ibid., pp. 358ff.
15. In 1892 Pareto had raised similar doubts about the use of averages in economics: 'In primitive societies the socioeconomic unit may be the individual, but with a better and more perfect organization of work the unit becomes an aggregate of many people, all of them offering certain commodities and requiring some others. And we must take this circumstance into account. One should also add that Political Economy cannot be a science of averages, and it cannot aspire to predicting and explaining merely acts of single individuals'. V. Pareto, 'Considerazioni sui principi fondamentali della economia politica pura', *Giornale degli Economisti* (August 1892), p. 65.
16. Del Vecchio, 'I principii della teoria economica della moneta', p. 264.
17. Ibid., p. 265.
18. G. Del Vecchio, 'Il problema della stabilità del sistema capitalistico', *Economia*, 3:5–8 (1925), pp. 47–60, on p. 50.
19. Economic institutions fail when they are dominated by phenomena like bureaucratization, militarism, and syndicalism (Ibid., p. 57).
20. See Pareto, *Cours d'économie politique*.

21. R. Skidelsky, 'J. M. Keynes and the Quantity Theory of Money', in Blaug (ed.), *The Quantity Theory of Money*, pp. 80–96, on p. 80.
22. See Del Vecchio, 'Il problema della stabilità del sistema capitalistico'.
23. The Banca d'Italia became the Italian central bank in 1926. At the time in which Del Vecchio was writing the monetary issue was recognized to Banco di Napoli and Banco di Sicilia beside the Banca d'Italia itself.
24. See Fisher, *The Purchasing Power of Money*.
25. Cantillon's analysis concerned exchange by means of money among the main social groups in eighteenth-century France. See R. Cantillon., *Essai sur la nature du commerce en general* (1755; London: Macmillan, 1931), pp. 120ff. On this see A. Brewer, *Richard Cantillon. Pioneer of Economic Theory* (London: Routledge, 1992), ch. 6. Previously, William Petty and John Locke had discussed the same problem of the proportion between exchanged goods and circulating money.
26. Del Vecchio, 'I principii della teoria economica della moneta', p. 262.The idea of 'group', as stated by Del Vecchio, recalls the relation between the amount of goods sold and the share of goods not produced for the market. Arthur W. Marget, among others, subsequently discussed this point. See A. W. Marget, 'The Relation between the Velocity of Circulation of Money and the Velocity of Circulation of Goods', *Journal of Political Economy*, 40:3 (1932), pp. 289–313.
27. T. Aspromourgos, 'The Theory of Production and Distribution in Cantillon's Essai', *Oxford Economic Papers*, new series, 41:2 (1989), pp. 356–73, on p. 369.
28. Del Vecchio, 'I principii della teoria economica della moneta', p. 530.
29. Ibid., pp. 545–6, n. 1.
30. Cantillon, *Essai sur la nature du commerce en général*, part 2, ch. 4.
31. Del Vecchio, 'I principii della teoria economica della moneta', p. 263.
32. In a certain sense, by determining the quantity of money and implicitly guaranteeing the exchangeability of money, the 'main group' takes the place of the Walrasian auctioneer.
33. Del Vecchio wrote: 'If the commodities are more than two, the problem is more complex', certainly for the determination of the demand for money (Del Vecchio, 'I principii della teoria economica della moneta', p. 263).
34. G. Del Vecchio, 'Le variazioni periodiche dello sconto', *Giornale degli Economisti e Rivista di Statistica*, 46 (1913), pp. 342–408.
35. Del Vecchio, 'Un capitolo di teoria monetaria', p. 318.
36. In those years, some remarks on the importance of the distribution of money/wealth were made in a book which was much appreciated by Del Vecchio, *The Fundamental Problem in Monetary Science*, published by C. M. Walsh, in 1903. Walsh wrote: 'The argument from results [coming from monetary experience] concerns itself with the good and the evil which attend stability of money in exchange-value or in cost-value or esteem-value. The good and the evil resulting from the different functionings of money may manifest themselves in the distribution of wealth between the different classes of society, and in the production of wealth by and for the whole of society'. See C. M. Walsh, *The Fundamental Problem in Monetary Science* (New York: Mamillan, 1903), p. 337.
37. Del Vecchio, 'Un capitolo di teoria monetaria', pp. 317–8.
38. Del Vecchio, 'I principii della teoria economica della moneta', p. 261.
39. Ibid., p. 262.
40. W. S. Jevons, *Money and the Mechanism of Exchange*, 2nd edn (London: H. S. King & Co., 1876), p. 336.
41. Ibid.

42. A different perspective grounded on the idea of velocity as average was provided in the same year, 1909, by Irving Fisher, who published an article entitled 'A Practical Method of Estimating the Velocity of Circulation of Money' in the *Journal of the Royal Statistical Society* (1909), where he proposed estimating how many days money is held: 'money was held on the average about twenty days' (I. Fisher, 'A Practical Method of Estimating the Velocity of Circulation of Money', *Journal of the Royal Statistical Society*, 72:3 (1909), pp. 604–18, on p. 616). Clearly, Fisher's proposal was the opposite to Del Vecchio's. Fisher reached the conclusion that: 'money deposits plus wages divided by money in circulation will always afford a good barometer of the velocity of circulation' (Ibid., p. 617). He thus affirmed the importance of the average velocity, while Del Vecchio emphasized the importance of considering different velocities because of selling groups.
43. Fisher, *The Purchasing Power of Money*, p. 14.
44. Ibid., p. 17.
45. See K. Marx, *Capital. A Critique of Political Economy, Vol. I.*, German edition 1867; first English edition 1887, online version, p. 86. On this point see also M. W. Holtrop, 'Theories of the Velocity of Circulation of Money in Earlier Economic Literature', *Economic History*, 4 (1929), reprinted in M. Blaug (ed.), *Pre-Classical Economists*, 3 vols (Cheltenam: Elgar 1991), vol. 3, p. 19.
46. Holtrop, 'Theories of the Velocity of Circulation of Money in Earlier Economic Literature', p. 21.
47. W. E. Mason, *Classical versus Neoclassical Monetary Theory*, ed. W. E. Butos (Boston, MA: Kluwer Academic, 1996), p. 11.
48. Del Vecchio, 'I principii della teoria economica della moneta', p. 262.
49. A. W. Marget, *The Theory of Prices*, 2 vols (1938; New York: Kelley, 1966), vol. 1, p. 359.
50. Ibid., vol. 2, p. 379.
51. J. M. Keynes, *A Treatise on Money*, 2 vols (London: Macmillan, 1930), vol. 2, p. 20.
52. Ibid., vol. 2, p. 21.
53. Ibid., vol. 2, p. 22.
54. A not very dissimilar conception of money is attributed by P. Likitijsomboon to Marx, whose behavioural equation $M^d = PQ/V$ states that the quantity of money in circulation is determined by the money-velocity and the price-sum of commodities (see P. Likitijsomboon, 'Marx's Anti-Quantity Theory of Money: A Critical Evaluation', in F. Moseley, *Marx's Theory of Money* (Houndmills: Palgrave Macmillan, 2005), p. 161). In this case, an excess or shortage of money relative to the requirement of commodity circulation is adjusted by a decrease or increase in the quantity of money in circulation to restore equilibrium.
55. It should be stressed that Del Vecchio's monetary theory considers both the demand for money and its supply. It is neither a theory of demand alone nor a theory grounded on supply. But Del Vecchio argued that the approach based on supply alone lacks a 'causal link' between value and supply; consequently, the role of demand was absolutely the most important.
56. Although not cited by Del Vecchio, James Steuart in his *Principles*, stated that the demand for money had no influence on prices and that the excess or shortage of money was balanced by hoarding practices. Steuart was treated with much respect by Marx (see A. Arnon, *Monetary Theory and Policy from Hume and Smith to Wicksell. Money, Credit and the Economy* (Cambridge: Cambridge University Press, 2011), p. 323).
57. I have borrowed the term from Likitijsomboon, 'Marx's Anti-Quantity Theory of Money: A Critical Evaluation', p. 164.

58. See Fisher, *The Purchasing Power of Money*.
59. Del Vecchio, *Lezioni di economia applicata. Dinamica economica* (1933), p. 45.
60. Ibid., p. 46.
61. Del Vecchio, *Vecchie e nuove teorie*, p. 367.
62. Del Vecchio, 'I principii della teoria economica della moneta', p. 263.
63. This link was reaffirmed in 1933. See Del Vecchio, 'La teoria della moneta secondo W. Launhardt', p. 670.
64. Del Vecchio, 'Teorie dello sconto', p. 140.
65. Marshall, *Money, Credit and Commerce*, p. 14.
66. Del Vecchio, 'I principii della teoria economica della moneta', p. 549.
67. Ibid., p. 551.
68. V. Pareto, 'Programme et sommaire du Cours de sociologie', in *Ecrits sociologiques mineurs*, ed. G. Busino (1905; Genève: Droz, 1980), pp. 292–316, on p. 296.
69. V. Pareto, *Les Systèmes Socialistes*, (1902–3; Genève: Droz, 1965), p. 80.
70. See M. Morishima, 'Foreword' to *Vilfredo Pareto: Neoclassical Synthesis of Economics and Sociology*, in A. de Pietri-Tonelli and G. H. Bousquet, *Vilfredo Pareto: Neoclassical Synthesis of Economics and Sociology* (Houndmills: Palgrave Macmillan 1994), pp. xi–xxvi, on p. xi. Morishima added: 'so it is no easy thing to achieve a harmonious coexistence between these different equilibria' (Ibid.).
71. De Pietri-Tonelli, *Corso di politica economica. Introduzione*, p. 43.
72. Ibid.
73. G. Palomba, *Equilibrio economico e movimenti ciclici secondo i dati della sociologia sperimentale* (Naple: Jovene, 1935).
74. A. Bordin, *La teoria dell'equilibrio e gli schemi probabilistici* (Bellinzona: Leins & Vescov, 1933).
75. L. Amoroso, 'Ricerche intorno alla curva dei redditi', *Annali di matematica pura e applicata* (1925), pp. 123–57.
76. Del Vecchio, *Lezioni di economia applicata* (1933), p. 447.
77. Del Vecchio, *Introduzione alla finanza*, p. 225.
78. P. Jannaccone, 'Vilfredo Pareto, il sociologo', in L. Amoroso et al., *Vilfredo Pareto. L'economista e il sociologo* (Milan: Malfasi, 1949), pp. 20–34, on pp. 29–30.
79. Del Vecchio, *Lezioni di economia applicata* (1933), pp. 447ff.
80. Ibid., p. 450.
81. W. P. Cockshott et al., *Classical Econophysics* (London and New York: Routledge, 2009), p. 143 and ch. 6.
82. Del Vecchio, *Lezioni di economia applicata* (1933), pp. 450–1.
83. Cockshott et al., *Classical Econophysics*, p. 143.

4 Supervising Monetary Balance

1. Del Vecchio, 'Questioni fondamentali sul valore della moneta', p. 164.
2. Del Vecchio, 'Teorie dello sconto', p. 115.
3. Del Vecchio, 'Questioni fondamentali sul valore della moneta', p. 164.
4. See A. A. Porcelluzzi, *Walter Bagehot and the Open Money Supply Approach to Monetary Theory* (Saarbrüchen: VDM Verlag, 2009), p. 101.
5. Del Vecchio, 'Un capitolo di teoria monetaria', p. 315.
6. Del Vecchio, 'Teorie dello sconto', p. 216.
7. Del Vecchio, *Ricerche sopra la teoria generale della moneta*.

8. A. Zanni, 'Walras's Theory of Money: A Scientific Debate between Marget and Del Vecchio', *Economists' Archives* (1990), pp. 5–12, on p. 10.
9. Del Vecchio followed Francesco Ferrara in stating that money is a lengthening of the production process. Consequently, general equilibrium is the obligatory presupposition of any specific monetary theory.
10. F. Ferrara, *Opere complete*, vol. 5: *Della moneta e dei suoi surrogati*, ed. B. R. Ragazzi and F. Caffè (1856; Rome: Associazione Bancaria Italiana, 1961).
11. Wicksell, *Interest and Prices*.
12. G. Del Vecchio, 'Ritorni alla teoria ferrariana del credito' (1930), reprinted in Del Vecchio, *Ricerche sopra la teoria generale della moneta*, pp. 107–18, on p. 109.
13. Del Vecchio wrote: 'At given times, the credit expansion can sustain production'. Ibid., pp. 117 –8.
14. R. G. Hawtrey, *Credit and Currency* (New York: Longmans, 1928), p. 5.
15. Del Vecchio, 'Teorie dello sconto', p. 113.
16. Ibid., p. 115.
17. In this point, we found interesting D. Laidler, 'The Definition of Money: Theoretical and Empirical Problems', *Journal of Money, Credit, and Banking*, 1: 3 (1969), pp. 508–25, on pp. 510ff.
18. Del Vecchio, *Vecchie e nuove teorie economiche*, p. 266.
19. Del Vecchio, 'La teoria economica del credito. A proposito del libro del Prof. Fanno sul mercato monetario', p. 207.
20. Del Vecchio, 'Questioni fondamentali sul valore della moneta', p. 137.
21. Ibid., p. 138.
22. Holtrop wrote: ' in the struggle between the partisans of the 'currency' and those of the 'banking' theory, the phenomenon of the velocity of circulation was of no strategic value, as neither of the two schools succeeded in deriving from it an efficient argument for its own point of view' (Holtrop, 'Theories of the Velocity of Circulation of Money in Earlier Economic Literature', pp. 514 –5).
23. Del Vecchio, *Vecchie e nuove teorie economiche*, p. 366.
24. Del Vecchio, 'Teorie dello sconto', pp. 149ff.
25. Ibid., p. 156.
26. F. H. Knight, *Risk, Uncertainty, and Profit* (Boston, MA and New York: Houghton Mifflin Co, 1921), p. 131.
27. In this article, Del Vecchio reviewed Jevons's statistical study on the discount rate which singled out the following three causes of variation: *artificial conditions* depending on the division of the year; *seasonal* reasons connected to harvests; and *economic cycle* factors.
28. Del Vecchio, 'Le variazioni periodiche dello sconto', p. 404.
29. Ibid., p. 379.
30. Ibid., p. 401.
31. Ibid., pp. 397ff.
32. Ibid., p. 399.
33. Del Vecchio, 'Teorie dello sconto', p. 140.
34. Ibid., p. 121.
35. See, for example, R. G. Hawtrey, *The Art of Central Banking* (London: Longmans, 1932).
36. See also G. Del Vecchio, 'Il mercato monetario', *Annali di Economia* (1927), pp. 311–24.
37. Del Vecchio, 'Le variazioni periodiche dello sconto', p. 360.
38. Del Vecchio, 'Teorie dello sconto', p. 142.

39. Wicksell stated that: 'As the German author, Emil Struck, justly says in his well-known sketch of the English money market: in our days demand and supply of money have become about the same thing, the demand to a large extent creating its own supply' (K. Wicksell, 'The Influence of the Rate of Interest on Prices', *Economic Journal*, 17: 66 (1907), pp. 213–20, on p. 215). Wicksell and Struck made reference to a monetary market where borrowings are fed by deposits from sales. That was a quite different market from the Italian one.
40. Del Vecchio, 'Teorie dello sconto', p. 143.
41. Ibid., p. 134.
42. Del Vecchio, 'Le variazioni periodiche dello sconto', p. 405.
43. G. Del Vecchio, 'Induzioni statistiche per la teoria della circolazione', *Giornale degli Economisti e Rivista di Statistica*, 46 (1913), pp. 510–37, on p. 529.
44. Ibid., pp. 529 –30; original italics.
45. Del Vecchio's monetary paradox has some similarities with Fisher's analysis of the relationship between forecasted prices, reserves and rate of interest developed in his 1907 *The Rate of Interest*. But the theoretical framework is different. See Fisher, *The Rate of Interest*, pp. 322ff. and the footnote n. 1 p. 284.
46. Del Vecchio, 'Induzioni statistiche per la teoria della circolazione', pp. 530–1.
47. Ibid., p. 531.
48. Ibid.
49. Marget, *The Theory of Prices*, vol. 1, p. 173.
50. Del Vecchio, 'Teorie dello sconto', p. 144.
51. Del Vecchio, 'Questioni fondamentali sul valore della moneta', pp. 168ff.
52. Del Vecchio, 'Teorie dello sconto', p. 157.
53. Ibid., p. 160.
54. Ibid., p. 172.
55. Ibid., p. 185.
56. Actually, Ferrara was in favour of the competition among issue banks (see Del Vecchio, *Vecchie e nuove teorie economiche*, p. 259).
57. Del Vecchio, 'Questioni fondamentali sul valore della moneta', p. 154.
58. G. Del Vecchio, 'Credito', *Enciclopedia italiana* (1931), vol 11, reprinted in G. Del Vecchio, *Capitale e interesse*, p. 306.
59. Ibid.
60. Del Vecchio, 'Il mercato monetario', p. 313.
61. Del Vecchio, 'Teorie dello sconto', p. 173.
62. Ibid., p. 145.
63. G. Del Vecchio, 'Problemi del Tesoro e della circolazione', *Giornale degli Economisti e Rivista di Statistica*, 46 (1913), pp. 1–12, on p. 3.
64. Ibid.
65. Ibid.
66. At first sight, Del Vecchio's treatment in those years of 'expectations' is deeper than that by Fisher in 1911 when he tied the new concept mainly to prices: '... the expectation of a future rise or fall of prices causes an immediate rise or fall of prices' (Fisher, *The Purchasing Power of Money*, p. 263).
67. Del Vecchio, *Ricerche sopra la teoria generale della moneta*, p. 10.
68. G. Del Vecchio, 'Contributi alle dottrine della circolazione', *Giornale degli Economisti e Rivista di Statistica*, 47 (1914). Reprinted in *Ricerche sopra la teoria generale della moneta*, p. 338.

69. Del Vecchio, 'Contributi alle dottrine della circolazione', p. 339.
70. G. Del Vecchio, 'Teoria della esportazione del capitale', *Giornale degli Economisti e Rivista di Statistica*, 41 (1910), pp. 120–52, on pp. 133ff.
71. Ibid., p. 123.
72. Ibid., p. 136.
73. Ibid., p. 145.

5 Making Monetary Wealth Circulate

1. Del Vecchio, 'Lineamenti generali della teoria dell'interesse', p. 273, n. 1.
2. See A. Landry, *L'intérêt du Capital* (Paris: Giard 1901).
3. Suranyi-Unger, *Economics in the Twentieth Century*, p. 200.
4. On this aspect, see S. Tomo, 'Böhm-Bawerk's Objectivism beyond Menger's Subjectivism', in Y. Ikeda and K. Yagi, *Subjectivism and Objectivism in the History of Economic Thought* (Abingdon: Routledge, 2012), pp. 108–25.
5. Fisher, *The Rate of Interest*.
6. In the literature of the time, see also H. G. Brown, 'The Marginal Productivity versus the Impatience Theory of Interest', *Quarterly Journal of Economics*, 27:4 (1913), pp. 630–50.
7. Del Vecchio, 'Lineamenti generali della teoria dell'interesse', p. 284, n. 1.
8. Ibid., p. 284.
9. Ibid., p. 298.
10. Ibid., p. 286.
11. Ibid., p. 295.
12. Marginal productivity depends on the length of production processes, appearing to be independent from the value of the capital. However, this statement was presented as a simplification of the economic reality, in which capital value continuously changes because of competition in capital markets, both real and financial. If capital changes, also its productivity varies.
13. Del Vecchio, 'Lineamenti generali della teoria dell'interesse', pp. 298–9.
14. Ibid., pp. 297ff.
15. J. A. Schumpeter, *Die Theorie der wirtschaftlichen Entwicklung* (Leipzig: Duncker & Humblot, 1912).
16. Del Vecchio, 'Lineamenti generali della teoria dell'interesse', p. 324.
17. Ibid., p. 291
18. Ibid., p. 322, n.1.
19. Ibid., p. 325.
20. Ibid., p. 321.
21. The 'psychic' or psychological conception of time was introduced by Del Vecchio to highlight the difference between economic dynamics and those typical of the hard sciences: 'It is sufficient to remember that time in [classical] mechanics is reduced to space, whilst economics adopts a concrete time, which cannot be dealt with using the tools adopted by physics' (Del Vecchio, *Vecchie e nuove teorie economiche*, p. 248). It can also be said that time in economics does not flow independently from the perceptions that individuals have of their own economic relationships.
22. Del Vecchio, 'Lineamenti generali della teoria dell'interesse', p. 304.
23. Ibid., p. 299.
24. Ibid., p. 300.

25. When Del Vecchio wrote on this topic, this position, very common at that time, was taken by E. Cannan in *Wealth. A Brief Explanation of the Causes of Economic Welfare* (London: King & Son, 1914). In his *Treatise*, Keynes would write that savings are exactly the differences between money-incomes and money-expenditure, taking profits separately from any discourse on savings (*A Treatise on Money*, vol. 1, p. 126).
26. Del Vecchio, 'Lineamenti generali della teoria dell'interesse', p. 315.
27. Ibid., p. 369.
28. Ibid.
29. Ibid., p. 326.
30. Ibid., p. 368.
31. See G. Tusset, 'Individual and Market Inertia in Luigi Amoroso's Cycle Model', *History of Economic Ideas*, 20:2 (2012), pp. 43–63.
32. Del Vecchio, 'Lineamenti generali della teoria dell'interesse', p. 370.
33. Ibid., p. 371.
34. Ibid., p. 376. Although Dl Vecchio did not explicitly quote Ricardo, he certainly knew that the point had been discussed by David Ricardo in one of his pamphlets: '"If ... considerable portions of the currency were taken from the idle, *and those who live upon fixed incomes*, and transferred to farmers, manufacturers, and merchants, – the proportion between capital and revenue would be greatly altered to the advantage of capital; and in a short time the produce of the country would be greatly augmented". It is no doubt true "that it is not the *quantity*" of circulating medium which adds to the national wealth, "but the *different distribution* of it". If, therefore, we could be fully assured that the effects of the abundance, and the consequent depreciation of the currency, would diminish the powers of consumption in the idle and unproductive class, whilst it increased the number of the industrious and productive class, the effect would undoubtedly be to augment the national wealth'. D. Ricardo, *The Works and Correspondence of David Ricardo*, III. *Pamphlets and Papers 1809–1811*, ed. P. Sraffa (Cambridge: Cambridge University Press, 1951), pp. 120ff.
35. See Pareto, *Cours d'économie politique*.
36. See R. Benini, 'Di alcune curve descritte da fenomeni economici aventi relazioni con la curva del reddito e con quella dei patrimoni', *Giornale degli Economisti* (1897), pp. 177–214.
37. Del Vecchio, 'Lineamenti generali della teoria dell'interesse', p. 382.
38. Ibid., p. 387.
39. Ibid., p. 390.
40. Ibid.
41. Ibid., p. 383.
42. Ibid., p. 384.
43. Del Vecchio, 'I principii della teoria economica della moneta', p. 519.
44. On Del Vecchio's distinction between the discount rate as a monetary variable and the interest rate as a financial variable, see Realfonzo, 'Gustavo Del Vecchio', p. 53.
45. Del Vecchio, 'Lineamenti generali della teoria dell'interesse', p. 292.
46. Del Vecchio, 'I principii della teoria economica della moneta', p. 536.
47. Ibid., pp. 521ff.
48. The interest rate 'represents the economic boundary' of monetary circulation (1909, p. 526). Del Vecchio gave to the notion of monetary *circulation* a meaning that sums up all the aspects concerning the use of money. For example, the postponement of consumption is part of this theory because it is influenced by the real interest rate. Similarly,

institutional decisions concerning the discount rate affect the circulation of money. The theory of circulation is, therefore, broader than the theory of money, strictly speaking.

49. Del Vecchio, 'I principii della teoria economica della moneta', p. 537.
50. Del Vecchio, 'Questioni fondamentali sul valore della moneta', p. 121.
51. Mention has been made of Cantillon, who, in 1755, wrote that prices – and consequently the value of money – can change because of individual psychological reactions.
52. Marshall, *Money, Credit and Commerce*, p. 14.
53. Del Vecchio, 'Lineamenti generali della teoria dell'interesse', pp. 306ff.
54. Del Vecchio, *Lezioni di economia applicata* (1933), p. 222.
55. Sombart, "Versuch einer Systematik der Wirtschaftskrisen', *Archivfür Sozialwissenschaft und Sozialpolitik*, 19 (1904), pp. 1–21.
56. Del Vecchio, *Lezioni di economia applicata. Dinamica economica* (1933), p. 150.
57. Del Vecchio's evolutionism seems to show only marginal contacts with social Darwinism, which in Italy was sustained at that time by Salvatore Cognetti de Martiis (see F. Cognetti de Martiis, 'L'economia come scienza autonoma', *Giornale degli economisti*, 9 (1886), pp. 166–203; R. Faucci, *L'economista scomodo. Vita e opere di Francesco Ferrara* (Palermo: Sellerio, 1995) p. 261). This is because the evolution of economic systems was not considered to be the outcome of conflict among species, but the result of continuous changes in the economy.
58. Faucci, 'La cultura economica fra le due guerre mondiali', p. 201.
59. Del Vecchio, 'Sulla teoria economica delle crisi'.
60. Ibid., pp. 426ff.
61. Ibid., pp. 426–7.
62. Ibid.
63. A. Aftalion, *Les crise périodiques de superproduction* (Paris: Rivier, 1913).
64. Del Vecchio, 'Sulla teoria economica delle crisi', p. 430.
65. Ibid., p. 437. In his book pany years later, he stressed the monetary origin of economic crises (G. Del Vecchio, *Economia generale* (Turin: Utet, 1961), p. 195).
66. Ibid., pp. 437–8.
67. Ibid., pp. 436–7.
68. Ibid., p. 442.
69. Del Vecchio theorized that continuous change is an intrinsic feature of capitalist production – the capitalist system gives rise to variations (*Lezioni di economia applicata. Dinamica economica* (1933), p. 55) – which, in their turn, generates uncertainty. Such change is not only a possibility; it is a necessary condition for the economic system's development. In a 'stationary condition', 'capitalism would be bound to end' ('Il problema della stabilità del sistema capitalistico', p. 49). The *normal* condition of an economic system is dynamism, whilst the stationary state is episodic.
70. Del Vecchio, 'Sulla teoria economica delle crisi', p. 445.
71. Ibid., p. 446.
72. See G. Del Vecchio, *Aspetti teorici della crisi mondiale* (1932), reprinted as 'Theoretical Aspects of the World Crisis', in H. Hagemann (ed.), *Business Cycle Theory: Selected Texts 1860–1930* (London: Pickering & Chatto, 2002), pp. 261–76.
73. Del Vecchio, *Vecchie e nuove teorie economiche*, p. 402.
74. Ferrara, 'Delle crisi economiche', p. 385. See the articles by James Wilson on *The Economist* between 1845 and 1847 and collected in J. Wilson, *Capital, Currency, and Banking* (London: The Economist, 1847).
75. Ferrara, 'Delle crisi economiche', p. 389.

76. Ibid.
77. Ibid., p. 390.
78. C. Supino, *Teoria della trasformazione dei capitali* (Turin: Bocca, 1891).
79. Supino, *Le crisi economiche*. In 1907, Camillo Supino published an analysis of economic crises which aroused interest also abroad, as proved by Wicksell's citation ('The Influence of the Rate of Interest on Prices', p. 336).
80. G. Masci, 'Alcuni aspetti odierni dell'organizzazione e delle trasformazioni industriali', in *Nuova Collana di Economisti Italiani e Stranieri*. Vol. 7, *Organizzazione industriale* (Turin: Utet, 1934). The 1934 essay developed the content of a previous work, *The Laws of Industrial Changes* (*Le leggi delle trasformazioni industriali*), published by Masci in 1922.
81. Masci, 'Alcuni aspetti odierni dell'organizzazione e delle trasformazioni industriali', p. 940.
82. Ibid., p. 942.
83. Ibid., p. 932. According to Masci: 'Briefly, capital liquidity is the tendency of capital to disappear as capital and to re-appear as consumption goods: the level of liquidity is measured by the inverse of the ratio between the time taken by a capital good to transform itself into a consumption good, and the duration of the production process' (Alcuni aspetti odierni dell'organizzazione e delle trasformazioni industriali', p. 941). Masci affirmed that the notion of 'liquidity' means the transferability of capital from one process to another, and that it must not be confused with that of 'attitude to consumption' (consumabilità) (Ibid., p. 942).
84. Ibid., p. 953.
85. M. Resta, *Il capitale fisso e le trasformazioni industriali* (Padua: Cedam, 1938).
86. V. Pareto, *Manuel d'économie politique* (Geneve-Paris: Droz, 1909), p. 327.
87. Resta, *Il capitale fisso e le trasformazioni industriali*, p. 23.
88. It must not be forgotten that Ferrara had thoroughy analyzed the links between high-order and low-order firms (*Esame storico-critico di economisti e dottrine economiche.*, p. 250, vol. 1).
89. Resta, *Il capitale fisso e le trasformazioni industriali*, p. 49.
90. In 1933, Foà proposed a concept of 'capital liquidity' with the same meaning as Resta's 'capital mobility' (B. Foà, *Il capitale nell'equilibrio economico* (Messina: Industrie Grafiche Meridionali, 1933), p. 25).
91. Resta, *Il capitale fisso e le trasformazioni industriali*, p. 68.
92. Ibid.
93. Ibid., p. 121.
94. Caffè, 'L'opera economica di Gustavo del Vecchio' (1961).
95. Del Vecchio, 'Lineamenti generali della teoria dell'interesse', p. 387.
96. Ibid.
97. Incidentally, this explains why Del Vecchio was called the 'Italian Schumpeter'.

6 Dealing with Irreducible Risk

1. Mises, *The Theory of Money and Credit*.
2. A. C. Pigou, *Industrial Fluctuations*, 2nd edn (London: Macmillan, 1929).
3. On this topic, see P. Bini, 'Captains of Industry and Masters of Thought: The Entrepreneur and the Tradition of Italian Liberal Economists from Francesco Ferrara to Sergio Ricossa', *Rivista Italiana degli Economisti*, 18:1 (2013), pp. 87–130.

4. Schumpeter, *Die Theorie der wirtschaftlichen Entwicklung.*
5. W. Sombart, *Der Bourgeois* (München und Leipzig: Duncker & Humblot, 1913), translated in English as *The Quintessence of Capitalism* (New York: Howard Fertig, 1967).
6. J. B. Clark, *The Distribution of the Wealth* (London: Macmillan, 1899).
7. C. Bresciani-Turroni, 'Le variazioni "cicliche" dei prezzi', *Annali del Seminario giuridico della R. Università di Palermo*, vol. 2 (Palermo: Gaipa, 1912), pp. 227–82, on p. 269.
8. Bresciani-Turroni wrote on innovation in 1912, before or simultaneously with publication of Schumpeter's *Theorie*. Bresciani met Schumpeter in 1913 (see P. Bini, *Costantino Bresciani-Turroni. Ciclo, moneta e sviluppo* (Civitanova Marche: Otium, 1992), p. 75) and started to cite him in the following years. One may ask whether the entrepreneur as innovator would have existed in Bresciani-Turroni before publication of Schumpeter's work.
9. C. Bresciani-Turroni, 'Oscillazioni fra sconto e prezzi durante i cicli economici' (1916) in Bresciani-Turroni, *Saggi di economia* (Milan: Giuffrè, 1961), pp. 371–420, on p. 410.
10. C. Bresciani-Turroni, 'Le vicende del marco tedesco', *Annali di Economia*, 7 (1932), pp. 1–596, on p. 355.
11. C. Bresciani-Turroni, *Corso di economia politica. Teoria generale dei fatti economici* (Milan: Giuffrè, 1953), p. 284.
12. Ibid., p. 285.
13. Bresciani-Turroni, 'Le vicende del marco tedesco', p. 378.
14. Ibid., p. 388.
15. In his depiction of the entrepreneur-speculator, Bresciani-Turroni evoked the description previously proposed by Sombart in around 1910, when he had argued that the 'spirit of speculation' should be considered an 'expression of the capitalist firm's essence'. See Sombart, *Der Bourgeois*, p. 129.
16. Knight, *Risk, Uncertainty, and Profit*, p. 308.
17. Pigou, *Industrial Fluctuations.*
18. Pigou wrote: 'industrial conditions are neither stationary nor yet progressive in a continuous line, but that productivity and desire move in jerks. In a sense this fact may be regarded as the cause of errors; because, if everything were absolutely stable, recurring every year with exact similarity or in a perfectly regular progression, people could not fail to be aware of the relevant facts and to form correct judgments'. See *Industrial Fluctuations*, p. 74.
19. U. G. Papi, *Lezioni di economia politica. III*, 8th edn (Padua: Cedam, Padova, 1950), p. 28.
20. U. G. Papi, *Lezioni di economia generale e corporativa* (Padua: Cedam, 1934), p. 41.
21. Ibid., p. 53.
22. Ibid., p. 55.
23. Papi, *Lezioni di economia politica. III*, p. 54.
24. U. G. Papi, 'Trend e punti di inversioni in una fluttuazione economica', in Società Italiana degli Economisti, *Atti della prima riunione scientifica* (Milan: Bocconi University, 1952), pp. 39–51, on p. 47.
25. Papi, *Lezioni di economia generale e corporativa*, p. 73.
26. Ibid., p. 74.
27. See Papi, 'Trend e punti di inversioni in una fluttuazione economica', p. 39. That Papi treated his theory as dynamic is proved by his concept of error: the latter was explained as a consequence of the temporal characterization of the production process, during which the initial inputs may change without compensatory movements (Papi, *Lezioni*

di economia generale e corporativa, p. 106). Time is not an abstract factor, but rather the background against which entrepreneurial errors occur.

28. M. Fanno wrote: 'the economic models proposed since the thirties are mainly founded on the assumption that economies are steady. And this is the cause of their theoretical failures. To understand business fluctuations we should examine progressive economies' ('Le teorie delle fluttuazioni economiche', in *Società Italiana degli Economisti, Atti della prima riunione scientifica* (Milan: Università Bocconi, 1952), p. 20).
29. M. Fanno, *La teoria delle fluttuazioni economiche* (Turin: Utet, 1947), p. 77.
30. Ibid., p. 297.
31. E. Slutsky, 'The Summation of Random Causes as the Source of Cyclic Processes', *Econometrica* (1937), pp. 105–46.
32. G. Yule, 'On a Method of Investigating Periodicity in Disturbed Series with Special Reference to Wolfer's Sunspot Numbers', *Transactions of the Royal Society* (1927), pp. 267–98.
33. Fanno, *La teoria delle fluttuazioni economiche*, p. 45.
34. The reference is to J. Tinbergen, who grounded the cycle on investments.
35. H. L. Moore, *Synthetic Economics* (New York: Macmillan Co. 1929).
36. A. Magliulo, *Marco Fanno e la cultura economica italiana del Novecento* (Florence: Polistampa, 1998), p. 169.
37. The distinction between potential development and secular development refers to the substantial literature on net investments originated by the gap between expected capital and real capital. Such proposals, which go back to Schumpeter, were common in Anglo-American lines of inquiry during the 1940s and the 1950s. See R. M. Goodwin, 'Secular and Cyclical Aspects of the Multiplier and the Accelerator', in *Income, Employment and Public Policy. Essays in Honor of Alvin H. Hansen* (New York: W.W. Norton & C., 1948), pp. 108–32.
38. Fanno pointed out that full employment did not involve all the production sectors, but only some of them. See Fanno, *La teoria delle fluttuazioni economiche*, p. 177.
39. Fanno, *La teoria delle fluttuazioni economiche*, p. 180.
40. Since growth may be interrupted before it reaches full employment, the downward trend may be halted before it reaches its theoretical minimum. This may happen because of: 'a) new discoveries ... ; b) new markets ... ; c) a reduction of consumption good prices greater than that of incomes; d) the introduction and spread of sales on installments; e) the resumption of building construction; f) renewal of public works; g) military expenditure'. See Fanno, *La teoria delle fluttuazioni economiche*, p. 330. As we see, Fanno believed in a mix of endogenous and exogenous factors.
41. It is a characteristic of dynamic theories to be grounded on entrepreneurial initiative or to adopt a Schumpeterian view mixing micro and macro analyses. See G. Mensch, 'Micro-Macro-Modelling (MMM) of Schumpeterian Dynamics 1950 1984', in P. Flaschel and M. Krüger (eds), *Recent Approaches to Economic Dynamics* (Frankfurt am Main Peter Lang, 1988), p. 178. It has become customary to distinguish at least three layers of the economy, denoted micro, meso and macro. It is the hallmark of 'Schumpeterian thought that change processes on all three levels go on simultaneously yet at different speeds of change'. See also Tusset, *La teoria dinamica nel pensiero economico italiano*, chs 2, 6.
42. The upward limit is based on full employment, while Fanno ignored the increase in productivity. However, this does not affect the basis of his theoretical scheme.
43. Caravale, *Cicli economici e trend* (Milan: Giuffrè, 1961), p. 139.
44. Ibid.

45. T. Cozzi, 'Marco Fanno e la teoria moderna del ciclo', in M. Manfredini Gasparetto (ed.), *Saggi di economia nell'attualità di Marco Fanno* (Padua: Cedam, 1982), pp. 227–38.
46. Fanno, *La teoria delle fluttuazioni economiche*.
47. M. Fanno, 'Considerazioni sullo sviluppo dei sistemi economici', in *Società Italiana degli Economisti, Atti della seconda riunione scientifica* (Milan: Bocconi University, 1956), p. 16.
48. A. H. Hansen, *Business Cycles and National Income* (New York: Norton, 1951).
49. To paraphrase Frisch, entrepreneurial initiative and disequilibrium correspond to impulse and to propagation respectively. But, contrary to what the Norwegian economist affirmed, here initiative and propagation reinforce themselves in a fluctuating movement ('Propagation Problems and Impulse Problems in Dynamic Economics', in *Economic Essays in Honour of Gustav Cassel* (London: Allen and Unwin, 1933), pp. 171–205).
50. F. Perroux, *La pensée économique de Joseph Schumpeter. Les dynamiques du capitalisme* (Genève: Droz, 1965), subsequently wrote that the notions of asymmetry and of agent's creating power are concepts fundamental for the analysis of economic dynamism.
51. The notion of endogenous cause is disputed. Here it means a change not completely arising within the economic system and involving both internal and external impulses.
52. L. Lugli, *Nuovo schema del processo economico* (Padua: Cedam, 1953), p. 67.
53. Knight was referring to the article published by Del Vecchio in German in 1928, 'Untersuchungen zur Theorie des Unternehmergewinnes', in H. Mayer, F. A. Fetter and R. Reisch (eds), *Die Wirtschaftstheorie der Gegenwart* (Wien: Verlag, 1928). That article was partially translated into Italian and published in *Capital and Interest* (*Capitale e interesse*) with the titles 'L'assicurazione' (1928, pp. 317–55) and 'L'impresa' (1928, pp. 356–69). Federico Caffè wrote that Frank Knight ('Profit', in *Encyclopaedia of the Social Sciences*, ed. Seligman and Johnson, vol. 11, p. 283) recognized Gustavo Del Vecchio's primacy in studying the relation between time passing and uncertainty.
54. See G. Del Vecchio, 'Teoria economica dell'assicurazione', *Annali di Economia* 4:1 (1928), pp. 43–86.
55. G. Del Vecchio, 'Untersuchungen sur Theorie des Unternehmergewinnes', in H. Mayer, F. A. Fetter and R. Reisch (eds), *Die Wirtschaftstheorie der Gegenwart* (Wien: Verlag, 1928), p. 282.
56. Del Vecchio, 'Untersuchungen sur Theorie des Unternehmergewinnes', p. 282.
57. Ibid., pp. 282–3.
58. Ibid., p. 287.
59. Ibid.
60. Ibid., p. 289.
61. Ibid., pp. 291–2.
62. Ibid., p. 292.
63. Ibid.
64. Del Vecchio, *Economia generale*, p. 128.
65. Ibid., p. 129.
66. Del Vecchio, *Lezioni di economia applicata. Dinamica economica* (1933), p. 53.
67. Ibid., p. 55.
68. Del Vecchio, 'Il problema della stabilità del sistema capitalistico', p. 49.
69. Del Vecchio, 'Introduzione' to Del Vecchio (ed.), *Economia pura*, p. 92.
70. G. Demaria, 'Sul concetto di tempo', *Archivio scientifico del R. Istituto superiore di scienze economiche e commerciali di Bari* (1931), republished in *Giornale degli Economisti e Annali di Economia* (1974), pp. 684–706. Stating that time is change enables us to

understand Demaria's interest in Heisenberg's quantum theory and his subsequent attempt to introduce the concept of 'indeterminacy' into economics. This marks the beginning of Demaria's reflections on the opposing concepts of determinism and indeterminism, as demonstrated by his earlier article 'Di un principio di indeterminazione in economia dinamica' (*Rivista Internazionale di Scienze Sociali* (1932), pp. 597–636). However, Demaria never considered economics to be a natural or mechanistic science. In fact, as Georgescu-Roegen noted, Heisenberg's indeterminacy proved that the idea of science without man had progressively lost ground (*Analytical Economics* (Cambridge MA: Harvard University Press, 1966), p. 104). Recognizing that indeterminacy marks any economic analyses means admitting that economics could never be based on the notions of static equilibrium and predictable facts, but rather on the concepts of change and uncertainty. In fact, on referring to the philosophical image of 'time as change', G. Demaria argued that the dynamic order is always 'original, new, creative, hesitant, and unpredictable' and that 'only the boundary of change, and not change itself, may be determined *a priori*' ('Le basi logiche dell'economia dinamica nel clima scientifico odierno', *Giornale degli economisti e Annali di economia*, 79 (1939), pp. 51–98, on p. 83). See also G. Tusset, 'Giovanni Demaria and the Economic Change', *International Review of Economics and Business*, 46:3 (1999), pp. 401–21.

71. Del Vecchio, *Lezioni di economia applicata. Dinamica economica* (1933), p. 55.
72. Ibid., p. 30.
73. Del Vecchio, 'Il problema della stabilità del sistema capitalistico', p. 52.
74. Ibid.

Epilogue

1. Faucci named Del Vecchio the 'Italian Schumpeter'. Faucci, *L'economia politica in Italia. Dal Cinquecento ai giorni nostri*, p. 293.
2. Dal Pane, 'Commemorazione di Gustavo Del Vecchio', p. 835.

WORKS CITED

Aftalion, A., *Les crise périodiques de superproduction* (Paris: Rivier, 1913).

Allais, M., 'The Psychological Rate of Interest', *Money, Credit and Banking*, 6:3 (1974), pp. 285–331.

Amoroso, L., 'Ricerche intorno alla curva dei redditi', *Annali di matematica pura e applicata* (1925), pp. 123–57.

Anderson, B. M., *The Value of Money* (New York: Macmillan Company, 1917).

Antonelli, G., 'Gustavo Del Vecchio', in D. Mirri and S. Arieti, *La cattedra negate. Dal giuramento di fedeltà al fascismo alle leggi razziali nell'Università di Bologna* (Bologna: Cleub, 2002), pp. 177–83.

Arnon, A., *Monetary Theory and Policy from Hume and Smith to Wicksell. Money, Credit and the Economy* (Cambridge: Cambridge University Press, 2011).

Aspromourgos, T., 'The Theory of Production and Distribution in Cantillon's Essai', *Oxford Economic Papers*, n. s., 41:2 (1989), pp. 356–73.

Bagiotti, T., 'Giulio Salvatore Del Vecchio teorico della causalità sociale', in *Studi di economia finanza e statistica in onore di Gustavo Del Vecchio* (Padua: Cedam, 1963), pp. 83–110.

Benini, R., 'Di alcune curve descritte da fenomeni economici aventi relazioni con la curva del reddito e con quella dei patrimoni', *Giornale degli Economisti* (1897), pp. 177–214.

—, 'Sull'uso delle formule empiriche nell'economia applicata', *Giornale degli Economisti*, 35 (1907), pp. 1053–63.

—, 'Una possibile creazione del metodo statistico "L'economia politica induttiva"', *Giornale degli Economisti* (1908), pp. 11–34.

Bini, P., *Costantino Bresciani-Turroni. Ciclo, moneta e sviluppo* (Civitanova Marche: Otium, 1992).

—, 'Captains of Industry and Masters of Thought: The Entrepreneur and the Tradition of Italian Liberal Economists from Francesco Ferrara to Sergio Ricossa', *Rivista Italiana degli Economisti*, 18:1 (2013), pp. 87–130.

Blaug, M., 'Why is the Quantity Theory of Money the Oldest Surviving Theory in Economics?', in M. Blaug (ed.), *The Quantity Theory of Money. From Locke to Keynes and Friedman* (Aldershot: Elgar, 1995), pp. 27–49.

—, 'Ugly Currents in Modern Economics', in U. Mäki, *Fact and Fiction in Economics. Models, Realism and Social Construction* (Cambridge: Cambridge University Press, 2002), pp. 35–56.

Böhm-Bawerk, E. von, *Rechte und Verhältnisse vom Standpunkte der volkswirthschaftlichen Güterlehre* (Innsbruck, 1881).

—, *Capital and Interest*. II. *Positive Theory of Capital* (South Holland: Libertarian Press 1959).

Boianovsky M., and V. J. Tarascio, 'Mechanical Inertia and Economic Dynamics: Pareto on Business Cycles', *Journal of the History of Economic Thought*, 20:1 (1998), pp. 5–23.

Bordin, A., *La teoria dell'equilibrio e gli schemi probabilistici* (Bellinzona: Leins & Vescov, 1933).

Bresciani-Turroni, C., 'Le variazioni 'cicliche' dei prezzi', *Annali del Seminario giuridico della R. Università di Palermo*, vol. 2 (Palermo: Gaipa, 1912), pp. 227–82.

—, 'Oscillazioni fra sconto e prezzi durante i cicli economici' (1916), in Bresciani-Turroni, *Saggi di economia* (Milan: Giuffrè, 1961), pp. 371–420.

— 'Alcuni effetti economici dei prestiti esteri in Germania negli anni 1924–1929', *Giornale degli Economisti e Rivista di Statistica* (1929), pp. 994–1067.

—, 'Le vicende del marco tedesco', *Annali di Economia*, 7 (1932), pp. 1–596.

— 'Le previsioni economiche', in *Nuova Collana di Economisti Italiani e Stranieri*, vol. 6 (Turin: Utet, 1932), pp. 209–364.

—, Corso di economia politica. Teoria generale dei fatti economici (Milan: Giuffrè, 1953).

Brewer A., *Richard Cantillon. Pioneer of Economic Theory* (London: Routledge, 1992).

Bridel, P., *Money and General Equilibrium Theory. From Walras to Pareto (1870–1923)* (Cheltenham: Elgar, 1997).

Brown, H. G., 'The Marginal Productivity versus the Impatience Theory of Interest', *Quarterly Journal of Economics*, 27:4 (1913), pp. 630–50.

Caffè, F., 'L'opera economica di Gustavo Del Vecchio', *Giornale degli Economisti e Analisi di Economia*, 20:9–10 (1961), pp. 631–9.

—, 'L'opera economica di Gustavo del Vecchio', *Studi di economia finanza e statistica in onore di Gustavo Del Vecchio*, 2 vols (Padua: Cedam, 1963), pp. 701–9.

—, 'Vecchio, Gustavo Del', in J. Eatwell, M. Milgate and P. Newman (eds), *the New Palgrave. A Dictionary of Economics*, 4 vols (London: Macmillan, 1987), vol. 4, pp. 800–1.

Cannan, E., *Wealth. A Brief Explanation of the Causes of Economic Welfare* (London: King & Son, 1914).

Cantillon, R., *Essai sur la nature du commerce en général* (1755; London: Macmillan 1931), with an English translation.

Caravale, G., *Cicli economici e trend* (Milan: Giuffrè, 1961).

Cavalieri, D., 'L'analisi economica tra causalità e interdipendenza: elementi per una valutazione storico-critica', *Quaderni di Storia dell'Economia Politica*, 5–6 (1987–8), pp. 9–56.

Clark, J. B., *The Distribution of the Wealth* (London: Macmillan, 1899).

—, *The Philosophy of the Wealth* (Boston, MA: Ginn & Co., 1907).

Cockshott, W. P., et al., *Classical Econophysics* (London and New York: Routledge, 2009).

Cognetti de Martiis, F., 'L'economia come scienza autonoma', *Giornale degli economisti*, 9 (1886), pp. 166–203.

Cozzi, T., 'Marco Fanno e la teoria moderna del ciclo', in M. Manfredini Gasparetto (ed.), *Saggi di economia nell'attualità di Marco Fanno* (Padua: Cedam, 1982), pp. 227–38.

Dal Pane, L., 'Commemorazione di Gustavo Del Vecchio'. *Giornale degli Economisti e Annali di Economia*, 32:11–12 (1973), pp. 826–36.

Del Vecchio, G., *Prodotto netto e monopolio* (Bologna: Noè, 1905).

—, *Ricchezze immateriali e capitali immateriali* (Alessandria: Società poligrafica Alessandrina, 1908).

—, 'I principii della teoria economica della moneta', *Giornale degli Economisti e Rivista di Statistica*, 39 (1909), pp. 255–72, 507–53.

—, 'Teoria della esportazione del capitale', *Giornale degli Economisti e Rivista di Statistica*, 41 (1910), pp. 120–52.

—, 'Il problema storico del valore della moneta', *Archivio storico italiano* (1912). Reprinted in Del Vecchio, *Ricerche sopra la teoria generale della moneta* (1932 and 1967), pp. 171–7.

—, 'La teoria economica del credito. A proposito del libro del Prof. Fanno sul mercato monetario', *Giornale degli Economisti e Rivista di Statistica* 46 (1913), pp. 200–13.

—, 'Le variazioni periodiche dello sconto', *Giornale degli Economisti e Rivista di Statistica*, 46 (1913), pp. 342–408.

—, 'Induzioni statistiche per la teoria della circolazione', *Giornale degli Economisti e Rivista di Statistica*, 46 (1913), pp. 510–37.

—, 'Problemi del Tesoro e della circolazione', *Giornale degli Economisti e Rivista di Statistica*, 46 (1913), pp. 1–12.

—, 'Sulla teoria economica delle crisi', *Giornale degli Economisti e Rivista di Statistica* 48 (1914), pp. 425–52.

—, 'Teorie dello sconto', *Giornale degli Economisti e Rivista di Statistica*, Supplement (1914). Reprinted in Del Vecchio *Capitale e interesse* (Turin: Utet, 1956), pp. 108–207.

—, 'Contributi alle dottrine della circolazione', *Giornale degli Economisti e Rivista di Statistica*, 47 (1914). Reprinted in *Ricerche sopra la teoria generale della moneta* (Padua: Cedam 1967), pp. 323–43.

—, 'Lineamenti generali della teoria dell'interesse', *Giornale degli Economisti e Rivista di Statistica*, 51 (1915), pp. 272–327, 367–408.

—, 'Questioni fondamentali sul valore della moneta', *Giornale degli Economisti e Rivista di Statistica*, 55 (1917), pp. 117–74.

—, 'Un capitolo di teoria monetaria', *Rivista bancaria*. (1925), reprinted in G. Del Vecchio, *Ricerche sopra la teoria generale della moneta* (1932), 2nd edn (Padua: Cedam, 1967), pp. 313–22.

—, 'Il problema della stabilità del sistema capitalistico', *Economia*, 3:5–8 (1925), pp. 47–60.

—, 'Il mercato monetario', *Annali di Economia* (1927), pp. 311–24.

—, 'Untersuchungen sur Theorie des Unternehmergewinnes', in H. Mayer, F. A. Fetter, and R. Reisch (eds), *Die Wirtschaftstheorie der Gegenwart* (Wien: Verlag, 1928).

—, 'L'assicurazione' (1928) in *Capitale e interesse* (Turin: Einaudi, 1956), pp. 317–55.

—, 'L'impresa' (1928) in *Capitale e interesse* (Turin: Einaudi, 1956), pp. 356–69.

—, 'Prefazione', to G. Demaria, *Le teorie monetarie e il ritorno all'oro* (Torino: Bocca, 1928), pp. v–xiii.

—, 'Teoria economica dell'assicurazione', *Annali di Economia*, 4:1 (1928), pp. 43–86.

— 'Le teorie economiche di Rodolfo Benini', *Giornale degli Economisti e Rivista di Statistica* (1929), pp. 957–66.

—, *Lezioni di economia applicata. Dinamica Economica*, 3rd lithographic edn (Padua: Cedam, 1930).

—, *Grundlinien der Geldtheorie* (Tübingen: Verlag, 1930).

—, 'Ritorni alla teoria ferrariana del credito' (1930), reprinted in Del Vecchio, *Ricerche sopra la teoria generale della moneta*, pp. 107–18.

—, 'Credito', *Enciclopedia italiana*, vol XI (1931), reprinted in Del Vecchio, *Capitale e interesse* (Turin: Einaudi, 1956), pp. 305–14.

—, *Ricerche sopra la teoria generale della moneta* (1932), 2nd edn (Padua: Cedam, 1967).

—, *Aspetti teorici della crisi mondiale* (1932), reprinted as 'Theoretical Aspects of the World Crisis', in H. Hagemann (ed.), *Business Cycle Theory: Selected Texts 1860–1930* (London: Pickering & Chatto, 2002), pp. 261–76.

—, *Lezioni di economia applicata. Dinamica economica* (Padua: Cedam, 1933).

—, 'La teoria della moneta secondo W. Launhardt', in *Economic Essays in Honour of Gustav Cassel* (London: Allen & Unwin, 1933), pp. 665–71.

—, 'Review of Mises L., Robbins L, and Conrad O.', in Del Vecchio, *Progressi della teoria economica* (Padua: Cedam, 1936), pp. 151–4.

—, *Progressi della teoria economica* (Padua: Cedam, 1936).

—, 'Introduzione' to G. Del Vecchio (ed.) *Economia pura. Nuova collana di economisti italiani e stranieri* (Turin: Unione Tipografico – Editrice Torinese, 1937), pp. vii–xxxi.

—, *La sintesi economica e la teoria del reddito* (Padua: Cedam, 1950).

—, 'La costruzione scientifica della dinamica economica', *Giornale degli economisti e Annali di economia*, 11:9–10 (1952), pp. 584–91.

—, 'Risposta al questionario indirizzato agli economisti della Commissione parlamentare di inchiesta sulla disoccupazione', *Atti*, 4:4 (Rome 1953).

—, *Introduzione alla finanza* (Padua: Cedam, 1954).

—, *Vecchie e nuove teorie economiche*, 2nd edn (Turin: Utet, 1956).

—, *Capitale e interesse* (Turin: Einaudi, 1956).

—, *Economia generale* (Turin: Utet, 1961).

Demaria, G., 'Sul concetto di tempo', *Archivio scientifico del R. Istituto superiore di scienze economiche e commerciali di Bari* (1931), republished in *Giornale degli Economisti e Annali di Economia* (1974), pp. 684–706.

—, 'Di un principio di indeterminazione in economia dinamica', *Rivista Internazionale di Scienze Sociali* (1932), pp. 597–636.

—, 'Le basi logiche dell'economia dinamica nel clima scientifico odierno', *Giornale degli economisti e Annali di economia*, 79 (1939), pp. 51–98.

—, 'La moneta nell'equilibrio economico generale'. Preface to Del Vecchio, *Ricerche sopra la teoria generale della moneta* (Padua: Cedam 1967), pp. 17–29.

De Pietri-Tonelli, A., *Corso di politica economica. Introduzione* (Padua: Cedam, 1931).

Dietzel, C., *Das System der Staatsanleihen in Zusammenhang der Volkswirtsschaft betrachtet* (Heidelberg: Mohr, 1855).

Dopfer, K., 'Evolutionary Economics: Framework for Analysis', in *Evolutionary Economics: Program and Scope* (Boston, MA, Dordrecht and London: Kluwer A.P., 2001), pp. 1–44.

Fanno, M., Cicli di produzione, cicli del credito e fluttuazioni industriali, *Giornale degli Economisti*, 71 (1931), pp. 329–70.

—, *La teoria delle fluttuazioni economiche* (Turin: Utet, 1947).

— 'Le teorie delle fluttuazioni economiche', in *Società Italiana degli Economisti, Atti della prima riunione scientifica* (Milan: Bocconi University, 1952), pp. 1–38.

— 'Considerazioni sullo sviluppo dei sistemi economici', in *Società Italiana degli Economisti, Atti della seconda riunione scientifica* (Milan: Bocconi University, 1956), pp. 7–25.

Faucci, R., 'La cultura economica fra le due guerre mondiali' in G. Becattini (ed.), *Il pensiero economico: temi, problemi e scuole*, 11 vols (Turin: Utet, 1990), vol. 3.

—, *L'economista scomodo. Vita e opere di Francesco Ferrara* (Palermo: Sellerio, 1995).

—, *L'economia politica in Italia. Dal Cinquecento ai giorni nostri* (Turin: Utet, 2000).

Ferrara. F., *Opere complete*, vol. 5: *Della moneta e dei suoi surrogati*, ed. B. R. Ragazzi and F. Caffè (1856; Rome: Associazione Bancaria Italiana, 1961).

—, 'Delle crisi economiche' (1864), in *Opere Complete*, vol. 4: *Prefazioni alla Biblioteca dell'Economista*, ed. B. Rossi Ragazzi (Rome: Istituto Grafico Tiberino, 1956), pp. 343–420.

—, *Esame storico-critico di economisti e dottrine economiche*, 2 vols (Turin: Utet, 1889–91).

Fisher, I., *The Nature of Capital and Income* (New York: MacMillan, 1906).

—, *The Rate of Interest. Its Nature, Determination and Relation to Economic Phenomena* (New York: MacMillan, 1907).

—, 'A Practical Method of Estimating the Velocity of Circulation of Money', *Journal of the Royal Statistical Society*, 72:3 (1909), pp. 604–18.

—, *The Purchasing Power of Money* (New York: MacMillan, 1911).

Foà, B., *Il capitale nell'equilibrio economico* (Messina: Industrie Grafiche Meridionali, 1933).

Fossati, E., *The Theory of General Static Equilibrium* (Oxford: Basil Blackwell, 1957).

Frisch, R., 'Propagation Problems and Impulse Problems in Dynamic Economics', in *Economic Essays in Honour of Gustav Cassel* (London: Allen and Unwin, 1933), pp. 171–205.

Georgescu-Roegen, N., *Analytical Economics* (Cambridge, MA: Harvard University Press, 1966).

Gini C. 'Prezzi e consumi', *Giornale degli Economisti e Rivista di Statistica*, 15 (1910), pp. 99–114; 235–49.

Giva, D., 'Gustavo Del Vecchio', in *Dizionario Biografico Italiano* (Rome: Istituto dell'Enciclopedia Italiana, 1990), pp. 397–402.

Gioia, V., 'Il contributo epistemologico di Gustavo del Vecchio', *Quaderni di Storia dell'Economia Politica*, 8 (1990), pp. 147–67.

Goodwin, R. M., 'Secular and Cyclical Aspects of the Multiplier and the Accelerator', in *Income, Employment and Public Policy. Essays in Honor of Alvin H. Hansen* (New York: W.W. Norton & C., 1948), pp. 108–32.

Hansen, A. H., *Business Cycles and National Income* (New York: Norton, 1951).

Hawtrey, R. G., *Credit and Currency* (New York: Longmans, 1928).

—, *The Art of Central Banking* (London: Longmans, 1932).

Helfferich, K., *Das Geld*, 2 vols (1903). English translation: *Money* (London: E. Benn Limited, 1927).

Hermann, von F. B. W., *Staatswirtschaftliche Untersuchungen* (1870; München: Werber, 1932).

Hicks, J. R., 'A Suggestion for Simplifying the Theory of Money' *Economica*, 2:5 (1935), pp. 1–19.

Holtrop, M. W., 'Theories of the Velocity of Circulation of Money in Earlier Economic Literature' *Economic History*, 4 (1929), reprinted in M. Blaug (ed.), *Pre-Classical Economists*, 3 vols (Cheltenam: Elgar 1991), vol. 3, pp. 503–24.

Jannaccone, P., 'Vilfredo Pareto, il sociologo', in L. Amoroso et al., *Vilfredo Pareto. L'economista e il sociologo* (Milan: Malfasi, 1949), pp. 20–34.

Jevons, W. S., *Money and the Mechanism of Exchange*, 2nd edn (London: H. S. King & Co., 1876).

Keirstead, B. S., *The Theory of Economic Change* (Toronto: Macmillan, 1948).

Keynes, J. M., *A Treatise on Money*, 2 vols (London: Macmillan, 1930).

—, *The General Theory of Employment Interest and Money* (London: Macmillan, 1936).

Knies, K., *Geld und Kredit* (Berlin: Weidmann, 1873).

Knight, F. H., *Risk, Uncertainty, and Profit* (Boston, MA and New York: Houghton Mifflin Co, 1921).

—, *The Economic Organization* (New York: Kelley, 1967).

—, 'Profit' in *Encyclopaedia of the Social Sciences*, ed. E. R. A. Seligman and A. Johnson, 17 vols (New York: Macmillan, 1959), vol. 11, pp. 480–7.

Kuenne, R. E., *The Theory of General Economic Equilibrium* (Princeton, NJ: Princeton University Press, 1963).

Labriola, A., *Saggi sul materialismo storico* (1925; Milan: Editori Riuniti, 2000).

Laidler, D., 'The Definition of Money: Theoretical and Empirical Problems', *Journal of Money, Credit, and Banking*, 1:3 (1969), pp. 508–25.

Landry, A., *L'intérêt du Capital* (Paris: Giard 1901).

Likitijsomboon, P., 'Marx's Anti-Quantity Theory of Money: A Critical Evaluation', in F. Moseley, *Marx's Theory of Money* (Houndmills: Palgrave Macmillan, 2005), pp. 160–74.

Loria, A., *Dinamica economica. Studio sulle leggi delle variazioni* (Turin: Bocca, 1935).

Lugli, L., *Nuovo schema del processo economico* (Padua: Cedam, 1953).

Macleod, H. D., *Principles of Economical Philosophy* (London: Longmans, 1872).

Magliulo, A., *Marco Fanno e la cultura economica italiana del Novecento* (Florence: Polistampa, 1998).

Marget, A. W., 'Léon Walras and the "Cash-Balance Approach" to the Problem of the Value of Money', *Journal of Political Economy*, 39:5 (1931), pp. 569–600.

—, 'The Relation between the Velocity of Circulation of Money and the Velocity of Circulation of Goods', *Journal of Political Economy* 40:3 (1932), pp. 289–313.

—, *The Theory of Prices*, 2 vols (1938; New York: Kelley, 1966).

Marshall, A., *Money, Credit and Commerce* (1923; New York: Kelley, 1965).

Martello, T., *La moneta e gli errori che corrono intorno ad essa* (Florence: Le Monnier, 1883).

Marx, K., *Capital. A Critique of Political Economy, Vol. I*, German edition 1867; first English edition 1887, online version.

Masci, G., 'Alcuni aspetti odierni dell'organizzazione e delle trasformazioni industriali', in *Nuova Collana di Economisti Italiani e Stranieri*. Vol. 7, *Organizzazione industriale* (Turin: Utet 1934), pp. 929–58.

Mason, W. E., *Classical versus Neoclassical Monetary Theory*, ed. W. E. Butos (Boston, MA: Kluwer Academic, 1996).

Menger, C., 'Geld', in *Handwörterbuch der Staatswissenschaften*, III vgl, No. 24 (1892).

—, *Grundsätze des Volkswirtschaftslehre* (Wien: Holder-Pichler-Tempsky, 1923).

Mensch, G., 'Micro-Macro-Modelling (MMM) of Schumpeterian Dynamics 1950 1984', in P. Flaschel and M. Krüger (eds), *Recent Approaches to Economic Dynamics* (Frankfurt am Main Peter Lang, 1988), pp. 177–92.

Mises, L. von, *Theorie des Geldes und der Umlaufsmittel* (München, 1912), translated and reprinted as *The Theory of Money and Credit* (New York: Foundation of Economic Education, 1971).

Moore, H. L., *Synthetic Economics* (New York: Macmillan Co. 1929).

Morishima, M., 'Foreword' to *Vilfredo Pareto: Neoclassical Synthesis of Economics and Sociology*, in A. de Pietri-Tonelli and G. H. Bousquet, *Vilfredo Pareto: Neoclassical Synthesis of Economics and Sociology* (Houndmills: Palgrave Macmillan 1994), pp. xi–xxvi.

Mortara, G., 'Recensione a C. Bresciani-Turroni. Le vicende del marco tedesco', *Giornale degli Economisti e Rivista di Statistica* (1932), p. 286.

Palomba, G., *Equilibrio economico e movimenti ciclici secondo i dati della sociologia sperimentale* (Naple: Jovene, 1935).

Pantaleoni, M., 'Osservazioni sulla semiologia economica', *Revue d'Economie Politique* (1892), reprinted in *Scritti varii di economia* (Milan: Sandron, 1904), pp. 423–75.

—, *Pure Economics* (New York: Macmillan, 1898).

—, 'Caratteri delle posizioni iniziali e influenza che esercitano sulle terminali', *Giornale degli Economisti*, 23 (1901), pp. 333–55.

—, 'Una visione cinematografica del progresso della scienza economica' (1907) in Pantaleoni, *Scritti vari di Economia. Erotemi* (Bari: Laterza, 1925), pp. 211–22.

—, 'Di alcuni fenomeni di economica', in Pantaleoni, *Scritti vari di Economia. Erotemi* (Bari: Laterza, 1925), translated into English as 'Some Phenomena of Economic Dynamics', in A. T. Peacock, W. F. Stolper, R. Turvey and E. Henderson (eds), *International Economic Papers No.5*. (London and New York: Macmillan, 1955), pp. 26–57.

—, *Scritti vari di Economia. Erotemi* (Bari: Laterza, 1925; Padua: Cedam, 1963).

Papi, U. G., *Lezioni di economia generale e corporativa* (Padua: Cedam, 1934).

—, *Lezioni di economia politica. III*, 8th edn (Padua: Cedam, Padova, 1950).

— 'Trend e punti di inversioni in una fluttuazione economica', in Società Italiana degli Economisti, *Atti della prima riunione scientifica* (Milan: Bocconi University, 1952), pp. 39–51.

Pareto, V., 'Considerazioni sui principi fondamentali della economia politica pura', *Giornale degli Economisti*, August (1892), translated in English as 'Consideration on the Fundamental Principles of Pure Political Economy, III', in R. Marchionatti and F. Mornati (eds), *Considerations on the Fundamental Principles of Pure Political Economy* (Abingdon: Routledge 2007), pp. 45–74.

—, *Cours d'économie politique* (Genève: Droz, 1896–7), vols 1 and 2, new edn, ed. G. H. Bousquet and G. Busino (1964).

—, *Les Systèmes Socialistes*, 2 vols (1902–3; Genève: Droz, 1965).

—, 'Programme et sommaire du Cours de sociologie', in *Ecrits sociologiques mineurs*, ed. G. Busino (1905; Genève: Droz, 1980), pp. 292–316.

—, *Manuale di economia politica con una introduzione alla scienza sociale* (Milan: Società Editrice Libraria, 1906; Rome, Edizioni Bizzari, 1965).

—, *Manuel d'économie politique* (Geneve-Paris: Droz, 1909).

Perroux, F., *La pensée économique de Joseph Schumpeter. Les dynamiques du capitalisme* (Genève: Droz, 1965).

Pigou, A. C., 'The Value of Money', *Quarterly Journal of Economics*, 32:1 (1917), pp. 38–65.

—, *Industrial Fluctuations*, 2nd edn (London: Macmillan, 1929).

Porcelluzzi, A. A., *Walter Bagehot and the Open Money Supply Approach to Monetary Theory* (Saarbrüchen: VDM Verlag, 2009).

Prévost, J.-G., *A Total Science: Statistics in Liberal and Fascist Italy* (Paris: McGill Queens University Press, 2009).

Realfonzo, R., 'Gustavo Del Vecchio: Critical Conscience of the Italian Neoclassical School', in W. J. Samuels (ed.), *European Economists of the Early 20th Century* (Cheltenham: Elgar, 2003), pp. 37–58.

Resta, M., *Il capitale fisso e le trasformazioni industriali* (Padua: Cedam, 1938).

Ricardo, D., *The Works and Correspondence of David Ricardo*, ed. by P. Sraffa. III. *Pamphlets and Papers 1809–1811* (Cambridge: Cambridge University Press, 1951).

Rist C., *History of the Monetary and Credit Theory: From John Law to the Present Day* (New York: Kelley, 1966).

Russett, C. E., *The Concept of Equilibrium in American Social Thought* (New Haven, CT and London: Yale University Press, 1966).

Salin, E., *Politische Ökonomie. Geschichte der wirtschaftspolitischen Ideen von Platon bis zur Gegenwart* (Tübingen: Mohr, 1923).

Scazzieri, R., 'Del Vecchio, Gustavo', Treccani, online at http://www.treccani.it/enciclopedia/gustavo-del-vecchio_(Il_Contributo_italiano_alla_storia_del_Pensiero:_Economia)/ [accessed December 2013], p. 13.

Schumpeter, J. A., *Die Theorie der wirtschaftlichen Entwicklung* (Leipzig: Duncker & Humblot, 1912).

—, *History of Economic Analysis* (New York: Oxford University Press, 1954).

Schultz, H., *The Theory and Measurement of Demand* (Chicago, IL: University of Chicago Press, 1938).

Shackle, G. L. S., *Time in Economics* (Amsterdam: North-Holland Publishing Co., 1967).

Skidelsky, R., 'J.M. Keynes and the quantity theory of money', in M. Blaug (ed.). *The Quantity Theory of Money. From Locke to Keynes and Friedman* (Aldershot: Elgar, 1995), pp. 80–96.

Slutsky, E., 'The Summation of Random Causes as the Source of Cyclic Processes', *Econometrica* (1937) pp. 105–46.

Sombart, W., *Der Bourgeois* (München und Leipzig: Duncker & Humblot, 1913), translated in English as *The Quintessence of Capitalism* (New York: Howard Fertig, 1967).

Spiethoff, A., 'The "Historical" Character of Economic Theories,' *Journal of Economic History*, 12 (1952), pp. 131–9.

Starr, R. M., *Why is there Money?: Walrasian General Equilibrium Foundations of Monetary Theory* (Chelthenam: Elgar, 2012).

Stigler, G. J., 'The Early History of Empirical Studies of Consumer', *The Journal of Political Economy*, 62 (1954), pp. 95–113.

Supino, C., *Teoria della trasformazione dei capitali* (Turin: Bocca, 1891).

—, 'Scienza economica e realtà economica', *La Riforma Sociale*, 5 (1896), pp. 397–415.

—, *Le crisi economiche* (Milan: Hoepli, 1907).

Suranyi-Unger, T., *Economics in the Twentieth Century: The History of its International Development* (New York: Norton, 1931).

Tomo, S., 'Böhm-Bawerk's Objectivism beyond Menger's Subjectivism', in Y. Ikeda and K. Yagi, *Subjectivism and Objectivism in the History of Economic Thought* (Abingdon: Routledge, 2012), pp. 108–25.

Tusset, G., 'Giovanni Demaria and the Economic Change', *International Review of Economics and Business*, 46:3 (1999), pp. 401–21.

—, *La teoria dinamica nel pensiero economico italiano. 1890–1940* (Florence: Polistampa, 2004).

— 'The Italian Contribution to Early Economic Dynamics', *European Journal of the History of Economic Thought*, 16:2 (2009), pp. 267–300.

—, 'Individual and Market Inertia in Luigi Amoroso's Cycle Model', *History of Economic Ideas*, 20:2 (2012), pp. 43–63.

Walras, L., *Eléments d'économie politique pure, ou théorie de la richesse sociale*, 2 vols (Lausanne: Corbaz. 1926), translated in English as *Elements of Pure Economics* (Homewood: Irwin, 1954).

Walsh, C. M., *The Fundamental Problem in Monetary Science* (New York: Mamillan, 1903).

Wicksell, K., *Geldzins und Güterpreise*. (Jena: Fischer, 1898). Engl. Transl. *Interest and Prices* (London: Royal Economic Society, 1936).

—, 'The Influence of the Rate of Interest on Prices', *Economic Journal*, 17:66 (1907), pp. 213–20.

Wieser, von F., *Natural Value* (1893; New York: Kelley, 1971).

Wilson, J., *Capital, Currency, and Banking* (London: The Economist, 1847).

Yule, G., 'On a Method of Investigating Periodicity in Disturbed Series with Special Reference to Wolfer's Sunspot Numbers', *Transactions of the Royal Society* (1927), pp. 267–98.

Zanni, A., 'La teoria monetaria di Walras: una polemica scientifica tra Marget e Del Vecchio', *Quaderni di storia dell'economia politica*, 7 (1989), pp. 135–45.

—, 'Walras's Theory of Money: A Scientific Debate between Marget and Del Vecchio', *Economists' Archives* (1990), pp. 5–12.

—, 'La "Nuova Collana di Economisti" di Bottai ed Arena', *Annali della Fondazione Luigi Einaudi*, 45 (2011), pp. 99–112.

INDEX